CW00742356

PLAYING UP WITH POMPEY

THE STORY OF THE PORTSMOUTH 6.57 CREW

BOB BEECH

HEADHUNTER BOOKS
www.headhunterbooks.co.uk

First published in August 2007 by Head-Hunter Books

ISBN 978-1-906085-02-5

Head-Hunter Books
www.headhunterbooks.co.uk
www.myspace.com/headhunterbooks

CONTENTS

Dedicated to:
Linda, Mum & Dad, but especially
To Charlotte, Lloyd & Claire.
Forever in my thoughts.

Acknowledgements

I would like to thank the following people without whose help, support and encouragement this book would not have been possible.

My wife and soul mate Linda for having enough confidence in me to allow me to put our money where my mouth is. My good friend Dave T whose boundless energy and enthusiasm helped push the project to its final conclusion. Chas, Enj & Sweeny who had to endure endless emails and phone calls but answered every one; they especially helped out with the England chapter as well as sorting out some photographs. Jez W, Bish, Kev G & Jake Payne who also helped out with photographs. Dave F, Richie B, Tony B & Jon Cobb who have always shown me true friendship, Darren L & Eddie C who helped out with a few details. Thanks also goes to Mike S, Georgie Wipeout, Ian Jenkins, Tim Hanks, Paul Finnegan, Ernie E, Cass Pennant, whose advice was much appreciated, Pete B, Brian Curtis, Andy H, Martin D, Spurs Andy, Johnny Madgewick, the staff at Portsmouth Central Library and my sister Beverly who many years ago encouraged me to be a writer and who also gave up a lot of her time to proof read the finished article. There are also those whose help has been invaluable but wish to remain anonymous - you know who you are, thanks. As well as those individuals already named, I would like to give a special mention to all of the lads from Salisbury with whom, I am sure everyone connected with the 6.57 Crew will agree, an unbreakable bond of friendship has been forged over the years, the Hayling Island crew from the 1980's along with the Fareham lads from the same era and also to Ian O, Raffles & Mark T, I spent many a Saturday with these three over the years but I've not seen them for some years.

It would be impossible to name everyone from the days gone by, so I would just like say to everyone who, over the years, has contributed in some way to some great days out. Those were the days my friends, I just hope I have done OUR story some justice.

BUSINESS AS USUAL

FOREWORD

By Jon Cobb

I met Jon via a mutual friend both of whom are fanatical about Portsmouth Football Club despite neither having ever lived in the city. Jon has never been involved in hooliganism although, over the years, has been on nodding terms with the odd well-known face at away games. While preparing this book, I was very interested to hear what he thought about the antics of the 6.57 Crew. Here is what he had to say.

There is something unique about the people of Portsmouth. I was first attracted to this hardy, passionate population back in 1980 when I saw thousands of them converge on Oxford for a league game at the Manor Ground - well come on, you didn't think it was anything to do with the football back then did you?

I was born and raised in a village in Hertfordshire and have always had a love for football. Trouble was my choice locally was either Watford or Luton. Luton have some great fans and I have lived there for some years now but, in my formative years, a trip to Kenilworth Road was something of a risk due to its proximity to the M1. Being so close to the motorway system meant there was usually a big away turnout come match day and the London clubs in particular used to terrorise the town. There was however a tasty crew called the MIGS who could put on a show. Trouble was none of them lived in my village when I was growing up and so I would have to go on my own. On alternative Saturdays, I would go to Vicarage Road to see Watford. I did this for quite a few years as the football was pretty exciting with the attacking partnership of Luther Blisset and Ross Jenkins usually meaning a few goals. Funny that I never saw either of the Brimson brothers when I used to go, although I remember a total annihilation of the Watford end by West Ham in the early eighties which, from the safety of the away end with the West Ham fans (I wasn't stupid!), was spectacular. It's amazing how you can tell from over 100 yards that there are 300 shaven headed ICF just to the right of the middle of the home end.

Watford!! Clap, Clap, Clap, wait for it... 'EEYEE CEEE EEEFFF'.

For those that stood, it was both brutal and swift. I couldn't support a team with half hearted fans so, when I was 16, I started to venture to London as a mate of mine was a Spurs fan. I went a few times, even going away with them to Aston Villa and Ipswich but there was still something missing. Unless you live in Seven Sisters, you're not really supporting something that represents more than a football team. That's the difference with Pompey. As a fan, it's a representation of more than the team; it's your team and, equally important, your City. Pompey will always be well supported because the football club is just a vehicle for men in particular to show their pride in the town from which they come. A City which doesn't necessarily deal a fair hand, a City which is aesthetically not that pleasing, cold and misty in Winter, too hot in the Summer, lacking a decent hospital, rough housing estates and its most famous resident in the past fifty years being a children's TV presenter. However, it is a City that is theirs and they are proud to be a part of it.

After spending my time drifting around various grounds watching different teams, just out to watch a good game of football on a Saturday afternoon, I had become good friends with a guy who had moved into the village. He was a few years older than me and we would often talk about football. Tim used to live in Nottingham as a kid and he told me how one day he got off the bus in Nottingham town centre and heard a booming chant coming from the City Ground. 'I thought that it was the sound of Big Ben' is how he described the moment to me. He insisted to me that Pompey fans were the only ones to ever take the Trent End and he followed Pompey ever since. At the first opportunity, he invited me to a game.

'We're going to Oxford tomorrow, wear your England scarf, its blue, white and red so you'll be safe enough' were his words.

For the life of me, I couldn't see the point of going to a university town to watch a Division Three match between two teams that I had no interest in but, hey, what's the worst that could happen?

The worst did happen! At about one minute past three, my love affair with Portsmouth Football Club started. I stood there on the packed away terrace, surrounded by blue and white painted faces (sixteen years before Euro 96 made that a trendy accessory), as, at the other end, the home fans were sent scattering as they realised they had been infiltrated. There was an unusual passion with these fans; their team contained no players that were instantly recognisable to fans of other teams other than that of goalkeeper Peter Mellor whose mistakes as Fulham keeper had allowed West Ham to win the 1975 FA Cup final. At first, I couldn't understand what it was that made them so excited about this dull football. The same reason they do every week, they are representing their city. This was taken to extremes the following Wednesday when an estimated 13,000 of them descended on Liverpool for a League Cup match. Back in 1980, this sort of support was unprecedented and the papers were full of the fact that the famous Anfield Kop was 'out sung'. The following week came my first ever visit to Fratton Park. As a footballing spectacle, the game was memorable only for a youthful Peter Beardsley scoring a cracking individual goal for Carlisle which, I'm sure, will stay forever in the memory of the thirteen Carlisle fans stood at the Milton End. I was hooked on Pompey. I had walked through the football wilderness and suddenly my team had found me. I still go today with the same lad that took me all those years ago. He lives in Northamptonshire now. The name of his house? Fratton Park, what else? We meet up every Saturday and travel home and away together although a lot of the away games are closer to home for us.

Its funny, as I travel throughout the UK with my job, I've come to realise that Pompey fans are like born again Christians. Before you know anything else about them, you know they are Pompey fans; it will come out sooner rather than later because although we may not have the most fashionable team, we are proud of it. People love to pontificate about football hooligans but violence is going to happen between young men. They don't need much of an excuse. However I appreciate that grounds are now a lot safer since the hooligan element has begun to die out but I can still think of many occasions when I was glad to have the Pompey boys around. One such instance was when we played Hereford in the League Cup on a Tuesday night. Four of us were on holiday in Torquay but left mid-afternoon to get up to the game.

The evening passed off without incident. We lost 3-2 but went on to win the second leg 3-1 to go through on aggregate. We decided that we would have a couple of jars before heading back because Torquay would be shut down for the night by the time we got back. We gave the first two bars a miss and entered the third that had a healthy mix of drinkers and perhaps ten Hereford lads in the corner. These lads immediately clocked us and start giving us the old 'slit throat gesture'. The youngest of the four of us started to get worried but I told him to look untroubled and give an air that we could handle ourselves as I was pretty confident that they would wait for us to leave before they made their move. We'd cross that bridge when we needed to. As the tension mounted the bright headlights of a coach shone through the pub windows, although it never registered that the cavalry had arrived. Two minutes later, 52 of Pompey's finest strolled in; the 10 Hereford took one look and made a hasty exit, out of the back door. Bye lads! There was no trouble, other than the thieving of a big brass horse and I don't think the lads on the coach realised that they saved us from what was looking like a one sided toeing.

When I first started watching Pompey, the 6.57 Crew was not a named, organised mob but the hoolies following Pompey were still very much in evidence. One cup game in Colchester, another humiliating defeat on the pitch, paled into insignificance by the scenes of violence off it. An equal number of around a dozen Pompey and what were rumoured to be Millwall fans (although there were always these types of rumour) battled for what seemed like ages. With only what appeared like two policemen in the ground, they were left to get on with it. I think it would be fair to say that honours were even. As the final whistle blew, the Pompey end emptied onto the pitch and headed straight towards the Colchester end. Pitch invasions used to happen quite regularly back then and MOTD would happily show them. It used to make me laugh because there would be an invisible line about twenty yards from the centre circle, whereby the invaders would stop and taunt but rarely move forward. If their opponents were up to it and would encroach onto the pitch, it gave those high waist baggies, scarf around the wrist, side burned wannabes who were all bravado enough distance to retreat without facing any real danger. However, the Pompey fans just hurdled this imaginary line and kept heading towards the Colchester fans. Once over the advertising hoardings, they were presented with retreating human wall of Essex boys who simply had no appetite for the fight. Outside the ground, as we walked past the home end, a lone Pompey fan stood in front of the exit, legs apart, arms outstretched and bellowed

'Whose man enough to admit they support Colchester?'

The silence was deafening.

As the years moved on and the 6.57 became known across the country, I found myself in the seats away at Leeds United. There were a 100 or so in there and it was quite evident that, as a 'non-hoolie', I was very much in the minority. The Leeds firm spotted us although, to be honest, the 6.57 lads made no attempt to hide who they were. At the end of the game, the Leeds lads were waiting at the exit gate heavily outnumbering us. Now I'm thinking that it would be a great time to wait for a police escort but my fellow fans thought different. The look on the Leeds fans faces when Pompey didn't stick to the script! There was one lad who I never spoke to but I knew we would be all right if he was around. He was totally unfazed and looked like he didn't have a care in the world despite the long walk back to the station with a Leeds mob that, in some cases, quite literally had had their noses put out of joint waiting to even the score. With me however it was a case of 'TAXI!!!!'

Because of my geographical location it is sometimes easier to get to away games, especially mid-week matches. So I sometimes find it funny when I'm at Fratton Park or wherever and I listen to Pompey fans, not casuals but the type of fan that seems to spend most of his day on the Internet following up a rumour about the latest signing. This type of supporter refuses to believe that anyone else is a bigger fan than them. I hear them say how the hooligans aren't real fans like they are but I sometimes think, hang on I didn't see you at Tranmere on Tuesday night; the 6.57 lads were there but you weren't and there wasn't a hint of bother; they were there supporting Pompey.

It's inevitable that, at times, you are going to be mistaken for a rival fan and I've always been able to talk myself out of the few occasions. However, if you are a regular at Fratton Park, you get known and start to feel one of the crowd. It was interesting therefore that I got a glimpse of how an away fan must feel on visiting Fratton and wandering around the area. There was some pretty serious trouble at Coventry a couple of seasons ago which saw a good old fashion taking of the Coventry end. This lead to rumours a plenty that

Coventry were going to even the score the following season when they visited Pompey. The pubs were full and Pompey were waiting. I had been given a real quality shirt the week before by a good mate who treats me like his own fashion charity case and I was keen to wear it to the match that week. The penny never dropped that this top was a turquoise colour closely matching that of the Cov home kit. I would like to think that three lads, one a shirter, would not get picked on by a gang but the intensity of the looks as I walked down Fratton Road past the packed pubs was scary. Portsmouth is still a town that a visitor needs to watch his back and certainly treat with respect. I have been coming down here for over twenty years. I love the people, I love the place but I know in my heart of hearts that I am not a Pompey lad, however much I would love to be. However, the uniqueness is its attraction. There is no place like Pompey and that's the way I want it to stay. Pompey are now in the Premiership but its fans have been in the top league for years. Portsmouth will never be a prawn sandwich experience, a knuckle sandwich on the other hand..........

INTRODUCTION

Portsmouth, a city on the South coast of England, first settled over a thousand years ago, probably most famous for being home of the Royal Navy. The City received its Royal Charter from King Richard the Lion Heart in 1194. The city coat of arms that was later adopted by the club was also a gift from the King. There has been for many years speculation as to how the city got its nickname of 'Pompey', which as everyone knows is even carried by the club. There are many reasons given although the most likely answer comes from the city's naval heritage. One of the hulks laid up in the Solent, used as a floating billet, was the captured French ship "*La Pompée*", so the sailors who were stationed on it were known as 'Pompey' sailors. Another version is that some of the Portsmouth based sailors took to climbing to the top of Pompey's pillar in Egypt. Although the reason that would probably appeal most of those involved in the activities of the 6.57 Crew, is an old naval expression 'to play Pompey' which means to wreak havoc. There is a spirit about Portsmouth people maybe due to being literally in the front line whether the country be at war with Hitler or Napoleon, both of which did their best to destroy the City (some would say they didn't try hard enough) but Pompey is a rough town populated by some rough people. It's one of those places that if you want a fight on a Saturday night then you won't have to look far for somebody happy to oblige.

In 1898, a group of local businessmen got together and decided to form a professional football club. They brought some land off Goldsmith Avenue on which was built Fratton Park and, despite the best efforts of the club in the past couple of decades, this still remains our home. Since being formed, the club have gone up and down the divisions with great highs and terrible lows. Portsmouth is a football city whose townsfolk are passionate about their team although the city has a large student population who can sometimes be seen wearing the shirt of whatever team they support. Portsmouth shirts are very much the majority in the streets around the city. Pompey have always been known for their supporters and the way we get behind our side. There is also another set of fans that are known up and down the country; known, sometimes feared, but always respected by our peers - we went by the name 6.57 Crew. For many years Portsmouth Football Club has had associated with it what the popular press may describe as an unruly element. From the days when ends were the vogue at football, it was the Fratton End boot boys. Even in those days there was a group attached to the Fratton Enders that went under the name Pompey Blue Platoon - they were seen causing trouble at many away games including when they charged the Milton Road end at The Dell in the early 1970's or, around the same time, when they rampaged at Oxford. As the years went on, so football firms evolved. There was a group at Fratton Park known as 'Harry's Gang' who took up their position in the South enclosure, right next to the away supporters' pen. Many games saw Harry's Gang in action. I can remember games against Barnsley where there were battles mainly against the police and one match against Chesterfield which saw fighting all afternoon. At the time, Pompey were in the old Third and Fourth Divisions and many games were marred with the sort of violence inside Fratton Park which nowadays is totally unimaginable. The early 1980's saw the emergence of the 'casual'.

The casual scene was a fashion born as a direct result of football hooliganism whereas, before, it was the other way round. The 6.57 Crew was one of the football gangs that prided itself on being at the forefront of the dresser stakes. What the firm was wearing became as important as running the opposition, sometimes more so. There was a case at the Portsmouth magistrates where one of the Pompey lads took in a range of designer shirts and jumpers as part of his defence. He had been arrested during a game against Leeds United. In court, he claimed that the charge of threatening behaviour was wrong as all he was doing was making fun of what the Leeds lads were wearing compared to what the southerners wore. He had brought the range of clothing to prove his point that the Leeds supporters were eighteen months behind. He was found not guilty. Along with the designer labels came fancy names as fans saw fit to add an identity to their particular firm whether it is after their own mode of transport to matches or for some other reason. No matter what the team, there is a story of how their firm got its name. West Ham seem to think that they were the ones that started this trend and that the rest of the country followed their lead after the documentary about them was shown on national television. I can't vouch for anyone else but I do know that the 6.57 Crew tag was being used by Pompey a good while before the programme went to air.

The very first game my Dad ever took me to at Fratton Park was against Hull City. I would have been about eight years old at the time and I remember that it was a warm sunny day so I suppose that it would have been at the start of the season. I don't remember very much about the game but I can picture clearly sitting on one of the crush barriers at the Milton End watching four or five Hull fans run around the pitch with a tiger skin. I have a lot to be thankful for to my Dad, not least of which he instilled my two sporting passions into me, boxing and Portsmouth Football Club. My Dad started supporting Pompey as a boy. He was lucky enough to be following them all over the country when they were undoubtedly the best team in the land. Dickinson, Froggett, Reid etc. were household names winning back to back championships, one of only a handful of teams to do this but sadly that was a lifetime ago. As well as being an avid fan of God's own team, Dad was a very accomplished boxer and went on to be an excellent coach. He was a trainer at a very good club in Portsmouth and even taught me the art of pugilism. Years later we worked together and on the long cold nights when we were at work, we would chat about the best and worst Pompey games we have seen and whether Rocky Marciano would have beaten Muhammad Ali (I still think you are wrong about that one though Dad!) We were more like very good mates than Father and son; we have always got on well but, when we worked together, it seemed to bring us closer. My Mother and Father have retired now and have moved down to Cornwall and, while I miss not being able to pop around and have a cup of tea with them (or borrow the odd tenner) whenever I'm at a loose end, I wish them both every happiness and, besides, their place will make a great base when Pompey have their annual pre-season West country tour.

My first ever away game was at Aldershot, just up the road when I was eleven or twelve. I saved my school dinner money that week and jumped on the train. The problem was I neglected to tell anyone. My parents and Portsmouth police searched the City for me. Meanwhile I was having a great time at the Recreation Ground; however the game was soon up when, at half time, a message came over the PA system to phone home. My Dad had guessed where I was after searching out most of my other haunts. My cousin Paul who is about four years older than me saw me and gave me a bit of a bollocking but I managed to give him the slip. I thought to myself well I'm here now I'll worry about the consequences later. I arrived home that evening happy as Larry after watching Pompey win 2-1. Fortunately I threw my hands up and pleaded guilty as charged when questioned by Dad. I say fortunately because I didn't know he had a crucial and damming piece of evidence for on the front page of the Sports Mail, which was bought religiously every Saturday, was a photograph of me wildly celebrating Pompey's winner next to two very pissed off looking Aldershot fans.

Dad and I always went to Fratton Park as well as the occasional away game. This however came to an end on 23rd of February 1980. A crowd of nearly 20,000 gathered to watch Pompey take on Huddersfield Town in a top of the table Division Four match. We had taken up our usual place on the Milton End terrace alongside a group of Dad's friends. The game was about ten minutes old when a group of Huddersfield fans stood in front of us. There was nothing unusual about that as the Milton End was always and still is the away end with Pompey mixed in (although the mixing part is now a thing of the past). Things were a little bit different today though. Suddenly it went off big time. A few Pompey boys had got amongst the Town fans and away it went. The big mistake the Yorkshiremen made however was to include my Dad and his mates in the fight. Now like I said, he was a good boxer but he can also have a fight outside the ring and I can see him smacking the mouthy northerners now, his pipe between his gritted teeth. The fight that day had wildly differing effects on both Dad and I. For me, it was the most exciting thing that I had ever seen and wanted to see some more; for Dad though it was the end. He had seen the very best Pompey could offer and over the years the worst. He had witnessed the very best team in England slump down the leagues until they were in Division Four. This though was the last straw for him. After the match we went home and Dad has never been to another game since.

The events in this book are true although some of the names have been changed in order to protect the guilty; however it should be remembered they are taken from the perspective of Pompey. They were how I and those around me saw things at the time. If you were there and were on the opposing side, you may well have a contradictory view of things. This doesn't make either of us wrong as all football fans, especially those who were involved in the proceedings described, tend to view things with rather rose tinted glasses. There may well be incidents that are omitted but this isn't careful spin doctoring on my part. There are three main reasons for this; either they have been discussed in depth elsewhere or there wasn't enough room in these pages (after all, over the years there have been many hundreds of incidents) or, more likely, I wasn't there and can therefore not confirm the details either way, which is not to say I was an eye witness at all of the incidents but have been able to get first hand accounts from those that can be described as reliable sources. Neither is this book a rival to Rolling with the 6.57 Crew. That book looked mainly at the Air Balloon mob who can rightly be thought of as a major part of the 'original' 6.57 Crew. I was never part of the Air Balloon lot; in fact I can only ever recall drinking in the pub on two occasions. I was part of the generation that came onto the scene slightly later just as the casual movement started to take hold across the country. Most of the Air Balloon lads were still very much involved but as their story was excellently told in Rolling, I have chosen to concentrate on the things that my generation got up to in the name of the 6.57 Crew. Over the years, whether or not we cared to admit it, there has never been a football firm who at some point or another was on the wrong end of things. Sometimes it was when we were against one of the 'top firms', sometimes it was when we visited some backwater and were taken completely by surprise and I don't care how much others try and deny it, we have all come unstuck. I don't try and say that the Portsmouth 6.57 Crew were the best or hardest football firm in the country. We weren't which is not to say we couldn't mix it with the best of them and on our day we could be a formidable force, although more times than not we couldn't organise the proverbial in a brewery. It has to be said however that for years the Six Five Seven constantly punched above its weight when you take into consideration the size of the City. Neither is it meant to glorify the incidents that are portrayed, I see it more as part of the jigsaw that makes up the era between the late 1970's and the early 1990's which was seen by many as the 'golden age' of football hooliganism. After all, during the 1950's the Teddy Boys terrorised 'ordinary' people while into the 1960's Mods and Rockers would regularly do battle. At the time, these events were greeted with horror and outrage but now they are looked back on and remembered fondly as part of British social history. Maybe one-day football hooliganism will be thought of in the same way......

Nah, I don't think so either.

1
IN THE BEGINNING, THERE WERE THE BOOT BOYS

While there was an emergence of football hooliganism towards the end of the 1960's when newspapers carried stories about football rowdies, it wasn't until the following decade that the phenomenon saw the emergence of the boot boys. While the notorious Manchester United Red Army grabbed most of the headlines closely followed by the legendary Millwall F-Troop who were made infamous by the Panorama documentary about them, supporters of clubs up and down Britain were on the rampage. The Glam rock song 'Teenage Rampage' by The Sweet was never more appropriate as clubs seemed powerless to stop this new trend of aggro, Pompey was no exception. The name of the game in the 1970's was to take the home teams end and there were a number of ways this could be achieved although to be really able to claim to have 'taken' the end should mean that the terrace in question had been stormed and the home occupiers forcibly removed. For instance, when Arsenal completed their first League and Cup double in the early 1970's, they played Pompey in one of the early rounds of the FA Cup. Some Arsenal fans claim that the Fratton End was taken that day; in truth they got in the ground more than an hour before kick-off and when the Fratton Enders finally left the pub, they mobbed up and steamed into the north Londoners. A police line was placed between the two hostile groups and sporadic fights kicked off throughout the game. So while there is no doubt that the Arsenal mob had indeed occupied the Fratton End, can they claim to have taken it? It's debatable. After the particular match in question though, Arsenal fans were terrorised as they made their way back to Fratton railway station, so probably regretted their trespass anyway. Many years later I watched a spectacular end taking at Craven Cottage and not a punch was thrown. Pompey fans forced the gate under the main stand that runs along the river. Before they had reached the other end, the Fulham fans had already fled in terror. The sight and sound of Pompey aggro was a feature at nearly every match home and away in the early 1970's. In 1972, when Pompey played Brighton for the first time in years, there was fighting inside the ground at Fratton Park and police made what they described as numerous arrests and ejected over 80 from the ground. At the return fixture the following April, fans were involved in clashes inside the ground and in the surrounding streets after the match. A very good friend and someone whom I have the utmost respect for, Johnny Madgewick, recently told me this story from that day.

'While it was going off in the town, some people were smashing windows and what have you. That wasn't my style. If we bumped into a few Brighton and they wanted it, then fair enough but I could never see the point in smashing stuff up. A friend and me ended up having a few beers where we bumped into three others from Pompey. Eventually we walked to the ground and figured that we would find everyone else in the Brighton end. We paid our money and went in to find that we were the only ones in there. Being so heavily outnumbered, we said to each other to keep a low profile. Unfortunately one of the others forgot himself when Pompey had a shot at goal and jumped up. The Brighton lot now knew who we were and it was pretty obvious that they would fancy their chances because there were only five of us. The thing was, we also knew that all of us could have a fight so we'd be able to take a couple with us. We went back to back and sure enough, in they came. The first couple to have a go were put down, then the next, it didn't take long for the rest of them to start doubting themselves and begin to back away. You have to remember that when it goes off at football the first ones to go in are the game ones, the top lads. Those that aren't so sure of themselves hold back waiting for the top boys to do some damage and then steam in to pick off the stragglers. These are the pushers and shovers. I used to love getting hold of one of these and drag them in to the punch up with me. They could either get stuck in or be used as a shield taking punches meant for me, some of them weren't much use for anything else. Besides, I've always found that the ones that are all swagger and telling everyone how hard they are, are usually the ones who can always be found at the back when it went off. After seeing their top lads go down, the rest of the Brighton mob started to hesitate and not come at us. Soon there was a big gap where we had managed to back them off. I said to my mate that if we run at them they are going have it on their toes, so we charged and to our amazement everyone one of them took off. Five of us had taken the Brighton end, we had expected the rest of the Pompey mob to charge onto the pitch and give us a hand but as it turned out, we didn't need them.'

Three and a half years on, I remember a game at Fratton Park on 27th December. I was 10 and sat transfixed as I watched hundreds of Pompey fans run across the pitch from the South enclosure and attack the Brighton fans in the Milton End. Dad and I were in the North Stand, we were usually on the terrace but I remember that this particular match he got some tickets from my Great Grandfather who for years worked on the player's entrance at Fratton Park. It was a Third Division game and a crowd of nearly 33,000 turned up to see Pompey win 1 – 0 with the darling of the Pompey fans, Dave Kemp, scoring the only goal. Kemp scored 17 goals that season after signing from Crystal Palace in November; he went on to score 32 goals in 63 appearances for the blues when, typical of Pompey, they sold him to Carlisle. A few weeks before the Christmas time clash with Brighton, Pompey had played away to Aldershot in the FA Cup first round. So serious was the fighting that police had to draft in re-enforcements from all over Hampshire and parts of Surrey before the trouble was quelled. In 1974, fighting on the Milton End terrace marred the home game with Nottingham Forrest. Afterwards the Pompey board announced measures to prevent further trouble in the stadium. These included the digging of moats at either end of the ground in order to stop pitch invasions. It didn't and what John Deacon described as a 'revolutionary' step against hooliganism by putting up fences to divide up the ground and prevent movement around it, this didn't work either. Having beaten York City 3 – 1 at Fratton Park on the previous Saturday, a win that guaranteed that Pompey wouldn't be relegated from Division Three, the blues travelled to Swindon for the final match of the season. The 1976/77 season would end as it had started in Wrexham back in August. That day, Pompey had arrived in the north Wales town in two coaches while most of the Welshmen were still sleeping off their Friday night out. By opening time, pub windows were being smashed and shops looted. Eventually the English hordes were rounded up and taken to the Racecourse Ground but this wasn't the end of the trouble. Pompey fans invaded the pitch and charged into the Wrexham end. One of the Pompey supporters appeared in court the following Monday minus his trousers which he had ripped off when he got caught on the spiked railings around the pitch. Those who appeared in front of the bench were fined a total of £525. Back in Wiltshire, 15 minutes before the kick-off, hundreds of Pompey fans swarmed over the fences and into the Swindon end. The police spent well into the first half battling with the fans and eventually forced them back to the away end. During the game, Pompey fans invaded the pitch three times causing the game to be delayed. A fan also ran onto the pitch and tried to attack referee Malcolm Sinclair. Swindon Town was the venue for Pompey's first Saturday away game the following season. Once again, there was trouble before kick-off when Pompey fans charged through the streets causing damage and chanting 'we are the greatest football hooligans'. Just before kick-off, around 150 lads paid to get into Swindon's County Road End and charged into the home fans scattering them. Despite the best efforts of the police the Pompey fans stayed in the end the whole afternoon.

Much of the 76/77 season was marred with violence. 2 Pompey fans were jailed for 3 months after Palace fans were attacked and chased following a match at Selhurst Park. This followed the week after Sheffield Wednesday had visited Fratton Park and there was serious fighting in the Milton End. After the match, Pompey fans attacked the Wednesday coaches parked in Rodney Road. Several vehicles had to make the long journey back to Yorkshire with broken windows. The relentless march of the terrace terrors went on. Once again Brighton was on the wrong end of it after Pompey fans invaded East Sussex and went on what was described by the Sussex police as 'a ten-hour wrecking spree'. Hours before the Wednesday night fixture, the trains taking them along the south coast were very badly damaged. On arrival in Brighton, the rampaging Pompey mob made their way to the seafront causing trouble and more damage in several pubs. Before the game, the Brighton lads had wisely kept a low profile but, once inside the Goldstone Ground, there was nowhere for them to hide as they were repeatedly attacked. At one point the Pompey mob took the Brighton end, running both the opposition fans and the constabulary. Although there were 100 members of the Sussex force on duty, they struggled to keep control, eventually being forced to call in extra manpower. Once the match ended with a 4 – 0 victory to Brighton, hundreds of Pompey fans surged onto the streets. House and shop windows were smashed and cars turned over as they rampaged down the street. Brighton's lads didn't want to know and, long before the final whistle blew, melted away into the darkness before the marauding mob saw them. In all, there were just 31 arrests made - all of them Portsmouth supporters. Just for good measure, the trains home were also ransacked. This truly was the age of the boot boys. Years later, nothing much had changed when, after Pompey were beaten by a single goal in a 1994 FA Cup game, Pompey and Brighton fans were involved in fighting on the pitch. Brighton fans had run onto the pitch but were sent scurrying back onto the terraces after around thirty Pompey fans went into them. It was clear that the authorities needed to stamp out the anti social behaviour on the terraces, so, in a move that in today's world would be called a zero tolerance approach, police promised to get on top of the hooligan element at Fratton Park. In home games as bizarre as Peterborough, there were 10 arrests and 14 ejected from the ground; against Port Vale the statistic was 15 arrested and, when Pompey played a mid-week match against Chester, there were 3 arrests and 4 ejections. Part of the crackdown saw a 17 year old fined £75 for swearing at the police although, to be fair, his actual words to the policeman in question were 'I'll smash your fucking nose in' so there couldn't really be any complaints. The Club also did their part by introducing a members-only travel club for away games. This was more a cosmetic campaign by the Club because, although members had to provide passport size photographs and other details when they joined, of course the vast majority of the hooligans never travelled on club organised coaches anyway as the preferred method of transport was the special trains and coaches organised by Martin Fooks. The 'Fooksie' special to Bradford is particularly legendary. Those that were on it to this day claim it was one of the best mobs that Pompey ever took away.

The train was over subscribed with hundreds making the trip. Bradford fans were waiting in a pub nearby for the special to pull in. As the column of Pompey's finest came close, they piled out of the pub clearly not expecting the numbers that greeted them. The battle was as one sided as it was brutal. Fooksie is a legendary figure among Pompey fans and is still a respected individual. During the early 1970's he was one of the first to hit upon the idea of organising transport to away games. Soon his coaches and trains were a constant feature of Pompey days out. He even hit upon the idea of organising a boat to Bournemouth. The trip was going to be a ferry leaving Portsmouth Harbour to Lymington where coaches would then take everyone on to Dean Court. Unfortunately the police got wind of the plans and the ferry company cancelled the booking. Not every game went in favour of the Pompey fans such as the time they travelled to Luton in 1974 where far stiffer opposition than expected was waiting for them in the town centre. For a while the Police clamp down started to have the desired effect. There was still trouble at away games, as Reading, Oxford, Plymouth and other places found out but, at home, at least the air of anarchy for a while began to fade away. While these events unfolded, I was just a wide-eyed kid. I witnessed the proceedings from a safe distance then re-enacted them in the playground with my friends on Monday. I decorated my bedroom with newspaper clippings much to the annoyance of my parents. Not just Pompey. I trawled the Sunday papers for reports from across the country. I was far too young and small to get too close to the real action. My time would come soon enough and eventually I'd become accepted by the 'Pompey Boys'. Until then, it would be a case of biding my time. Come Saturday, I would be stood on the Fratton End in my ten hole Ox Blood Doc's which were probably as big as I was, along with my tonic trousers and crombie overcoat, getting on the very fringes of the action after the match, without actually doing anything but as far as I was concerned I was one of the boys, a Fratton Ender. The Fratton End was the place to be, standing at the top on the right hand side as you looked down on the pitch. The atmosphere there was electric, songs such as Knees Up Mother Brown with everyone jumping up and down as one and Those Were The Days My Friend, will be forever etched onto the memory of those who gathered there.

Towards the end of the decade, the Fratton End lost some of its pulling power for the 'hardcore' boot boys as the Pompey hooligan element began to split into two factions. There were those who wanted to sing at the match yet, if the opportunity arose, get involved in the action, still massing at the top of the terrace, while those with more skulduggery in mind began to drift into the South enclosure next to the away fans in the Milton End. From here they launched assaults as well as missiles at those next to them. Myself and a few school friends loved going into this section of the ground and, while we thought we were getting in on the action, the reality of it was we weren't and most likely we were in the way. Eventually there was a distinct split in the formation of the Pompey support. There were those that loved to go to the match to support the team and have the added buzz of a good row and everyone else! Those that knew the score had this aloofness about them. We began to dress different with a distinct lack of team colours. We had our own codes of standard. Everything about us was somehow different. The 1970's were consigned to the pages of history, it was now the 1980's and the terrace culture was about to take a new direction. Along with many of those who were leaving school the same time as me, the Pompey Boot Boys were about to evolve into the 6.57 Crew, a style conscious gang of casuals as announced in The Face. It wouldn't be long before we were getting up to mischief up and down the country. This new casual look attracted a younger element so, while some of the older lads kept going, a lot of the boot boy types dropped away and the baton was passed to a new generation.

2
RITES OF PASSAGE

In the years gone by, the majority of teenage boys would leave school and immediately start a trade apprenticeship. In Portsmouth, the place to get an apprenticeship was the Dockyard which had just about every skill imaginable on offer. Along with learning skills, the first few months naive boys would run the gauntlet of pranks and of course get to do all the worst jobs on offer. There isn't a Dockyard apprentice who didn't get sent to the stores for a long weight - the store man would come back an hour or so later and ask if he had waited long enough. These sort of silly jokes were the very least the youngsters would have to face up to. At the end of the apprenticeship, the newly qualified tradesman would then face a rite of passage peculiar to the given trade, whether this is being placed in a barrel and being rolled down the steps into one of the dry docks once the cooper apprenticeship had finished or one of the many other mainly barbaric rituals. In the football hooligan world, youngsters also have to wait for their own rite of passage. Many are barely tolerated by the older more established hooligans, even though some are as game as those they look up to and, in many cases, aspire to be like. Down in Pompey during the mid to late eighties, the young firm went by their own name of 6.58 proclaiming that they were 'just a minute late'. The 6.58 were very game with a few nasty individuals amongst them. A few of them went on to be well established in the ranks. Recently a lot of the youngsters called themselves 'The House of Burberry'. The name started as a bit of a joke when their little firm came walking up the road and one of the older fellas said here comes the House of Burberry, digging them out because of their matching designer clothes. After Dad stopped going, I started to go to away matches with my Uncle Ted, travelling up and down the country in his Datsun car. However, as I got older, I started going away with my mates. My regular travelling companion was a guy named Ian, a good friend from school days. I haven't seen him for a few years but I do know that he joined the army and served with some distinction during the first Gulf War back in 1991.

Ian and myself travelled all over the country. It was the 1982/83 season, a good season for Pompey fans as we had a great side and on the way to winning the Third Division title. Money being tight, our regular method of transport was to travel to the match on club run special trains and then blag our way home on regular trains with the rest of the crew. If we were ever stopped by a train guard, we would give them some sob story of how we were told by a nasty policeman to get on this train. Given our age, the guard would understand and tell us it was alright. This of course was before the Persil Revolution where there was a deal on the Persil soap powder offering cheap rail tickets. While the bosses at Persil must have been delighted with the amount of soap powder they shifted, I wonder what they would have thought had they known that they were helping gangs of football hooligans go to war all over the country each Saturday. Eventually one of our 'must have' items was the Young Person's Railcard, an invaluable item that cost a few pounds but entitled the owner to half price travel anywhere in the country. It wasn't long before the card had paid for itself many times over. We had some great days out. One match at Preston, it went off outside Deepdale with Pompey running the home fans. Four of us were walking through the park next to the ground when we were approached by two Preston fans that were twice our age. They obviously fancied their chances with us being youngsters and started giving us the come on. Ian punched one with a sweet right hand and then booted him for good measure. The two ran off with us taking the piss out of them. Another match was Doncaster Rovers. After the game, Pompey's sizeable mob ran through the Town centre. There was no real trouble as small groups of Donny fans were off before we got too close but it did keep the coppers fit. On Doncaster station, there was a bit of a wind up of the police and Pompey scarfers that were waiting for the special. The mob started chanting 'United', 'United' and making out that we were Sheffield fans and made out as if to go for the scarfers. The police really started to panic but were even more confused when, during it, the London bound train arrived and everyone got on. It was also quite funny watching the scarfers on the platform giving it the wankers sign and shouting come on then Sheffield as the train pulled away. On the way home, it went off with Tottenham outside the Griffin Pub in Charring Cross. One Spurs lad really copped for an unfortunate one but, luckily for the Tottenham lads, the Metropolitan police's own firm, known at the time as the Special Patrol Group, waded in quickly to prevent it escalating. Later on in the season we travelled to Orient. As we came out of the ground, the police had a real sense of humour failure which made the events even funnier to us. The match was a few days after the Met had mistakenly shot Stephen Waldeck who they thought was a man by the name of David Martin who was on the run after shooting a policeman. The police stopped a yellow mini they thought was being driven by Martin and, during the arrest, shot the man five times causing a big outcry in the media. After the match which the blues lost 2 – 1 the police tried to give us an escort. As always, we had other ideas and instead broke away and started running down the street chanting 'Don't stop, you'll get shot'. The police had the right hump and started riding horses into us and whacking anyone who they got close to with their truncheons.

Pompey started a fantastic run after the defeat against Orient. The following Saturday, we beat Oxford 1 – 0 at Fratton Park then lost only twice from then to the end of the season. Included in this run was a 0 – 0 draw with Cardiff at Fratton Park in a clash between the top two teams in the division. The match was played out against a backdrop of serious crowd disorder. For such an important match it was clear that there would be a big following from South Wales. There were one or two incidents in a couple of pubs before the match but it was inside the ground that saw the worst of the bother. The match was fifteen minutes old when Pompey fans on the North terrace started fighting with the police. Everyone had turned out for this one because we knew that Cardiff would arrive in force. There was an attempt to get on the pitch in order to assault the Milton End where the 3,000 Cardiff fans were gathered and the police used dogs to force us back onto the terraces. Not that many had managed to get on anyway but the game was held up for a few minutes. The hostile atmosphere continued throughout the afternoon but the main trouble inside the ground was between Pompey fans and the police. At one point, a pig's head was thrown at the line of police facing the North terrace. At the final whistle, there was a more determined effort by our lot to attack the Milton End but again without success. Pieces of concrete were hurled at the Cardiff contingent. At first the Welshmen backed away but they then started to smash up the clock and old scoreboard that used to stand at the back of the Milton End and returned the fire. For some reason, the Cardiff fans seemed to think that the clock had some great sentimental value to Portsmouth supporters. Even years later they would chant 'Pompey, Pompey, what's the time?' In fact the clock had only been there for a couple of seasons. Originally this was where the half time scores were put up but the scoreboard fell into disrepair. Some advertising boards were nailed to it and the clock added for good measure. It was a good half hour after the final whistle that police managed to push the majority of us towards the exits. Outside the ground, there were more battles with the police as we tried to make the area safe to escort the Cardiff fans to Fratton train station with a lot of running up and down the side streets off Goldsmith Avenue to try and outwit the coppers. Eventually the police managed to get the Welshmen onto their trains and point them towards the valleys. This wasn't the end of the violence though. As the trains pulled out of the station, they were bombarded with a hail of bricks. One train in particular was badly damaged with one of the Cardiff fans suffering serious eye injuries from flying glass. It has to be said though that a lot of the Cardiff fans were more than up for it. They had brought a massive mob determined to settle a score from when Pompey had played at their place earlier that season. We had taken a mob of 400 plus to Ninian Park and had taken it to the Soul Crew all day. It was the start of a bit of a feud between the 6.57 and the Soul Crew with both turning out large firms whenever the two sides met. A few weeks later, promotion was finally clinched during a mid week match at home to Southend with Pompey beating the Essex boys 2 – 0. Now the Third Division championship was up for grabs and all we needed to do was beat Plymouth Argyle away on the last day of what had already been a very eventful season. It wouldn't be the first time that Pompey fans had brought terror to the West Country city only a couple of years before when we played at Home Park on the opening day of the 1980/81 season in a League Cup first round match. Pompey fans had started arriving in the city during the early hours of Saturday morning and trouble was erupting in many town centre pubs by lunchtime. There was fighting outside the ground as fans made their way to the match. Just before kick-off, around 200 Pompey fans scaled the fences and invaded the pitch in order to attack the Plymouth fans. One pulled up the corner flag and threw it javelin style in to the Plymouth mob. Collapsible wooden chairs were then thrown back and forth as the fans clashed. During the second half, Pompey fans on the away terrace surged forward causing part of the perimeter fence to collapse. Fortunately nobody was seriously hurt. This time thousands of Pompey fans made the trip. The whole day was billed as a time to party but in the end there was widespread mayhem. Trouble started on Friday night with fighting in both Plymouth and Torquay where there was a major fight in a nightclub hospitalising four people. Three lads were arrested on Torquay train station where 40 boys were spending the night; the lads had broken into the inspector's office and thought it would be a laugh to keep the Devon resort town awake with a bit of Karaoke over the PA system. By Saturday morning, hundreds of Pompey fans were involved in fighting and looting as they took over Plymouth town centre. There was condemnation in the papers as, on the journey down, a group of Pompey fans stopped off at Stonehenge and spray painted 'PFC Kick to kill' on the stones. As a mob numbering around 400 moved towards the ground, it again kicked off with Plymouth fans trying to keep it together but time and again getting forced back by the marauding Pompey mob. During the carnage outside the ground, the Devon & Cornwall police helicopter landed in the park in order to airlift one fan to hospital with a suspected broken skull.

Our little group spent the day wandering around Plymouth town centre taking in the sights and sounds that was the Pompey Army on the rampage. At one point, there was a queue outside an off licence, however it wasn't fans patiently waiting to be served. The shop was being systematically looted and items were being passed down the line. It was a case of the last person in line got what ever came to them. We watched as one guy ended up with a Party Seven can. With no way of getting at the beer inside, the can was soon being thrown around until it ended up going through a shop window a little further up. Eventually Ian and I entered the large covered terrace that ran the length of the pitch at Home Park. There were a few other Pompey lads there and we gathered together. One of the Pompey fans climbed onto the shoulders of his mate and unfurled a well-drawn banner of a Pompey fan holding a head and at his feet was the headless corpse of a Scummer. They started chanting 'we want heads' 'we want heads'. There were only about 30 or so of us and the first Pompey to enter the Plymouth terrace that day although there were other Pompey lads coming through the turnstiles all the time so we didn't feel threatened even though we were attracting the attention of the Plymouth fans that moved forward and got around us. The Pompey lads who we were with were battle-hardened veterans, all at least 10 to 15 years older than Ian and myself. We would have been 16/17 at the time but we had been to enough games by now to know that it was about to go off. Soon the fifty Plymouth scattered when we charged at them, quickly the Police moved in and forced us to the bottom of the terrace and behind them the Plymouth fans regrouped; a few more punches were thrown until the police steamed in with their truncheons. We climbed over the perimeter wall and onto the pitch and with the constabulary in hot pursuit, ran across the pitch and onto the terrace opposite. As I was about to jump off the low wall on the terrace, a lad went to give me a hand but pulled a little too hard. I landed heavily on my ankle, the pain was instant and I honestly thought I'd broken it. Apparently though, it was only a severe sprain, either way it bloody hurt. That was it, my fun and games for the day were had come to a premature end. During the game, there were constant pitch invasions. I never took part as I was still sulking over my ankle. Ian however charged across the pitch during one and into the fighting that was taking place on the other side. The police had by now all but given up on segregation as Pompey fans had taken over the entire ground. During the melee, Ian was grabbed from behind only to shrug his would be attacker off but was then dived on by three of the policeman's colleagues and marched around the pitch. He appeared in Plymouth magistrates on Monday morning to be fined for his part in the proceedings that had left the Devon town shell shocked.

The match eventually finished, after many hold ups, 1 – 0 to Pompey. That was the signal for more pitch invasions. I limped onto the pitch but, as I left the ground, I had a look around me. The scene was one of utter devastation. Pompey fans had gone on the rampage in a similar way to when the Jocks took over Wembley in the 1970's. Amongst other things, they pulled up the pitch and broke down the goals, causing what must have been thousands of pounds worth of damage. On the terraces, there were buckled fences and fires burned in various places. Home Park looked like the aftermath of an air raid as many Pompey fans took bits of the ground as souvenirs. Outside in the park, there was more fighting as Pompey fans continued to run amok. During the night there were further outbreaks of violence as rival fans fought each other in the pubs around the town centre but, by that time I was on the train home, my ankle was throbbing and turning all sorts of colours and my travel companion faced a longer stay in the West country than he had intended. All things considered, perhaps not the best outcome for the day but we were crowned champions. In all, there were sixty five arrests made with all those nicked being kept in custody until the Monday morning when they appeared in front of the town's magistrates. Sentences ranged from £25 fines to two months inside with the fines totalling £3,400. It's funny how the road of life has so many twists and turns. After the Plymouth trip, Ian calmed down a lot. He still went to football and was still as game when the circumstances were right but the experience and fine seemed to knock a bit of sense into him. He eventually drifted away from the football scene altogether. Maybe, had it been me that was locked up that day, it would have been Ian's name on the front of this book and not mine.

The next season would be a massive one for us because we all knew that some of the big guns of the hooligan world were awaiting our arrival and what's more we were safe in the knowledge that most of them would be marking us down for extra special attention. The second Division contained some of the top firms in the country so we knew that we would be tested most weekends. To give the club its credit, they obviously saw that we would have some stiff competition so arranged a couple of good warm up games for us. The games against London opposition saw something that we had rarely faced up to now. It went off with West Ham outside the Milton Arms with some of the top I.C.F. boys during which one of our lads was stabbed. After the police broke it up, they found half a dozen discarded knives of varying description nearby and a few days later when Arsenal visited, a Gooner was arrested outside Fratton Park again with a knife. That afternoon it kicked off in Carisbrooke Road. Thirty or so Arsenal, which included some of their most well known faces of the time, broke down a garden wall as they were fronted by a Pompey mob. However, before it kicked off the police put a wedge between the opposing gangs. It wasn't a wasted journey for the Arsenal fans though as some of them went home richer than they started the day after they robbed a turnstile operator of his takings.

The opening match of the season saw Pompey at home to Middlesbrough. The Teesiders had been relegated the previous season. Off the pitch however they had a growing reputation so a few lads decided that they would go to Waterloo station and meet them, catching them by surprise. None of us youngsters was invited to this particular outing; it was one strictly for the Air Balloon boys. It was arranged that they would meet up at the Air Balloon pub at the crack of dawn. As the first couple of carloads arrived, a van was spotted parked up nearby. Rather than wait for the others to turn up, they attacked the van. During the brief fighting, the windscreen was smashed after the driver crashed into a wall while trying to escape. After the brief skirmish, they made their way back to the pub where they found the others waiting. The trip to Waterloo proved to be a wasted journey, no 'Boro lads were seen at all so they made their way back to Portsmouth but, as they entered the city, police motor cyclists pulled the fleet of cars over. All the lads were arrested for the attack on the van. The match itself saw Pompey go down 1 – 0 and saw some of the worst refereeing ever. The only goal was scored while goalkeeper Alan Knight was laying concussed in the penalty area. The crowd was stirred up and it wouldn't take much to spark it off. This game was also the first at Fratton Park where fences were put up around the pitch, mainly as a result of the trouble during the Cardiff match the previous season. As the final whistle blew, a handful of Boro fans climbed the fence and ran onto the pitch in celebration. With emotions already running high amongst the Pompey fans, it was like a red rag to a bull. Fans poured over the fences from the North terrace and onto the pitch to get at them. Seeing that they had stirred up a hornets nest, the Boro fans scampered back onto the away terrace like something out of a Tom and Jerry cartoon as the Pompey mob snapped at their heels. It wasn't long before police dogs were being used to drive the Pompey fans back onto the North terrace where it proceeded to go off between fans and police. As we eventually started to leave the ground, someone was heard to shout. 'Summers over then, business as usual' it was a phrase that would become well known by all of us over the coming years. The Pompey chairman, John Deacon, afterwards announced that he was 'declaring war on the hooligans' starting with life bans for all those arrested. Middlesbrough has always had a well-respected mob, especially in our part of the world. Pompey and 'Boro, have had a few tear ups and we were always pretty well evenly matched. We saw them as the '6.57' of the north if you like, game as anything and would cause you some severe damage if you took them lightly. Back in 1985, we played up there in the freezing cold. Most hadn't bothered making the trip because the majority of the country was under a blanket of snow and figured there was little point going all that way for a game that would be more than likely postponed. In all, there were a little over a dozen who braved the mid winter and set off, the bulk of which were still in their teens with maybe three who were in their twenties, not really the sort of mob that you'd really want to be taking to a place like Middlesbrough. It was a long trip to Darlington but the usual game of brag broke out to see away the hours of boredom. On arrival at Darlington, the police at the station informed us that the game was off due to the weather. While we decided what to do next, a couple of Darlington fans approached and asked to tag along as we were playing their arch rivals. It was soon agreed they could. Meanwhile one of the older lads had found a phone box and had called Ayrsome Park who had insisted the game was definitely going ahead. After a drink in the pub next to the station, we boarded our connecting train. Despite our lack of numbers, none of us were nervous because travelling with Pompey back then was a matter of fact thing. We had been to so many places even as youngsters and pulled off so many stunts that we had no fear of anyone or anywhere. Our train pulled into Dinsdale to be greeted with a white wilderness. Almost as if this were the first time any of us had seen snow, we leapt off the train and into an immediate snowball fight. The train continued without us so we made our way to a nearby pub, all the way lobbing snowballs at each other. We took advantage of the warmth of the pub and settled there for a few pints before a minibus taxi was ordered which drove us to the ground. We pulled up next to the main stand and almost immediately one of the 'Boro lads approached and told us that they had been waiting for us at the main station all morning. We simply told him that we were here now.

Not bothering with the away supporter's enclosure, we went straight into the main stand, sitting at the very front at pitch level. The first half of the match passed without incident, both off and on the pitch where the players seemed just happy to stay on their feet let alone play football as the pitch was a sheet of ice. Half time couldn't come quick enough although somehow one of our lot had managed to fall asleep across a row of seats. We retreated to the relative comfort of behind the stand and stocked up on hot drinks in an attempt to thaw out.

During the half time interval, a small group of 'Boro who were hanging around outside the ground began arguing with us through a black iron fence. Someone threw a coffee over the mouthiest of them which set the tone for later. With the game resumed, we retook our seats in the sparsely populated stadium Only 6000 or so had been foolish enough to brave the cold and the football on offer wasn't the type to get the blood pumping either. With twenty minutes to go, we began to notice 'Boro's mob starting to drift into the seats behind us. In particular, a tall black lad with an afro wearing a ski coat sat around ten rows behind us looking down with others in the seats around him. As more 'Boro began to come in, the tension began to mount and the adrenaline was starting to flow around our bodies for the first time that day. Eventually one of our older lads stood up and said that rather than wait for them to start, we should take the fight to them. We got up and went into the 'Boro mob, taking them a little by surprise at first. We held our own as the fighting began to spill out onto the pitch as more 'Boro began to join in. By this time, we were fighting around by the dugouts and one or two of the

Pompey players were trying to break it up. As the final whistle brought the dreary game to an end, a Mexican stand off ensued with Pompey on the edge of the pitch and 'Boro in the walk way at the front of the stand. Middlesbrough fans were now coming onto the pitch from all sides of the ground so we made a move to one of the goalmouths. 'Boro were soon there with us swapping punches but now their numbers were too much for us so we headed towards the safety of the away terrace. Once there, we began laughing as others now joined us to give their view of what had gone on. As was the norm at the time, we were held in the ground for a while. Eventually we headed into the street but, before we got too far, a group of 'Boro came across the road to meet us. A small scuffle broke out but it was soon brought to an end by the police. We were then escorted to the station and put aboard our train without further incident. We continued our journey home discussing the day's events and planning for the next trip. We got back to Waterloo and time for a quick pint in the Wellington, grab a bag of chips and jump on the last train home arriving back home 18 hours after leaving it for our 600 mile round trip but that is what we lived for, week after week.

The flash-point games kept coming thick and fast. September saw a trip to Ninian Park after which the South Wales police described the match as one of the worst they'd had to police. The constabulary also acknowledged that neither set of fans were innocent in the days proceedings. As if to labour that point, 44 arrests were made, 22 from each side. We arrived as usual by normal service train only to be stopped and searched by police waiting at the station for our arrival. There was also a large Soul Crew presence watching our every move. After we had been searched and given the usual warnings, our mob was pointed in the direction of a pub where it wasn't long before our hosts joined us. The pub was totally wreaked with every window, glass and stick of furniture smashed and what can only be described as a good old-fashioned toe-to-toe taking place outside. At the ground, the police claimed that they were 'tricked' by the hooligans who were wearing 'respectable' clothes as both mobs got into the main stand with each other but police, sensing something wasn't quite right, managed to move us out before anything happened. After the match, Cardiff fans threw stones into the away end from neighbouring gardens. They also lay in wait for us as we were being escorted to Cardiff Central train station. As the bricks rained down on us, we tried our best to try and break free from the police escort but were beaten back by the police who seemed as happy to crack our heads as the Soul Crew were. It was around this time, firms across the country started to hand out calling cards. Pompey were no exception. Ours summed up the mood of the time, it simply read Portsmouth 6.57 Crew, Business As Usual.

A couple of weeks later came the long trip to Newcastle. A big firm went up to North East and even though it meant leaving in the middle of the night, we arrived early and stormed into the Newcastle firm in a pub by the train station. The Geordies were incensed by the cheek of it. They clearly had not expected a mob to travel that far in enough numbers not only to take the battle to them but more than able to put them onto their back foot for a while. Throughout the match the Geordie fans hung over the fences, running their fingers across their throats and pointing towards the street. We just laughed at them. After all, we had them on their toes earlier so idle threats from behind a fence weren't going to frighten us. As usual, once the final whistle blew, we were kept in the ground while the police cleared the streets. They did a good job as we didn't see a soul until we got back to the main station in the city centre where it kicked off again. This time, honours were more even but by then we had already done what we had intended to do.

During the journey home, Chelsea's firm were taken by surprise as our train pulled into Doncaster station. They were waiting on the platform. A roar went up from the train which was amplified by the station roofing. The Chelsea lads must have wondered what the hell was going on. Many of them ran towards the exits without really knowing why. We tried to get off the train but were held back by the transport police who were franticly signalling the driver to get moving. The train pulled away leaving the Headhunters regaining their composure. We got back to Kings Cross first and waited for them knowing that they would be in on the next train but obviously the transport police were having none of it and made sure we were all cleared out of the station before the train arrived.

It had been a long and eventful day but we were well on the way to putting the 6.57 Crew on the map. Our confidence was sky high and we had a feeling of invincibility knowing we could muster big numbers for games just about anywhere in the country but, not only were we turning out in force, we could also inflict damage to our rivals.

It was during the home game against Newcastle later on that season that I really came of age. As usual in those days, I was in the main shopping centre just before midday with a few other lads my age when a couple of the older fellas came running down to say that a mob of Newcastle were on the way. It had gone off in a few of the pubs in Southsea the night before so really there should have been more of the older firm about. There could be no excuses. They knew they were in town because they had been fighting them. Ten of us started to walk up towards the train station when we saw this mob of around thirty Geordies running up back towards the train station. The Geordies had just set about three Pompey lads and had given them a bit of a kicking; the three lads joined us, one of them had a spilt a bit of claret and was itching to get his own back. We continued on to the City Arms pub opposite Portsmouth & Southsea train station. As soon as we got there, we could see that inside the Geordies were going to town on a handful of Pompey. We charged in led by the guy who had earlier been attacked to try and help the out. The Geordies were hefty guys and we were soon involved in desperate fighting. Us youngsters did as best as we could but were a bit out of our depth. We were wedged by the doors, the punches we landed bounced off them whereas theirs really hurt but at least we had given it a good go. It was noticeable that one or two of the established lads had shot off leaving the rest of us to it, something I know that to this day annoys the guy that led us into the fray as we have become good friends. During the battle, a few of the lads from Hayling turned up and soon pitched in. Glasses, ashtrays and stools flew around the pub. Police vans began to pull up and restore order. To be honest, nobody from our crowd were sorry to see the boys in blue turn up as I don't think we could have held our own for much longer. I looked around to make sure my mates were okay; they were although, like myself, they had the odd lump and bump but everyone was fine and even though we were showing the odd sign of battle, we were elated and were proud that we had stood our ground against the odds even if the temptation had been there to bolt.

We made our way to the Sir Robert Peel pub close by. While we couldn't say that we had beaten the Geordies, we were able to hold our heads up knowing we had done our bit. As more lads arrived, news of the earlier trouble spread. A guy that wasn't at the City Arms started making snide remarks about us young guns being in the way. However, one of the top boys who was involved in the earlier action defended us saying that we had done well. This made our day, our chests swelled with pride as we stood having a pint with them. A few lads our age came into the Peel and were gutted that they had missed out. We excitedly told our stories, adding bits for extra impact. We had arrived. The more recognised lads began to accept us. Before now, we had been involved but on a larger scale. Now we had proved that we would not take to our toes when the odds were stacked. Surreally, during the fighting, I can remember the Frankie Goes To Hollywood song Relax playing on the Juke Box in the City Arms; even now I get a headache when I hear this song.

After the match two mobs numbering around 40 or 50 went at it in Priory Crescent, neither side budged an inch. I've always rated Newcastle as being among the most game I have come up against over the years. I have been to St. James' Park on a few occasions and, while I don't buy into the media thing about them being the most passionate fans in the land, they love their football and it seems to me that most of them are up for a row.

Just after Christmas was a trip to Stamford Bridge, a game that we had all been looking forward to all season. Chelsea we knew were among the top firms in the country at the time and everyone had marked this game down to put on a show of force in the capital. We caught the nine o'clock train to Waterloo. As soon as the train started to pull into the station, people began to excitedly jump off the moving train as it slowly pulled up to the platform. We were fully expecting a welcoming committee from West London and couldn't wait. We rushed onto the concourse. At the same time, another large mob appeared at the other end of the station. The shout of 'Here they are' filled the air and, without hesitation, we ran straight at them. The two firms charged at each other at least both 300 strong. This was why we were here, our fledgling mob, in the capital to do battle with one the most established and respected mobs in the country on their own ground. At this point, a transport police officer was seen to dive for cover with the words 'Fuck this, let them get on with it'. As the two firms were about to do battle, we started to recognise faces on the other side, the other mob began to do the same. Suddenly, it began to dawn on us both, these mobs were Pompey. On the train we had been looking around at what was a good mob, now as the two mobs joined and went down towards the underground, we had an outstanding mob. Today we'd be untouchable. We had arrived.

The police understandably were having none of it. As our tube train pulled into Earls Court, only the front carriage pulled up to the platform. It was a good ploy by the police as it stopped us rushing out as a mob. Eventually we all managed to get out onto the street but we were being tightly marshalled towards Stamford Bridge. There was verbal coming from the Headhunter boys who stood watching and there were one or two half hearted attempts from both sides to get at each other. The police though were very much on top of the situation and we were put in the ground without too much fuss. The atmosphere inside the stadium was cracking. Either side of the away end there were Chelsea mobs in the seats chanting and taunting us. We were giving just as much back. This could get very interesting.

The game finished 2-2, after which like every where else in the country the police tactic was to hold us back in the ground. However, some of us had different ideas. We managed to get into the East stand. Looking back, we noticed others following and about 150 of us ran into the now empty Shed end. Unfortunately, the daring outbreak was thwarted when the police managed to roundup all of us again once we had got out into the street. The Chelsea firm was expected to be at Waterloo but it didn't happen. We were left feeling a little disappointed on the way home. We had taken one of the best mobs most of us had seen to Chelsea but nothing had happened. At least it showed that Pompey were now serious players on the hooligan stage. By the time April came around, and the season was beginning to draw to a close, Pompey were in a mid table position and the season was beginning to drag. On the other hand, Chelsea travelled to Fratton needing a win to secure promotion. Being so close to going up, the Londoners brought massive support with them; as a result there was trouble all over the town. As early as 10 o'clock in the morning, travelling fans hung around waiting for the pubs to open with the odd slap dished out. At this point Chelsea were in dribs and drabs all over the place and some were picked off. One lot were outside the City Arms and a couple of the Hayling lads went into them. Myself and another of the lads from Hayling had a bit of handbags with two Chelsea near Portsmouth & Southsea station. Apparently the two London boys had been split up from their mates and one of them had had his designer jumper nicked. They approached us but it was one of those nothing incidents and was broken up by a transport copper who told us to go away in no uncertain terms. During the afternoon, Chelsea fans were taking in the sea air on Southsea seafront, there were clashes all over the resort.

One clash saw around 30 or so of us chased for what seemed like miles by a top Chelsea firm. We had earlier left the Sir Robert Peel and made our way to Southsea. As we stood near South Parade Pier, a group of Chelsea lads came off of the beach. As we went towards them, a roar went up as their mates joined them. We wouldn't have stood a chance as we were outnumbered around three to one so the sensible thing was to go. At one point we made a stand near a building site. As they came around the bend, we threw bricks and other stuff at them. While they backed away at first, it simply seemed to make them angrier and they charged at us again. Another mob of Pompey met up by the fairground on the seafront and fared a bit better than us when they took it to some Chelsea on the common giving them a bit of a toeing. It would be impossible to say whether this was the mob that had chased us earlier as there were mobs of Londoners all over the place but reports were coming in all day of different battles. You would bump into someone who would say 'We've just run Chelsea's firm in Commercial Road' and two minutes later someone else would come along and say 'We've just been battered by Chelsea's firm in Palmerston Road' It was like that all day. Later on, the Chelsea's main firm containing all their well known faces, a good mob probably 200 plus, were in the Parade Pub opposite Southsea common. By now however, the Pompey numbers in the Sir Robert Peel had risen to the same and we were on the march. Avoiding the main roads so not to get spotted by the Police who, as you can imagine were out in force, we managed to get within striking distance of the Parade. At around 6pm, the attack went in. Being a hot day, a lot of the Chelsea were outside drinking and were the first to come under attack. The Chelsea mob poured out of the pub and both sets of fans went toe to toe. Not too long after the start of the battle, the first police units began to arrive and it wasn't long before the police had the situation under control. Some say honours were even, others Pompey were on the back foot; either way it was one of those battles that wasn't for the feint of heart. The Old Bill rounded up the Chelsea mob while they pushed us away from the area. The police then set about escorting both sets of fans towards Fratton Park. They took the Londoners down Waverley, Lawrence and Fawcett Roads while the Pompey lads were marched down Victoria Roads North and South and, while the police blocked off side roads that linked the two main routes, they had forgotten that the two roads merge at Fratton Bridge, Doh! One Chelsea fan was given a real beating after he had got cut off from his mates; I personally thought that the shoeing that he received was more than a little out of order. While all this was going on, it was going off between Pompey and Chelsea fans in Commercial Road. There was one nasty clash outside the Mighty Fine pub that left two Chelsea fans with stab wounds. Although neither were seriously injured, it still left a bit of a chill among many as it wasn't something a lot of us condoned.

Once inside the ground, neither set of fans could get near each other but, after Chelsea threw away the lead and blew their chance of promotion (it was great to know that it wasn't just Pompey that were masters of this fine art!), their fans were a little pissed off so much so those in the South stand decided to rearrange the furniture by throwing the seats on the pitch. I read recently that during this, there was a line of police on the touch-line to prevent a pitch invasion and while yes there were police on the touch-line, I would love to have seen the Chelsea fans invade the pitch from a stand that is thirty feet off the ground. Maybe it was the 1st Headhunter parachute division. While the Chelsea fans in the ground were pelting the police with all manner of objects, many of their acquaintances were being forced to run the gauntlet of our mob. We knew that it would soon be time for the main event though. Soon the proper Chelsea mob were coming at us in waves, literally hundreds of them steaming in, many flashing blades. We did as best as we could but soon found ourselves being overwhelmed as the Headhunters forced us backwards. Eventually we did start to get it together and started going back at them. Fighting was taking place everywhere. At one point a Chelsea fan was thrown through the window of an antique shop in Milton Road but their numbers took their toll and we were forced to retreat time and again. It was late into the night before the trouble died down with small fights taking place in Indian Restaurants and on Southsea seafront after the night-clubs closed. The violence had lasted all day and, while we had given it a good go, Chelsea had come down in such numbers that we found that we had been unable to cope We had a few minor victories but, on the whole, it was the Chelsea boys that could go home in satisfaction. I suppose you have to be in it to win and could hold our heads up that while we had been beaten on the night, it was Chelsea's proper firm that had done it and they had been given a run for their money.

3

THERE IS A TEAM IN HAMPSHIRE...

I feel it only fair to say that, while there is no love lost between the supporters of Portsmouth and Southampton Football Clubs, the far larger 'hooligan' element where these two teams are concerned is connected with Portsmouth. I have no idea why this is. The cities are roughly the same size in population and Southampton has some very tough estates, equally as rough as any in Portsmouth or any other city for that matter. Many of the hooligan type fans that follow Southampton have often mused as to why their club has never really had a large hooligan following while their hated rivals twenty or so miles down the road have. It should also be noted that the following chapter is of course from the Portsmouth 6.57 Crew perspective of things. It would be wrong to say that every time the two sets of fans have clashed that Pompey always had the upper hand as of course we didn't.

Local derbies are things of legend in football. No matter what team we support, we all have a rival that regardless of anything we simply must not lose against them. Some of the games are famous world-wide, such as Rangers versus Celtic or Liverpool against Everton. Others are more local affairs that pass almost unnoticed by everyone else. Regardless of the scale, every fan feels that their rivalry is bitterer, more fierce and far more passionate than anyone else's. On the South coast of course is the little matter of Pompey and Southampton. It is fairly well known that Pompey fans refer to Saints as Scummers and it makes me laugh when I hear supporters of other clubs that have started calling their rivals Scummers; there was an absolute storm in the papers when the half time scoreboard at Norwich proclaimed that the Scummers (Ipswich Town) were losing. Whereas other clubs may call their rivals this because they feel that it sounds good, in Portsmouth, it is much deeper seated. Both cities have large docks. A while back, there was there was a strike for better working conditions and better pay. The strike was solid and beginning to take effect but then one place started back to work and gradually the strike crumbled. The furious Portsmouth Dockers looked at the initials of Southampton Company Union Men, and immediately labelled these scabs, 'Scummers' and the docks and town in which they lived 'Scum', the name has stuck ever since. For many years there has been an enormous rivalry between the two ports but I am at a loss as to why. Portsmouth has for centuries been the home of the Royal Navy. Thousands of warriors have left our shores in order to do our country's bidding, the Empire was forged with Pompey gunboats. HMS Victory, HMS Warrior, HMS Ark Royal, all names synonymous with Portsmouth. The D-Day landings were planned and launched from here. Years later, HMS Hermes led the Task Force out of Portsmouth harbour to retake the Falkland Islands. Portsmouth's number one export has always been war; Southampton on the other hand is the home of fruit, veg and transit vans.

In September 1974, a train carrying around 300 Pompey fans to an away game at The Dell was wreaked. So bad was the damage that when the train pulled into Southampton station, all on board were arrested and held at Southampton Central police station until after the game had finished although only five were actually charged with any offences. This was a tactic that would be used in a Pompey vs. Southampton match thirteen years later. Smashing up trains nowadays would be frowned upon as being unnecessary but in the 1970's, it was part and parcel of the hooligan scene, much to the annoyance of British Rail. For instance, Brighton fans on their way to a match at Fratton Park in 1972 caused so much damage to two trains, they had to be taken out of service. September 1975 saw more serious outbreaks of trouble at a Hampshire derby, once again played at The Dell. Pompey were 3-0 down and, as the forth goal went in, around 300 Pompey boys left the ground and headed straight for the Scum end charging in and sending the Southampton fans scattering. After the police forced the Pompey fans back out onto the street, the fans went on the rampage smashing windows and fighting with police. The police were criticised that, despite having 250 officers on duty, they were unable to prevent the trouble. On the pitch, the Scummers would have the last laugh at us for a while. When they played at Fratton Park in April 1976, their 1-0 win relegated Pompey to the Third Division. Towards the end of the game when the exit gates were opened, hundreds of Portsmouth fans stormed into the away fans stood on the Milton End and many Southampton fans were hurt during the ferocious attack. Before the game, around 100 Southampton fans had cheekily gone into the Fratton End. Their audacity had become their undoing however because they were soon swamped by Pompey fans and were sent packing. After the match, Saints fans were forced to run the gauntlet of rampaging home fans and many were injured as they were attacked on their way back to their transport. To rub salt into the wounds while the blues were to finish bottom of Division Two, a matter of weeks later the Scummers went on to win the FA Cup with an off side goal by Pompey born Bobby Stokes. The sad demise of Pompey meant that the fixture was now a thing of the past. The Hampshire derby would not be played in a competitive match for another eight years.

The FA Cup is always special to football fans. There is nothing like waiting to see who your team draws. I remember being huddled around the radio with workmates one Monday lunchtime in 1984, fingers firmly crossed. Pompey came out of the hat first - great another home draw. In the previous round, we had beaten Grimsby at Fratton. Then we heard 'will play.... Southampton'. A cheer went up and that was it, not much work was done that afternoon as we discussed what we thought would happen both on and off the pitch. After the cup draw was announced, Portsmouth was buzzing. As soon as the tickets went on sale, the queues stretched back for what seemed like miles. Myself and another mate went AWOL from our work as trainee painters for the morning. We arrived at the ticket office well before dawn but were by no means at the front of the queue. As fans clamoured to get their place in the ground, the black market around the city pubs did a roaring trade with tickets changing hands for ten and twenty times their face value. Of course the papers had to have their say. The local Portsmouth evening paper went into detail night after night about what the police tactics would be. Even the tabloids got in on the act with a back page banner headline that screamed 'SCUM CUP RECORD BANNED'. A local comic/folk singer named Shep Woolley had made a record bestowing the virtues of all things Pompey. The ditty had a line in it which went something like 'You can keep your Scummers, you can keep your Aldershot, cause Pompey's got the lot' The moral majority were horrified. If this record wasn't taken off the shelves immediately, there would be riots on match day because of it. Pompey stopped selling the disc at the club shop until the offending line was removed. I felt it only right that the record be banned for being offensive to the ears. Mind you, when Shep jumped on the Championship bandwagon in the 2002/03 season by re-releasing the tune, it was sold in the Pompey shop, 'Scummer' line and all. Finally after weeks of waiting and preparation, it was match day. I had a driving lesson about 8 am that morning. I explained to the instructor that I would be busy after 10 o'clock so it would have to be an early start. I can remember that the city seemed a lot quieter than usual as if the whole town was holding its breath. By 11.30, reports that the opening salvos had been fired started coming over the grapevine. A train making its way into the city stopped at a red light next to the King George V playing fields in Cosham in the North of Portsmouth. Because of the big match that afternoon, the local league sides had elected to play in the morning. These games were in progress when the train stopped. A few Scummers inside the train leaned out of the windows and began to shout abuse at those playing football. The games came to an immediate halt as the players ran towards the train. Players, supporters and even a couple of the referees then proceeded to brick the train.

36,000 crammed into the ground. This was the official attendance although I know for a fact that a few lads without tickets dropped the turnstile operator a fiver each and jumped over in order to watch a tense game with few chances for either side. The Scummers were crammed into the Milton End terrace. For years they claimed that they had a mob of around two hundred pushed against the fence where they taunted the Pompey fans on the North terrace which was packed, sardine like with lunatics. Photographs however prove this to be wrong. While the Southampton support filled the other two sections of the Milton End to near bursting point, the section next to the north terrace wasn't full and there was a large gap where the two parts of the ground met with police only lining the Portsmouth side of the fence. This game, almost like no other before it, had attracted just about every face the City and beyond had to offer as if a clarion call had been made to rise up and repel a hated enemy. Throughout the entire match, both the Southampton players and supporters were bombarded with all manner of things; coins, golf balls, cans and bottles. At one point from somewhere behind where I was standing, somebody threw an empty beer bottle. As it arced through the air, the eventual victim watched as if hypnotised as the bottle sailed towards him, eventually hitting him on the forehead. The Scummer, like many others left the ground with the help of the St. Johns Ambulance.

The match went first this way and then the other, a typical blood and thunder local derby cup tie. There wasn't that much in it when the ball went out for a throw in. Mark Dennis stood with his back to the North terrace. As he went to take the throw, he dropped as if pole axed as a two pence piece bounced off his head. As he writhed around in agony, I half expected the bench to send over a priest to administer the last rites rather than the man with the magic sponge! Seeing the way this so called soccer hard man went down, I have often wondered why the Ministry of Defence spend billions of pounds developing various weapons when all they need do is issue each soldier with a catapult and a pocket full of loose change. Mind you, after the match, he did comment that as a Millwall fan he could kind of understand the Pompey fans. It was in the resulting injury time when Scum scored the only goal of the game. The goal was scored by Steve Moran who was once decked in a Southsea nightclub by Dave Leaworthy who at the time was on Pompey's books; he was later to play for Tottenham amongst others. The club along with the local paper later offered a £200 reward for information leading to the conviction of the coin thrower. The reward was never claimed.

Shortly after the final whistle, Pompey fans poured out of the ground and towards Goldsmith Avenue, an unruly mass intent on getting at its enemy. It was obvious that there was no way that the police were going to allow this crowd to hang around here for long so, after a short stand off, a line of police ten deep backed by dog handlers just itching to let their canine ball biters loose on the rabble in front of them, started to force us in the direction of Fratton railway station. It wasn't long before running battles broke out with the police. During this, a Naval Provost van appeared. The Naval Provost are a common sight in the town where they patrol, picking up errant matelots who have got themselves into some sort of bother. The NP's are also used by the police for back up on Friday and Saturday nights and so have police radios. The NP's are never used at football as they would become an automatic target. I can only assume that the NP's had heard what was going on, on their radios and decided to be nosey. Soon the van was engulfed in the Pompey mob, every window was smashed and it was only the fact that the driver floored the accelerator sending people diving for cover that they escaped without serious injury. It was very similar to the pictures of the Poll Tax riot in Trafalgar Square when the police car drove into the middle of a civil war and the officers inside were lucky to escape with their lives.

The human mass reached Fratton Bridge and tried to make a stand here but the law needed to get the Pompey followers well away from the area around the station as it would be obvious that as soon as there was any sight of the Southampton escort coming into view then the marauding mass would attempt to surge through the wall of police. The police really had no choice but continue to push the fans into Fratton Road battling every step as they came under constant attack from concrete paving slabs, bottles and all manner of other objects. Knowing that the ploy was to get them away from the station area, the horde suddenly broke away and ran down Fratton Road smashing shop windows as they went. Personally I have never seen the sense in doing this kind of thing so can honestly say I took no part in it. In minutes, thousands of pounds worth of damage was caused. The police were almost powerless to prevent this orgy of destruction and could only look on as the mob took on a momentum of its own, smashing everything in its path. The police were almost relieved that the events had taken this turn as now the Pompey mob had taken on two forms; those that were intent on getting at the Scummers and those that were intent on causing pointless damage. As the vandals continued smashing their way along Fratton Road, the 'hoolies' that weren't distracted from the job in hand attempted to get to Fratton station via the back streets. Our efforts were continually thwarted by the efforts of the police. At around 6.15, the police decided that it was now safe enough to allow the Southampton fans to leave the ground. Surrounded by hundreds of police, they were escorted the short distance from the ground to Fratton train station. While this was happening, other police officers were still stretched as the back streets around the station were still a battleground. It was getting on towards eight o'clock before the last police units could be stood down but the cost was huge. Thousands of pounds worth of damage had been caused; there had been 59 arrested and 18 fans and police taken to hospital. Some of those arrested were sentenced to 90 days inside at a special sitting of the Portsmouth Magistrate's Court. When quizzed about the relatively small amount of arrests, the officer in charge on the day of the match said that there were too many people committing too many offences and not enough officers to cope.

Due to the differing fortunes of the two clubs, Hampshire derbies for many years became the exception rather than the norm and given the severity of the violence that has occurred when the teams have played, it was probably wise that the police have taken the stance that, unless the two teams draw each other in the cup or play in a league match, the two clubs should not meet. This decision came about after Pompey goalkeeper Alan Knight had his testimonial game against the Scummers at Fratton Park. Before the game, a large mob had gathered in the Froddington Arms. We waited and waited for any sign of the Scum firm to turn up. They didn't. A couple of spotters had travelled to Southampton to keep an eye on movements. A few of their lot had gathered in a pub opposite the main train station and, early on, things looked quite promising, however for whatever reason they decided not to travel.

Back in Portsmouth, it soon became clear that today it just wasn't going to be, some drifted away to the game while others stayed in the pub. The match itself came and went peacefully. What support Southampton did have at the game were not lads and therefore didn't get a second glance, however afterwards, a large crowd gathered outside the away fans' exit. The majority of the 6.57 Crew lads couldn't see the point in all this as the Inside Crew were living up to their name and were safely inside their front rooms. The police became agitated by this crowd of mainly scarfers and onlookers chanting at the Saints support still in the ground and started forcing them into Goldsmith Avenue. there were one or two clashes in Goldsmith Avenue but nothing major. Soon most got bored and retired to the pub. Once again, the Froddington was packed with a line of police on the other side of the road. Later on, the police claimed that they were under a constant bombardment of bottles and glasses from the pub. While I am not in a position to say that nothing was thrown at the police, I can say I never witnessed this happening but then the police wouldn't make up something in order to justify their actions, would they? Soon the police entered the pub, truncheons drawn and demanded that it be cleared. What I saw next was almost unbelievable. A pitched battle erupted in the pub. Glasses, bottles and pub furniture were thrown backwards and forwards by both the Pompey fans and the some of the police with anybody unfortunate enough to get near a policeman being assaulted with a truncheon. The police reaction that evening was totally over the top. At one point, I was backed into a corner by a copper and despite the fact I was offering him no resistance, I was hit several times by him with his truncheon. I had always been brought up by my parents to respect those in authority but, after years of going to football and seeing the boys in blue acting like bully boys hiding behind their uniform, I can say that I have little or no time for any of them.

The pub was cleared but, needless to say, it just kicked it off in the street. If the police hoped that the incident would go unnoticed, they were wrong.

Sitting in the pub having a quiet drink were a group of local councillors who soon demanded to know why the police had taken the action they did. Despite a bit of an outcry in the local paper, the whole thing though was soon brushed under the carpet.

No matter what steps the authorities take, sometimes it seems fate brings the two sets of supporters together. Two such occasions were in London. England played a friendly against Holland. This match is widely documented in other books but, suffice to say, with wide rumours that the Dutch were going to turn up at Wembley mob handed just about every football firm in the country turned up in the Capital that day. On the whole, peace had broken out between the rival factions, apart from one or two domestic scores that were being settled around the West End. Once at Wembley, it soon became clear that the Dutch had not travelled over and the united England mob soon fractured and the scene around the national stadium soon resembled the 1970's film 'The Warriors' with crews of varying sizes looking to see what the next move would be. That night Pompey had a fair size mob so we weren't unduly worried. The majority of us didn't have tickets for the game so made our way to a pub for the evening and most didn't even bother when there was a surge on the turnstiles which resulted in a lot of people getting in for nothing. On the whole, the night was uneventful and so, after meeting up with those that had watched the game, it was back to Waterloo and to the Wellington pub, our regular watering hole before the last train home. While the first few pints were still being pulled, one of the boys came running into the pub shouting Scum are upstairs in the station. No one could quite believe it. There had been no sign of them in the usual haunts and certainly nobody had seen them at Wembley. We quickly made our way up onto the station concourse and there, true enough, looking up to see the time of their train was the Inside Crew. Straight away, we took the fight to them and a huge battle erupted. For a short while, the Scummers were giving as good as they got as chairs flew along with the fists. Eventually they started to back off. There was however little pockets of resistance as some of their more experienced lads attempted to rally the rest which kept sparking it off. In due course, the Saints fans were forced to try and seek refuge in their train. One of the our lads grabbed a step ladder and put through one of the windows but the Southampton boys weren't interested and stayed in the relative safety of the train while the transport police moved in.

Another time Pompey were drawn away to Crystal Palace in the FA Cup, not usually a game that attracts a big mob. This day however saw a massive firm travel to Selhurst Park. It had nothing to with anything the Eagles had to offer more to the fact that Scum were also in the Capital that day for their cup clash with Tottenham. The first clash of the day was in Covent Garden. As we were walking along Charring Cross Road, we were approached by a small group of what turned out to be Crewe Alexandra supporters. They asked a couple of lads if they were Pompey and, when they said they were, the Crewe fans explained they had just been fronted up by a large firm of Scummers outside the Nags Head pub. It appears that they had thought that the Alex lads were Pompey. Needing no second invite, everyone made their way to the pub and launched an attack. The Scummers came out of the pub led by one with a blade who was wildly waving it about trying to slash anyone who came near. The result of this being Pompey began to back away. One of the 6.57 lads went to CS gas him but the can was pointing in the wrong direction and he succeeded only in gassing everyone around him. For his troubles, he ended up receiving a minor slash wound on his hand which considering how bad it could have been, he got off lightly. It was then on to plan 'B'. Another lad grabbed a litter bin and smashed it over the knife wielding Scummers head. Everyone rushed forward and into the Southampton mob. The fighting raged back and forth. The Southampton mob throwing glasses and like as they came out of it. It was claimed elsewhere that the fighting in Covent Garden on this day was arranged beforehand. This however is not the case.

Once the game at Selhurst was over, everyone headed straight for Waterloo. Luckily, Millwall must have had a decent game away somewhere that day or else there would have more than likely the usual flare up with them at London Bridge. That particular rivalry would have to wait for another day. Not surprisingly, the Pompey mob got back to Waterloo long before the Scummers arrived from North London. So as not to attract the attention of the BTP, most of the lads waited around either by the taxi ranks or in the car park that used to be at the far end of Waterloo station. About half an hour went by then the Scum firm started to appear up the escalator from the underground. At first they seemed a little apprehensive but, when they saw there was no welcoming committee, they started to swagger. The Scummers mobbed up by WH Smiths and started to decide what their next move would be. Word went out around that they were here so about twenty of us walked onto the concourse and fronted up the Scummers in an attempt to lure them out. This was more like it, they must of thought, 100 of us, 20 of them. They started to take the bait as we quietly tried to walk them to the station exit by the car park. However, when they were still ten yards short of the exit, they must of sensed a set up. The Scummers started to bounce up and down; 'Come on Pompey, let's fucking have it' they screamed. We then tried to bring them to the car park but it was too late. In a millisecond, the BTP were on to it and were pushing the Scummers back towards the middle of the station. 'You're shit Pompey, you had it on your toes' they shouted. Yeah what ever. Suddenly, a massive roar went up as the rest of the firm came steaming into the station but, before anything could happen, the BTP had the situation under control and not a single punch was thrown. We regrouped in the Wellington while others went up to try and persuade the Scummers to come out to play. Despite several attempts by Pompey to get at the Scummers, the police thwarted all efforts and most of the Scummers got on their train and went home once it was clear that nothing more was going to happen.

In the nearby Hole In The Wall pub, three of the lads did do battle with a group of them in the doorway after most of our lot split into smaller groups and going out in the West End. As we made our way back to the station for the trip home much later on, about thirty of us bumped into a mob of Southampton with similar numbers by the Casey Jones burger place on Waterloo station. Most of the Saints fans legged it, leaving one of their mates to get a kicking. Just like they had when we clashed after the Holland game, they rushed onto a train. Fortunately for them the train was the type with electronic doors so, as we banged on the doors and windows, the guard kept the doors locked. The Scummers on the train didn't want to know. A couple hid behind chairs although some did gesticulate, locked safely inside. Surely, if they really want it, why had they so quickly taken to their toes barely two minutes after they had been swaggering across the station giving it the big 'un?

We were drawn with them again in the FA Cup in 1996, only this time at The Dell. This time, the day passed without incident. We had been given less than 2000 tickets but, in spite of this, many of us managed to get our hands on them. Talk in advance of the game was that we would have to keep it together or we could be in trouble. It wasn't that we were all that bothered about them; we just figured that they may try and take advantage of their bigger numbers. As it was, we had the place to ourselves. I remember sitting in Burger King in Southampton city centre, three hours before kick-off, recognising plenty of Pompey faces hanging around but no locals. How embarrassing for the Scummers. For crying out loud, they go around the country saying how much they hate Pompey yet, this day, firms of Pompey walked around their town as if it were a home game and the sight of one of the Pompey lads stood outside of The Dell on his own, arms folded, abusing each and every Scummer that walked past him without anyone so much as wanting to make eye contact with him just about summed up the situation. On the pitch, we were once again let down by the players and were on the end of a miserable 3 – 0 drubbing. During the match the home fans to our right looked like they had a few handy lads amongst them. Their anti Pompey songs and hatred for us was much more like it, surely after would be far livelier. We came out of the ground and a few of us got together. We spotted about twenty or so of their lot but they were unsure of themselves and one of their number was trying his best to keep them together. Stick together, nobody run, he kept saying as they walked away from the ground. We mixed in with them and they had absolutely no idea we were Pompey. We got what we thought was a decent distance from the lines of police and one of ours shouted 'Come on, let's do it' but was jumped on by the Portsmouth Police spotters. Nobody had seen them. We fanned out across the road but the Old Bill were on us in a flash. Looking at the Scummers, they had the look of 'Where did they come from?' on their faces.

As before, it was a long time before we played Southampton again, eight years in fact. Pompey's promotion to the Premiership would mean a visit to Southampton a few days before Christmas. A quirk of fate however meant that there would be a mid week appetiser only two weeks beforehand when the two sides were drawn together in the Carling (league) Cup. How times had changed. In the eight years, the Dell was a dim and distant memory with a brand new stadium built a few miles away which had already been host to an England international. The fortunes of the two sides had changed dramatically over the years. For a long time, Southampton had always been the poorer Hampshire relation; Pompey had a vast history of Championships and strong teams packed with international players but years of neglect by various boards had seen Portsmouth Football Club eroded. There had been little in the way of investment before the arrival of Milan Mandaric whereas Southampton were happy just to cling on to the Premiership by their finger tips, year after year. While most seemed to think that the Saints' board were happy to be a bottom five club every year, so long as they stayed in the Premiership, as soon as they had a good player, he was cashed in on, usually sold for big money as well. The difference being was the Southampton board were investing. First came the ground; the impressive St. Mary's Stadium. How Pompey fans sniggered when they were unable to sell out all of their seats when the ground first opened even though few would admit it, deep down we were green with envy. We had after all been promised a new ground for years without any sign of it ever happening. The fact that Southampton wasn't a sell out, week in week out, worked in the clubs favour. For the first time ever, Dads in the region were able to take their kids to watch football while, at first, they may well have been there only to watch the bigger sides, suddenly Southampton had a fan base on which they could build on. With Gordon Strachan as manager, Southampton were able to climb up the league. FA Cup finalists in 2003 saw them claim a place in the UEFA Cup as the winners Arsenal had already qualified for the Champions League. Undoubtedly, football on the South coast had turned full circle with Southampton being the bigger side and Pompey lagging behind. That was on the pitch however. What remained to be seen was with this new found wealth and support, could they finally give the 6.57 Crew a run for their money?

Despite being an evening kick-off, many off the lads started to meet up before 1 o'clock. By two, many had arrived in Southampton and were keen to make their presence felt. As more and more lads turned up, word was that the Southampton firm was mobbing up in the Joiners Arms. Yet, despite having spent hours in the enemy town, Pompey's mob had neither sight nor sound of them. It was common knowledge where the Saints fans were but the usual protocol is for the away team to gather in the town and for the home to come to them. It was clear that this would not be happening today. So once again it was down to the Pompey fans to make a move. Eventually arriving at the Joiners, the shout went up as they charged. The Southampton firm, with good numbers, came out of the side door but only as far as a side alley. As quick as a flash, sirens filled the air and the riot cops moved in. Bottles and glasses flew back and forth and even, at one point, a pushbike. The police began to push the Pompey mob back towards the ground, some however managed to get away from them and doubled back towards the Joiners. This time however the Saints fans, sensing their chance, steamed out towards them. Despite the best efforts of some, the Pompey lot they stood little chance. Some of the less experienced took to their heels and one or two were dished out. Saints suddenly had their victory, modest yes but to them it was something to be proud of.

In the days before the match, Southampton Football Club stalwart Ted Bates died aged 85 years old. Bates was a former player who had also served as manager, chairman, director and president working for the club for 66 years. A minutes silence was planned before kick-off; however things didn't go as intended. As the whistle blew to signal the start of the silence, a few Pompey fans started shouting 'Scummer' and other such things although the majority of the Pompey fans observed the silence with respect and indeed tried to quieten those who didn't, a few Saints fans started to shout abuse back at them. Soon what was meant as a moment to show consideration for one of football's greatest servants descended into farce. The police had warned the referee Graham Poll that this may happen beforehand and had been instructed on what to do; a sharp blow of his whistle brought the tribute to a premature end. Not surprisingly, this was greeted by a chorus of boos from the home fans and you really couldn't blame them. When the young Pompey goalkeeper, Aaron Flahaven, was killed in a car crash a few years before, a minutes silence was held at St. Mary's before a Southampton friendly, a game that didn't even involve Pompey. This was observed impeccably by the fans. It was a shame that Pompey fans couldn't have given the same courtesy. The following day in the papers, many people were quoted as saying that they were ashamed to be Pompey fans. I wouldn't say that although I was left feeling a little gutted by the incident as I had always thought that Pompey fans had more class than that. It was a bitter pill to swallow to find out that I was wrong.

The game was a poor one, neither side playing well, however the Pompey team showed little passion for a local derby shown live on the television going down 2-0 without so much as a whimper. During the second half, messages kept coming over the PA system saying that Pompey fans would be kept in the ground after the match, met by much derision. Maybe this was to give the Scummers a head start! As the final whistle blew, some fans tried to get out of the stadium. A line of riot police and stewards formed at the top of a set of stairs but the weight of the crowd pushed them down. One of the stewards was hurt and needed hospital attention. A police cordon was put across the car park behind which was a group of Southampton supporters. They started jeering at the Pompey mob, thinking that they were safe behind the police lines. Usually they would have been but then this was no ordinary night. The police line was quickly breached and the Saints lads were quickly sent scurrying into the night. Fifty or so lads continued in pursuit of the Southampton mob towards a car sales plot. There, a lone police woman with her dog, started saying 'Get back, get back'. It was clear she was pretty much out of her depth when, with a quivering voice, finally pleaded, 'Please just get back'. Everyone just went around her and continued on their way.

The walk back to Southampton Central Station was more of a triumphant parade for the 6.57 lads while the attack on the Joiners hadn't gone exactly to plan, the night was theirs. Once again, we turned up in the City of our biggest rivals, hours before kick-off, yet again taken it to the Southampton mob and now were taking a leisurely stroll straight through the City, totally untroubled, not a single Saints fan had the nerve to show themselves. As the Pompey procession reached the darkness of the park right by the city centre, they all peered into the shadows; surely this would be where the Scummers would come from, but nothing. There was more than a little disappointment. They could have at least put a little bit of a show on; still they'd all be back again in a couple of weeks for the league game.

The days following the game saw the internet go into melt down. Southampton fans crowed triumphantly about the Joiners but ignored their poor showing over all. Pompey fans made excuses and then asked why the Saints had run scared after the game. I'm willing to bet that, as usual, those that shouted (or typed) loudest were probably nowhere near anything that happened. For Hampshire police, the night was a great success. Yes, there had been a little trouble but, on the whole, it had been contained. For them, the timing couldn't have been better. They had used the game as a dress rehearsal for the league match. Four days before Christmas, Pompey once again made a trip West. This time, the police had things sewn up pretty tight. The Pompey fans tried but there was no way the police were going let them go walkabout amongst the festive shoppers. The day passed off peacefully.

By the time the two teams reached March, Pompey were, as predicted, struggling with Premiership life and looked in danger of relegation. It hadn't been a bed of roses for Southampton. A poor run of form saw them slump to the bottom half of the table and, added to this, Gordon Strachan had left the manager's job. The two teams met at Fratton Park, both desperate for a win.

Off the field, Pompey had planned a show of strength in order to show the pretenders from along the coast just who were the Premier firm in the county. On the pitch, while not the best spectacle of football you'll ever see, Pompey had more desire and took a deserved 1-0 win; at least for now, we'd be able to hold our heads a little higher after two dire passionless performances in Southampton. Off the field, it was all sadly predictable. Before the game, a mob of Pompey filled Goldsmith Avenue. Southampton fans had arrived about forty minutes before the kick-off. To their own disgust, many of the Scum mob had turned down the chance of a trip to not so sunny Portsmouth, leaving the few who were game enough to come to run the gauntlet of hate before them. Surrounded by riot police, who were attacked time and again, it took nearly half an hour to be escorted the short distance to the ground. To add insult to this and maybe to prove that even God hates them, a vicious hail storm started battering those being escorted to the ground and those in the open Milton End. As soon as the final whistle blew, as if by tradition, a mob started to fill the streets by the away end and, in an exact rerun of twenty years before, things took the precise same course. Instead of keeping the Pompey fans moving, the police allowed them to gather in a mob several hundred strong. When the decision to move them came, the inevitable happened.

Although backed up by horses drafted in from elsewhere, it was still over an hour before the Southampton fans could be escorted from the ground. In that time, the police had been under constant attack in Goldsmith Avenue and Fratton Road. There was also the same sorry trail of damage to shops and businesses. Most of the decent Pompey lads however had long left the scene. Seeing that there was no way that they were going to get near their rivals, they had left the vandalism and stone throwing to the many youngsters who had allowed themselves to be swept along and the mugs who had no concept of cctv. Everyone had seen what happened when Millwall took on the police and this would be no different. By the following day, the police launched operation Market, targeting all those that had been caught on camera. Soon the arrests started. Everybody from a 10-year-old child who was convicted for violent disorder to forty something's. By the end of the operation, nearly ninety people were jailed for their part in the trouble. To the disgust of many, nearly half of those jailed were juveniles, many of whom were put behind bars despite this being their first offence. It would be true to say that, while the rioting took place, the majority of the more switched on Pompey lads were in the pub. This surely is the final nail in the coffin for the 6.57 Crew as the police and courts now sent out a signal that there would no longer be any tolerance of trouble at football in Portsmouth. Personally, I feel that, while police now have state of the art technology at their disposal, a contributory factor into the trouble that day was that the police were using the same tactics that they have for just about every match at Fratton Park for the past 20 plus years. Everyone knew what the police would do and, as a result, the trouble that quickly escalated after the match was almost a mirror image of when the teams met in 1984 as if the police hadn't learned from the mistakes made in the past.

Perhaps the funniest punch-up with a group of Scummers that I have been involved with came after a boxing show in Southampton. I was leaving the venue with members of the club I was involved with at the time when a group in the car park obviously noticing 'Portsmouth' on our club tracksuits starting shouting abuse. It was out of order because quite a few of those with us were kids. As the abuse went back and forth, it was clear that it was going to kick off so I ushered the kids back inside the sports centre. One of the Scummers started to front up one of the senior boxers. I went across to try and intervene but was too late. The Scummer hit the floor and everyone was piling in to each other. As we traded punches, one or two of the locals ran inside to get help. A few more came running out but I had the feeling these were just pissed up locals jumping on the Portsmouth – Southampton band wagon and not necessarily football lads. Some of those that came running out were members of the various Southampton area boxing clubs but, to give them their due, none of them got involved in the fighting. To be honest, we were now starting to enjoy ourselves. It was like shooting fish in a barrel, it really was that easy for us. Before long the boys in blue arrived but, by then, the fighting had all but fizzled out. A police inspector could not keep the smile off his face when one of the Scummers showed him the blood down his best Burton's shirt and pointed out various people, myself included. The inspector simply shook his head and asked the Scummer 'So at which point did you think it would be a good idea to pick a fight with a boxing team?' He then turned to us and asked if we wanted to press charges which of course we didn't. We then climbed aboard our mini bus and were given a police escort out of the city.

Groups of Pompey lads would often travel to Scum during the summer to watch Hampshire play cricket. On a couple of occasions, it kicked off but nothing too serious. I do know that, on one occasion, at Lords for a Hampshire cricket match, a few Pompey bit off a little more than they could chew and were given a slap. There was also the incident when the Sunday league side from the Air Balloon pub were playing the Tabby Cat from Southampton in a Hampshire cup game. While the game was on, a firm of tooled up Scummers ran onto the pitch and began to attack the Air Balloon players, injuring a couple of them. Although heavily outnumbered, the Air Balloon lads gave as good as they got before being forced to take refuge in the changing rooms. The Scummers soon did the off when the police turned up. Obviously the referee abandoned the game and, after the Hampshire FA ordered the match to be replayed at the same venue, the people who ran the Tabby Cat side decided to withdraw from the competition rather than face what could well have turned into open warfare had the match gone ahead.

There are many urban myths surrounding Pompey – Saints matches, many of which have little or no truth to them. There are claims that an ambush was set for them on the M3, attacking Scummers on their way to the Zenith Data Systems Cup Final. An ambush would be a little over dramatic. Some of the '6.58' youngsters did go to the service station that day and did, in fact, come badly unstuck although whether the incident is worth more than a couple of lines is open to debate I suppose. The other questionable 'fact' is that Pompey fans took to bombarding Scum coaches on their way to away games with blue paint as they passed Portsmouth. I'm not going to say that paint has never been thrown at coaches but I have not been able to track down anybody who knows of it happening. As far as I can make out, the only time coaches would pass Portsmouth would be if they were going to or from Brighton. I do know that around thirty Scummers once stood petrified on Fratton railway station surrounded by police as twice that number of Pompey lads stalked them while they waited for their connecting train to take them to an away game at the Goldstone Ground. There are claims that there was a 1,000-a-side battle in Goldsmith Avenue after the FA Cup match; it never happened and neither were Scum's firm waiting on Southsea Common for an arranged meet before the FA Cup match in 1984; another fable that has cropped up since the internet was invented.

Over the years there have been many incidents between Portsmouth and Southampton fans. For most of the time that I have been watching football, it was Southampton who were the top side. While we were struggling in the lower leagues, they were always in the top division. Off the pitch, it was us who were the Premier team while they languished a long way behind. However, since the arrival of the internet, Southampton have suddenly reinvented themselves into a super firm although, in fairness to them, their true lads have never claimed to have a top firm. I have got to know a few of them through my boxing connections and they have always said that Saints were never in the same league as Pompey but they would always try and turn out when the sides played. They also bemoaned the fact that occasionally they would go to a match mob handed but were never consistent in their efforts and that was the difference between Pompey and Saints. While the blues would travel up and down the country in their hundreds most weeks, sometimes the deck chairs would struggle to pull out 20 for a home game. Of course, we helped relegate them a couple of seasons back. After listening to their lot gloating about being the better team for years, we have been able to lord it in a fashion. I don't know how long our current superiority will last but, as a Pompey fan, I will just enjoy every minute of it.

4

ZULU'S, THOUSANDS OF 'EM

Funny though it may sound, if you get a group of lads together who have been involved in the odd bout of fisticuffs on a Saturday afternoon, many will tell war stories of how they did this, that and the other, but many of the stories that are clearest in their memories aren't necessarily those where they had a great victory (unless, of course, it was against the odds) more those where they came unstuck. I have never thought that there has been any shame in admitting when we have come unstuck; it has happened to all of us at some time or other regardless of what some may say. After all, you have to be in it to win it.

By the mid-eighties, we knew we were a good firm and we knew that we could turn on the style, home and away. No matter who we played, we were turning out in big numbers and had taken it to some of the very best firms in the country. In turn, these firms were coming to Fratton Park, mob handed and getting a very warm reception. To us, it was a back handed compliment that the likes of Chelsea and Leeds were coming here with big firms because they knew, if they didn't, we would be far too much for them. Of course, we were heading for a fall at sometime although nobody cared. We were the lads as far as we were concerned and many thought, foolishly, that nobody could touch us.

One of the best firms I have ever seen come to Pompey, was Birmingham City's Zulu's and, on one particular Saturday, they came to town and gave us a lesson but, before I get to that, this is how it all started one Tuesday night when Pompey were away to Birmingham. Despite it being midweek, Pompey took a superb firm up to the Midlands that day. The two sides hadn't been in the same division for a while so I don't know if Birmingham didn't reckon on much opposition that night and maybe that played a major part in what unfolded at St. Andrews. We had played away to Birmingham on a couple of occasions in the 1970's mainly in the FA Cup with mixed results off the field and the differing fortunes of the two teams would keep us apart until the 1985/86 season. Long before the fixtures came out, we had all made a point of making sure we would travel regardless of it being a mid-week game. Most of us had got the train up early, spending much of the day around the Bull Ring Centre. Eventually we made our way to the ground and paid to get into the seats where the Zulu's usually gathered. Just before the match kicked off, the Zulu's took up their positions. The chant went up 'Zulu's Zulu's'. They kept up this chanting for a while in a way that really made the hairs on the back of your neck stand up. Suddenly, during all this noise, another chant went up, only this time it was from all around the area where the Zulu's were stood chanting. SIX - FIVE - SEVEN, SIX - FIVE - SEVEN. Before the Zulu's could react, we were into them from all directions. Caught like a rabbit in the headlights and before they knew what was happening, they had moved in mass towards the pitch and then onto it. Pompey had run Birmingham from their seats and they were not happy. They stood on the edge of the pitch open mouthed, looking up at us, a line of police between them and the Pompey firm who stood in their section of the ground, SIX - FIVE - SEVEN, SIX - FIVE - SEVEN, went the chant again. It was yet another scalp we had taken and we were loving it. The Zulu's could not believe what had happened and, to be honest, neither could we. Surely, after the match, they would get a much sterner test outside of the ground.

The game finished and, to everyone's astonishment, the police allowed both sets of fans to leave the ground straight away. Once on the street, the Zulu's could be seen massing towards the other end. Without waiting for an invite, we charged straight at them, blows were traded and then, for the second time that night, Birmingham began to back off, then to turn away until they were in full flight with us in pursuit. The police quickly came into the brawling mass with dogs and horses, arresting a few and restoring order quite quickly but, by then, as far as the Zulu's were concerned, the damage had been done. We were starting to think this football lark was easy. We had taken a few slaps on our travels but we were taking the piss out of more than a few of the better known firms up and down the country more and more. We were beginning to think we were invincible; we'd be brought down to earth sooner or later though. The Zulu's have since dismissed that night as a non-event but those that know, as they say, know. After all, we all have a bad day at the office from time to time.

Later on that season of course, we had to play Birmingham at Fratton Park. Come that day, a small group of us gathered on the opposite side of the road to Portsmouth & Southsea train station. At around 10 am, the invading Zulu's arrived and boy, did they arrive. To pinch a line from the film, Zulu's thousands of 'em, well hundreds anyway. Three hundred+ got off that train which had meant an early start in Birmingham. They walked out of the station and towards the shopping centre and into the Wimpy for breakfast. As they refreshed themselves, those of us that had witnessed their arrival, tagged along at a discreet distance. One or two were going into overtime in the telephone boxes (long before the days of mobile phones) getting people out of bed to report the news that not only had Birmingham arrived but in serious force. By lunchtime, the shopping precinct area was buzzing. Birmingham had taken up residence in the Park Tavern pub whereas we were keeping a low profile in the Sir Robert Peel in the Somerstown housing estate only a couple of minutes walk from where the Birmingham fans were gathered. Although a few of us debated going into them before we were totally mobbed up, we sensibly ruled it out. There would have been no point as we would have been battered for no reason. In any case, when going up against a top firm, there is no point going on the offensive until you are really ready. Prior Planning Prevents Piss Poor Performance as they say in the military or, to put it another way, stops you getting the shit kicked out of you.

The pub telephone rang and the landlord answered. It was the call that everyone was waiting for had finally come. One of the lads took the phone. Game on. The Zulu's were on the move and were in the Guildhall Square not quite sure what to do next. We left the pub with similar numbers to the Zulu's, two excellent mobs ready to go to war. As we crossed the main road and entered Guildhall Walk, they saw us and started to move our way, neither side running but more a confident fast walk towards each other. Suddenly a flare was fired by one of the our crowd. That was the signal though it wasn't pre planned as such. Both hyped up mobs charged but so did the police. About a dozen snarling dogs and more police than you would see at convention pushed both mobs back preventing an almighty battle from being waged. This was just the start though and the police intervention only postponed the inevitable. Having the upper hand of knowing the local geography, we went back down Guildhall Walk and into Winston Churchill Avenue.

Birmingham meanwhile were being pushed back into the Guildhall Square. They ran down past the library and on past the law courts where a few would be making a star appearance after this days events were complete. This route also took them into Winston Churchill Avenue. By now, both mobs were on a collision course at the speed of two, out of control, freight trains. Within seconds, the two mobs were into each other; the rival firms each at around 300 strong fought a pitched battle in the middle of a busy dual carriageway. Neither mob gave an inch; it was some time before the police could drive a wedge between the two. At the time, it was well known in Portsmouth that, if you were arrested at football, it usually meant serious trouble. A 6.57 member tells a story of when he was arrested during a pre-match punch up with Leeds at around the same time as the Birmingham game. Somehow he ended up in the same police van as a one of the Leeds fans arrested and, as kick-off time was getting closer, the more agitated the Yorkshireman was getting. 'We'll miss start of match, at this rate' he apparently whined. Going on to explain that 'up North' they would of charged and bailed them by now, not any of this messing about with holding cells. So the Pompey fan took great delight in telling him that here it was very much different and that he would not be seeing the outside world until after court on Monday if he was lucky and that if he had any form, especially football, connected he was facing anything from 28 days upwards. The Leeds fan paled as he sat crest fallen at the thought of a possible prison sentence but you know what they say about not being able to do the time.

With the police now going into an arresting frenzy, both the Pompey and Birmingham mobs thought it best to make good their escape. The majority of our lot made their way back into the Somerstown estate as did a few small pockets of Birmingham. Here sporadic fights took place as little groups of the original big gangs clashed with each other. It didn't take long for police vans to start tearing around the streets and, as 6.57 Crew and Zulu's were picking off one another, so were the police nicking anyone that they thought may have been involved.

During the game, the Zulu's made a lot of noise in the South stand as they witnessed their team hammer ours. Outside the ground, after the final whistle, the police were fully stretched as they battled, literally in some cases, to keep the two mobs apart. You really had to hand it to the Zulu's that day, they arrived in town mob handed and did what they set out to do although

1982, Cardiff away, always a lively day out

1982/83 season. 6:57 Crew try to get at the Cardiff Soul Crew in the Milton End at Fratton Park. Despite what they think, breaking the hands off a clock isn't a result.

1983. Middlesbrough at Fratton Park. A few 'Boro came onto the pitch and this was the reaction of the 6:57 Crew. 'Boro's Frontline are an underrated firm in my opinion.

1987. The Scummers at home. This is part of the riot but it's always the same against them. A hyped-up Pompey Firm end up having it with the police.

1987. The 6:57 Crew on a hunting mission going through the back streets to get at the Scummers.

1987. A Pompey fan is being put into the ambulance in the background after being attacked and knifed by the Scummers. Moments later the police lost all control of the 6:57 Crew who went looking for revenge.

Chas' 21st Birthday bash with special guests Vince Hilaire and Docker Hughes.

End of season at Fratton Park - the police take no chances.

The lads who took on 'Boro at Ayresome Park on that freezing day in the North East. The Darlington boys are on the far end.

1993. Away to Rotherham. With nothing going on, a few boys took the opportunity to inspect the pitch.

Vote Docker !

What other firm has put someone forward in a General Election ?

Le Havre away. The French had been persuaded that there would be no trouble but a 'sack the board' demonstration spilled onto the pitch.

Le Plod have had enough and point out that they feel we should start making our way home !

Me (left) and Pete at Stamford Bridge, early eighties I think.
I was young and had a full head of hair; those were the days.

Meeting early at Ellie Jays. This is the last game of the 1986/87 season against Sheffield United. We had been promoted to the top flight a few days earlier.

Police dogs stop us from getting at the Blades Business Crew. After meeting up early, everyone was out. We would have been far too much for them had we passed the dogs.

Scotland away 1989. The 6:57 Crew arrive in Glasgow to do our bit for England.

Italia '90. The police retreat from the English mob.

Enjoying the Turkish sunshine; the T-shirts are a Docker tribute. All smiles at the moment but, by the end of the trip, there wasn't one person without a battle wound.

Budgie with his blood spattered flag.

Back in Munich, some of the same Old Vic lads, older maybe wiser. This time, it was quieter off the pitch and far better on it. Germany 1, England 5.

Port Vale away. the police thought they had everything sussed but it didn't stop it going off outside the police station.

The Anglo-Italian Cup. A failure as a competition but a great excuse for a piss up when we travelled to Bari.

Yakubu always enjoyed a night out with the boys when he played for Pompey.

My very good friend John Cobb fulfilled a lifetime ambition when he took part in a charity boxing match recently. I was proud to be in his corner on the night.

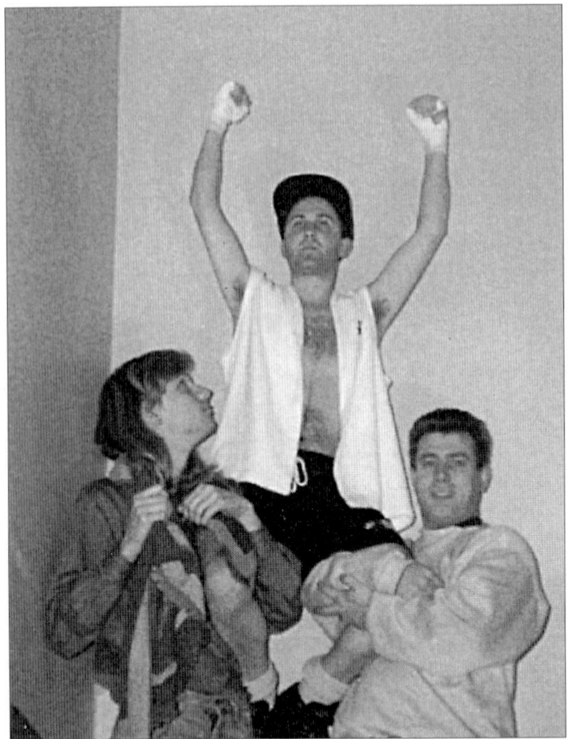

Boxing has always played a major part in my life. I have no idea when or where this picture was taken but it's safe to assume that I won !

The mad weekend trip to Carlisle. A few of us outside the ground feeling a little hung-over. I'm second right in the dubious hat.

they didn't fully set the record straight after they were knocked for six at St. Andrew's earlier that season. They had given it their best shot, however this wasn't going to be the end of the argument. The following season, the Zulu's would come to Fratton and embarrass us in such a way that it is still talked about today, even to the point that one or two of the top lads were so disappointed with the 6.57's performance they gave up altogether and began harnessing their energies into more profitable activities. Birmingham arrived in the city pushing for promotion and, with the previous season still fresh in everybody's mind, there was an air of anticipation. Although we had travelled to the midlands in fairly large numbers earlier in the season, apart from a fairly violent affair when around 20 or so 6.57 from the Fareham area were ambushed in a pub by a mob of Zulu's four times their number, not that much happened mainly due to high profile and aggressive policing. Today though was going to be different.

As always, on the morning of the game, a few of us started to gather in the town centre early. As the morning wore on, we were encamped in three different pubs, waiting. I sat in the City Arms with my usual group. We were getting inpatient. Everyone knew that they would be here. In fact, a guy I knew who supported Aston Villa had even called me the night before telling me that it was all the talk in Birmingham but nothing happened; no Zulu's around anywhere. About 1 o'clock, we started to make our way to pubs closer to the ground, still nothing. The game came and went and still absolutely nothing. As we made our way out of Fratton Park, some of the less knowledgeable and wannabes started to proclaim that Birmingham had 'shit out'. However, those who were somewhat more clued up knew that they were here somewhere. The buzz suddenly went around that they had been seen by Fratton Bridge. Pompey fans surged up Goldsmith Avenue towards the area but a nasty feeling was inside. Our mob had become too strung out and mingled in were too many lightweights, wannabes and even scarfers. We were about to do battle with what can justifiably be reasoned at the time to be one of the top 3 firms in the country but we were totally disorganised. As we reached Fratton Bridge, this mish-mash group of people started to gather speed, first into a trot then into a run, most having no idea why as no shout had gone up and the fact that the large amount of mugs that the crowd had attracted were still with us and not scattering in all directions shitting themselves was a definite indication that we hadn't run into the Zulu's. The momentum of the mob took us into Canal Walk and suddenly, there they were. The Zulu's stood their ground totally outnumbered but nowhere near out matched. The first few Pompey lads went straight in and the battle ensued. Unfortunately the wankers that had come along for the ride started to have second thoughts. While they talked a good fight moments earlier, now that it came to it, they had other ideas, turning and running for their lives despite never getting anywhere near to the front line. It was a little like watching one of those wildlife programmes on the television. You know where there are thousands of wildebeest grazing when a lion attacks. The wildebeest all run including the ones that haven't so much as seen a lion and are in no danger but they are running because all the other wildebeest are running. The usual shouts of stand etc. filled the air but it was too late, the damage was done Pompey were in full flight and Birmingham were starting to take the piss. Some of us managed to regroup and get rid of the idiots. The word went around to get to the Air Balloon pub. The Air Balloon was a popular pub near to the M275 motorway; well used by members of the 6.57 but never on a match day. The Zulu's had really done their homework on this one. It was rumoured that someone connected to the clubs had passed on the information but this was just speculation. We got to the Air Balloon only to find the Zulu's already waiting for us. Again it went off. This time, we had a much smaller mob as the hangers on had all melted away but we still faired little better; Birmingham had the upper hand. The police intervened, making the usual arrests and leaving us Pompey boys to limp away both body and pride battered. It would be easy to make excuses saying that we didn't have our mob together in Canal Walk but the fact is Birmingham done us; no excuses, they came to town and did the necessary, fair play to them. The defeat knocked some of the cockiness out of us. We had been beaten before. We had even been put on the back foot at home but this was the first time that we had been humiliated. For no particular reason, that was the last time there was a full mob-on-mob ruck with Birmingham. There have been a few skirmishes here and there but nothing on the scale that happened previously. It is as if both firms are happy to leave it at one win each and a draw.

Although the West Midlands is home to a cluster of clubs giving plenty of opportunity for derby matches and plenty of opportunity for their firms to flex their muscles, everyone I've spoken to at Pompey have only ever rated the Zulu's. This is because the others have never really given us any problems and, apart from one occasion against West Brom, none of them have ever brought it on at our place. During the 1983/84 season, we were drawn away to Aston Villa in the League Cup. The night of the game saw a massive mob turn out at Villa Park. It was a big game for us and, added to this, most of us had never been to Villa Park. Given how good The Zulu's were, we figured we would have a stern test from Villa, we were wrong . While the majority of the Pompey support were massed behind the goal, we had got into the old Trinity Road stand where we made our presence felt. After the game, we made our way onto the street behind the stand to see the Villa firm making their way down from the Holte End. Immediately we steamed into them. In the confusion, they turned and fled in utter panic. Having already got the upper hand, the attack was pressed home. Years later, I was talking to a few Villa lads who were all there that night. They all said they couldn't believe the numbers that Pompey had there and all admitted they were glad when the Police finally got the situation under control although not before we had run them all over the Aston area.

West Bromwich Albion is a side that haven't really featured much in the 'aggro' stakes over the years despite the fact that the two clubs have met many times. I can't count how many times I have been to The Hawthorns and just about all of them have been uneventful although they did come in good numbers to our place on the final day of the 1994/95 season. For once, it was the Baggies and not Pompey who needed to win in order to escape from relegation. Albion brought thousands down to Fratton Park with trouble beginning on the Saturday night before the game. West Brom fans and locals clashed in several of the pubs and clubs on the seafront. Come the day of the match, there were several fights outside the ground. A good friend of mine was given a good hiding by a group of West Brom lads by the White House pub. After being knocked down and taking a few digs, he simply told them 'Yeah, yeah you've done me'. The Baggies all backed off leaving him but there always seems to be one brave prick that wants to get a snide shot in. On this occasion, one ran in on the blind side and kicked my friend in the head before sneaking into the middle of the crowd to hide amongst his mates. My mate is still reminded of how he was more concerned about the fact his expensive designer sunglasses were smashed to bits although he seemed to be a little happier that the broken glasses he scrabbled around for weren't his as his were safely tucked away in his pocket. After being helped to his feet by an anxious policewoman, a mutual friend helpfully shouted to him, 'Don't tell her your name Rich' in a scene reminiscent of the famous Dads Army episode with Captain Mainwaring and Pike. Inside Fratton Park, it became clear that club officials had under estimated the amount of fans West Brom would bring with them and they were soon spilling out of the overflowing Milton End and onto the North Terrace. As a barrier to separate the two sets of fans, the police ran a piece of plastic tape down the terraces. Clearly this would not be enough especially given the high-octane atmosphere. It wasn't long before the tape was broken and fights started on the terracing. As the final whistle blew, the Midlanders charged onto the pitch celebrating the 1-0 win that they needed. Pompey fans also made their way onto the playing surface where a large brawl took place.

West Brom's huge rivals Wolves have a big reputation across the country although I have never really seen it as a game where you had to be on your guard when visiting and again I have been there on numerous occasions. Having said that, there was one trip there back in the 1980's when it went off big time. It was the usual early morning train and we arrived in Wolverhampton early. After spending an uneventful morning in the city centre, we reached the ground and went into the main stand. This was before the ground was redeveloped and was half falling down with many parts of the ground closed off. After the match, we came out of the ground and were met head on by the Subway Army. It was soon kicking off everywhere. We were too much for them though and we were soon forcing them backwards. The fighting resulted in one Pompey fan facing a lengthy prison term after one of the Wolves lads was thrown from the dual carriageway flyover. Nowadays, the Wolves firm have got the reputation for attacking scarfers and families as they leave Molinuex which has resulted in Wolves supporters getting a hot reception when they travel to away games. My feeling on this is that two wrongs don't make a right but can understand why some would see it as what goes around comes around. Wolves' Subway Army have never travelled to Fratton Park in any sort of numbers so there has not been any trouble of note. One time though, a van load did park up at the White House pub. At the time, not many lads were using the pub and, before the match, they were giving it large to a couple of blokes drinking in there. The Wolves boys were warned not to go back after but they took no notice. Word had got around what had happened and almost inevitably a few went back in case they did show their faces. It was a couple of brothers from Leigh Park who did most of the damage laying out the driver as well as serving up one or two others.

Following a match away to Sunderland, many of us made the short journey to Whitley Bay for a night out after. Although we were all just after a nights drinking, it was soon turned into a Wild West town. It was kicking off everywhere you looked. During the night though one of ours was set upon by a group from Coventry. The Pompey fan was left with serious injuries and in a coma for a while, fortunately, after a time, he did recover. Until that time, we never really had much of a history with them. The only other time we had come up against them was during our previous flirtation with the top flight in the eighties. On that particular occasion, we were sat in the seats next to the Coventry firm with a fence between the two of us. Sat in the Coventry section were a dozen or so 6.57 Crew lads who spent the afternoon talking with the City fans. Arrangements were made to meet at a certain place after the game. However, when the final whistle went, it is thought that, for the first time, the Coventry fans clocked the real size of the mob that Pompey had there that day and, rather than wait until outside, they decided to wade into the few that were in with them. The lads in the Pompey section started climbing the fences while police and stewards tried to quell the fighting. Once outside the ground, the Coventry fans were nowhere to be seen while Pompey fans walked to the train station unescorted. Before this match, I was run over by a police van while standing on the pavement. The driver thought it was hilarious; I just thought he was a wanker.

In September 2001, Pompey played away to Coventry City in a First Division fixture, a game that would usually get no more mention than half a dozen lines of match report in the national press. The events of that day were to leave football reeling back in shock. Had the 'bad old days' of the 1970's and 80's returned? The sight of hundreds of Portsmouth supporters climbing onto the pitch and charging into the Coventry mob at half time was definitely a snap shot from days gone by. It was if the fans had arrived by time machine from a time and place where this type of event was a weekly occurrence around the country. By the time the game came along, it was common knowledge around Portsmouth and the surrounding area that a considerable mob was going to make the trip to the Midlands. The week before the match, I was at work and a guy that I had never met before starting the job and certainly he cannot be connected with the 6.57 crew, was telling me all how this mob was going to Coventry on the train and how it was going to kick off big time up there. Although I didn't say much to him, careless talk and all that, I thought to myself typical Pompey, they aren't going to be able to move for police. During the mid 1980's and early 90's, we had to begrudgingly take our hats off to the police. If they weren't one step ahead of the mob, they were certainly up with play. On one game away to Port Vale in April 1990, Pompey took a massive mob by train and vans; the train mob was rounded up before they left Waterloo station whereas the road convoy that met up at the Air Balloon pub was pulled over as it pulled onto the M275 out of Portsmouth. The police had done their homework on this one. The local Stoke paper ran the front page lead 'Soccer thugs descend on city' and told alarmingly accurately how the fans were travelling to the area and that the police would be out in force to meet them. Regardless, it still went off. We steamed into their pub before the game whereas, after it, Port Vale were run down the road stopping in the police station car park thinking that it would deter the mob pursuing them. They thought wrong! A few of the Port Vale lads were really pissed off that they had been humiliated this way as they had fancied their chances. Mind you, it wasn't as if they didn't know we were coming.

I didn't travel to Coventry this time around however. The day before the match, I had an accident at work so was unable to travel but know many who did and, after listening to the reports of the violence, the days of that sort of police intelligence are long gone. It appears that Coventry City were treating the match as a low security risk and therefore had little or no police presence in the ground, relying on their own stewards. Surely they must have spoken to the Portsmouth police football intelligence officer whose, I would have thought, job it was to give a risk assessment based on the intelligence gathered. Neither can I get my head around the point of making a match all ticket for away fans while home fans are able to pay on the day, especially in the case of this particular game where we had sold out our allocation and were refused any more when they asked for them. Obviously there were more Pompey fans who wanted to watch the game so they simply travelled and paid at the turnstiles.

The bulk of the Pompey firm arrived in Coventry by train around 11.30. First of all, there was trouble at the Rocket pub in the city centre where the Coventry boys were gathering. The locals were chased away from the pub and regrouped elsewhere. There was further trouble at the Flying Standard. The police finally started to get their act together, rounding up many of the mob and bussing them to Highfield Road. By the time they were in the ground, feelings were running high. A few began to abuse the Coventry lads about the way they were easily bossed about earlier in the day. The response from the embarrassed Coventry lot was to start throwing coins and plastic bottles, undoubtedly not expecting the Pompey fans to spill onto the pitch and charge into them which is exactly what happened. Not surprisingly, the local media had a field day running several pages of stories and photographs. There was also the usual 'Was this violence orchestrated by right wing extremists?' In short, no it wasn't. It never is but then it always makes a good angle and, of course, it fills up a few extra paragraphs without the journalists needing to be original or informed. In short, the police, both in Portsmouth and Coventry had cocked things up. The initial police response in Portsmouth was swift and decisive. They decided to draft in an extra 60 officers for the following Tuesday's home game against West Brom and this helped because ? The laughable reason that the police spokesperson gave for the decision was because West Brom is close to Coventry. If the police really were going along this line of thinking then is it any wonder that they are unable to put a stop to the spiralling crime statistics in this country? Presumably further along this line of thought, there will be a massive police presence when Havant and Waterlooville play Kettering at some point in the future. The same tactic was used for Pompey's home game against Birmingham on a chilly November Tuesday. The lines of bored coppers in full riot gear in the ground was a ludicrous sight. The fact that there were barely 150 Birmingham fans at the match with next to nobody with even a thought about kicking it off in either set of fans, for me it summed up the police in Portsmouth making it up as they go along. By the time January came around, the West Midlands police launched Operation Rama and published photographs of 35 people they wished to question over the fighting. A web site was also launched as those involved waited with baited breath for front doors to start being booted in. Once the police had got their most wanted, came the court cases. The majority thought that they would be spending time behind bars; indeed had the events taken place at Fratton then that would have been almost certain, however everyone was taken aback by the sentences handed out, community service, fines and three year bans from all football, probably the severest part of the punishment. While it can be argued that the sentences were light, the writing was clearly on the wall. The majority of those who hadn't already decided to call it a day could not see the sense of carrying on. After all, in days gone by, if you didn't get pulled during the fighting itself, then you knew you were away free but it was now a totally different ball game.

Before we finish with the West Midlands, there needs to be mention of

Walsall. When Pompey were in the lower leagues during the late 1970's and early 80's, there were a couple of occasions when trips to Walsall became fairly violent affairs with clashes in the Walsall end. While they didn't have the numbers to cause us major problems, they were still game as they come so fair play to them.

Since the mid 1980's, Pompey have had a bitter rivalry with Leicester City's Baby Squad. It all started when the Leicester firm were battered in the Cockney Pride, in Piccadilly Circus, London. This was when CS gas was used for practically the first time. The Cockney Pride was a favourite haunt whenever Pompey played in London as was the nearby West One pub. On this particular day, we were away to Charlton and, as usual, once we arrived at Waterloo, made our way to the West End and in particular to the Cockney Pride, however Leicester had the same idea and it went off big time. During the fighting, one of the boys who had recently been on a day trip to France let off a CS gas canister that he had brought back with him. Chaos ensued with nobody knowing what the hell was going on. It was certainly the first time I had experienced the effects of CS gas. During the fighting, police officers that were on duty at the Libyan Embassy siege around the corner were called in to help restore peace. It was a busy day for us that day in London. After it went off with Leicester, we made our way to Chelsea and the infamous Gate 13 where we launched an attack on them. The Headhunters thought we had taken a liberty but secretly admired our cheek. We then went on to Charlton and steamed into them in their end. In the 1992/93 season, Pompey were within an ace of promotion to the Premier League. We were beaten by the difference of one goal by West Ham. For Pompey though, there was the safety net of the play-offs which saw us pitched against Leicester City. At the time, their ground was being redeveloped so the away leg was played at Nottingham Forest. Pompey took thousands and a very sizeable mob. To everyone's surprise, next to nothing happened. Maybe Forest and Leicester had arranged a local thing to which we weren't privy. Pompey lost the game 1 – 0 to a dubious off side goal. The second leg at Fratton would give us the chance to get back in the tie but we were missing leading scorer Guy Whittingham out injured, and Paul Walsh who had been on fire for us all season. Paul was suspended for chinning a Sunderland player at Roker Park a couple of weeks earlier. After this particular game, we ran Sunderland all over the place. I remember this long haired Sunderland lad bouncing in the middle of us saying, 'Come on Pompey, where are your boys?' One of the lads banged him out with the words, 'Here we are!' We went into them from every angle. There were so many of us that they just couldn't cope. We chased them all around the roads that were next to the stadium. Put simply, we just blitzed them. Come the evening of the play off second leg, Fratton Park was a complete sell out and the atmosphere was electric. An absolutely terrific match finished 2 – 2, not enough for Pompey who crashed out 3 – 2 on aggregate. After the match, fans invaded the pitch and went straight towards the Milton End. The Leicester fans, in an attempt to appease the Pompey fans, started singing Play up Pompey. Once outside, it was kicking off everywhere. There were running battles with the police as we tried to get at the Leicester supporters, several of which were injured and a couple of cars were turned over. For a while, the police were running around like headless chickens not really knowing what they were doing. In the confusion, many Leicester fans were attacked. Their bravado from before the match when they made a half hearted attempt on attacking the Milton Arms while Pompey fans were held back by the police, was now long gone. Many were just desperate to get away as fast as they could. Many of them tried to slip away in small groups unnoticed but they were easily picked off.

To give the Baby Squad their due, they have always turned up at Fratton Park. On one occasion, they thought they were getting a real result after the match when it went off outside the bookies on Milton Road. The Ladbrokes window was smashed as the group that had broken away fought with the small amount of Pompey that were there. At the same time in Goldsmith Avenue, the two main mobs were going for it and Leicester were getting a ragging. Every time they regrouped, Pompey were into them running them time and again. This has been conveniently forgotten while they brag about the bookies incident. Earlier that season, we had taken a great mob to Filbert Street and went straight into the stand where it was known that the Babies would be, mainly because they made a point of telling us. There were 40 or 50 of us in there but fairly scattered about. One or two little skirmishes were taking place while both mobs weighed up the situation. One of the Pompey lads was stood by the tea bar knowing that it was going to kick-off. It was just a case of who would start it. Looking to take the initiative, he went to grab hold of a cup of tea to throw at the big lump of a Leicester fan stood next to him but instead he took hold of a cup containing plastic stirrers and launched the contents at him. Thinking he was about to be badly scolded, the Leicester fan screamed and put his hands up to protect himself. Probably the only recorded incident of someone being spooned at football. This was the cue for everyone to wade in. Leicester were scattered in all directions. A very fat Leicester lad in a bright white jumper attempted to keep them together they regrouped and Pompey ran into them again. Fat bloke was jumping up and down (sort of) shouting 'Babies' 'Babies'. He became a target and was punched and kicked several times. Time and again Pompey ran at the Leicester mob, which was getting smaller and smaller and, every time Leicester scattered, fat bloke who had taken a bit of a battering was still there and still trying to keep his boys together. The Leicestershire Constabulary had decided enough was enough and ejected us all from the ground. One of the Pompey fans was nearly in tears when the police ejected him from Filbert Street. It wasn't his brush with the law that had him welling up nor was it that he had paid to get in but hadn't so much as seen his seat let alone a ball kicked. What had upset him so much was, as the constabulary grabbed him, he quickly placed his cube of cannabis in his mouth. As he was led through the ground, he faced a dilemma whether to swallow his illegal substance or not. He didn't relish the idea of sitting in a cell with the effects starting to take its toll but neither did he fancy being charged with possession. As he passed a group of Leicester fans, one gave it the big I am. As the policeman pushed the Leicester fan away, the Pompey lad took the opportunity to spit out the offending article. His face was a picture however when the police merely opened the doors and told him to fuck off. Pompey had a few results at Leicester over the years. One of the first times I went there, it kicked off before the game but it was afterwards that we had Leicester running when we chased them all the way up this long road from the ground. Every now and then a few would stop and turn and try and get the others to stand but without success. We simply ploughed into them and they were off again. Once on the main road, it was more of the same only this time, as a bus pulled up, they made out this was stopping them from getting at us. A futile face saving effort if ever there was one. One our lot merely went around the bus and into them on his own. As always, the local police soon put an end to our fun and games and rounded us all up. It was only then that we noticed that one of their lot had got mixed in with us. Our attitude was that he'd had a go and we weren't about to take a liberty with him. A couple of us ended up chatting with him, pointing out that he would be okay. He may have just been trying to keep us sweet but he said that our mob was the best that had been to Leicester for years.

The feud with the baby squad was fuelled by Pompey stopping off there while returning from games in the area on a couple of occasions. One such time, around 50 of us voted to pay them a visit. Getting off the train, we split into smaller groups so as not to attract unwanted attention and made our way out into the street. The adrenaline was pumping as we knew Leicester would be about because they had been at home that day. We would either have a spectacular result or would come badly unstuck; only time would tell. Once out of the station, our plan such as it was fell apart as, typical of Pompey, one group turned left and headed towards a pub at the top of the hill whereas the rest of us, much smaller in number, went the other way and went into the first pub that we came to. Unfortunately, our smaller group had now found the baby squad and hunter became hunted. They immediately knew that we were a football firm but as yet not who. Those were just mere details that could be sorted out later. Within seconds it went off, with us being pushed back towards the doors. Our master plan had gone out of the window as their superior numbers began to tell. We managed to get out of the pub more or less unscathed, pursued by the Leicester mob, lobbing bottles and glasses, as well as swinging pool cues. A good old-fashioned football pub fight! We were in danger of taking a real hammering and it soon turned into one of those situations where several attackers were swamping individuals at once, as we were forced back down the road. Luckily one of our number had a bit more common sense than the rest of us and had run back to find the others. The cavalry was on its way and not a moment too soon. The battle began to swing back in our favour as the rest of our lot charged down the hill and into the fray. I can vividly remember that earlier while they had the upper hand, they had been throwing all sorts at us, now the tables were turned and fire was being returned with interest. Someone from the back shouted 'Don't throw stuff, we're Pompey'. It's alright for you to say that mate, you haven't got someone in front of you trying to take your head off your shoulders with a pool cue! Some of the Leicester lads had a real go and the fighting was pretty intense for a while. The sheer momentum of the charge, when our reinforcements arrived, had forced Leicester back and, as we piled in, they kept going further backwards. It was one of those very rare occasions when you had all the time and space you needed without a copper in sight. Every blow was struck with feeling as the babies started to take a bit of a hiding. All around, there were private vendettas. One Leicester lad pulled out a blade and lunged at one of us. Our lad managed to dodge the knife and cracked him with a nice shot right on the button. In the end, even though they still outnumbered us, it turned into a rout with Leicester being chased all over the place. Eventually though, the police did arrive and started to round us up. One or two were arrested and, at one point, it looked like all of us were going to be spending the night but they seemed to be happy to get rid of us, taking us back to the train station and making sure we were put on a train South. A few weeks later, there was another away trip with a side order of Leicester although not on the same scale. Once again, Leicester were taken by surprise. Maybe they were thinking that lightning wouldn't strike twice. They were wrong and they must have been gutted!

Another time, when the boot was on the other foot so to speak, Pompey were due to play Leicester at Fratton Park. This particular match stands out as it is one of only a handful that I can remember in all the years I have followed Pompey to be called off at Fratton Park because of the weather. The game was postponed at around mid morning and, by that time, a lot of us had gathered in the City Arms. As news of the cancellation filtered through, many of the boys began to drift away, eventually leaving around 25 of us sitting having a drink and chatting. Of course the inevitable happened. A coach load of Leicester came around the corner, then another, then another and another. The Leicester firm got off their coaches and mobbed together. We made our way outside of the pub but soon began to go backwards. Some began to arm themselves with stools and glasses, ready for the inevitable attack. The Babies ran towards the pub but stopped outside. One of them picked up an A board but dropped it again. They seemed unsure of themselves as if they thought it was a set up and any moment hundreds of Pompey were going to appear from nowhere. We wished. We were looking at some serious pay-back here and we knew that there would be no way we would be able to hold them off for long. The Baby Squad did nothing. They had the chance for a result of sorts but instead all they did was get back on their coaches and go, leaving us inside wondering how we had got away with it. On the other hand of course, maybe they should have been credited in that realising they had massively superior numbers knew nothing would be gained from smashing up the pub and its occupants and decided to give us a pass. If this was the case then fair play to them. They didn't hang around in town long though, the coaches went off and were later involved in trouble in Newbury of all places.

It seems that whenever Pompey play Leicester City, the heavens open and there is torrential rain. When the two sides were drawn together in the FA Cup, it hammered down all day non stop, so bad that as Pompey goalkeeper

Alan Knight went down for a simple ball at the edge of the box, he continued travelling on his side through the mud and carried the ball out of the penalty area. Instead of using his brains, not only did the referee give the rightful free kick but he also sent Knight off. Before the match, we were mobbed in the Commercial Road area however Leicester had managed to hole themselves up in the Avenue Hotel pub on the northern outskirts. Around lunchtime, an impressive looking City firm started to walk into Portsmouth. They reached the Commercial Road area but, by now, we had moved towards Fratton Road. As the Leicester boys were escorted along Winston Churchill Avenue, a few tried to have a go at them but it came to nothing. The weather was no different during the league game when both sides were pushing for the First Division Championship. During the 2003/04 season, a game played in monsoon conditions which suited Leicester's, long ball, hit and hope style far more than it did a Pompey team who preferred to play a passing game, resulted in Leicester winning 2-0. Before the game, many of the Pompey boys were encamped in the pubs around Fratton Park knowing that the Leicester Baby Squad were in Havant surrounded by riot police but didn't know when they would be escorted to Fratton Park. Leicester were happy to be tightly escorted to the turnstiles at Fratton Park and claimed a massive result but, at least, they did better than Brighton of all teams. They camped in a pub in Chichester about twenty miles from Portsmouth and said Pompey should have come to them, hmm. Soon, sounds of police sirens filled the air as a car fought its way through the traffic. Sat bold as brass in the front seat was the officer in charge of match day policing with the Leicester police officer sat behind him. It didn't take much to work out that the next train in would have the Baby Squad on board. The Pompey lads poured out of the pubs and towards the station where police battled to keep the rivals apart. Had the car not come past with his 'Look at me, I'm in control' attitude the Pompey lads would have been none the wiser. The mob charged onto Fratton Bridge taking the police as much by surprise as anyone else but, with the Baby Squad tightly marshalled on the station, neither side got close to the other. As they were escorted to the ground, there was catcalling between the two groups but nothing else. After the game, fans spilled onto the streets around Fratton Park. There was little happening. Most drifted off to the pubs and the Leicester mob, such as it was, had little or no eagerness to leave the confines of the tight escort. The game, like most others, passed without incident.

5
MIXING IT WITH THE BIG BOYS (& GIVING IT TO THE SCUMMERS)

After years of missing out on promotion during the mid 1980's, Pompey finally managed to go up into top-flight football, courtesy of Shrewsbury Town beating Oldham. Typical of Pompey that they were in the top two for most of the season, yet nearly choked for the third consecutive season right at the death. One of the biggest games that season was the First versus second clash away to Derby County. The DLF had thrown down the gauntlet earlier in the season. They turned up in two mini buses and encamped in the back bar of one of the pubs in Milton Road, early on. Myself and a couple of others, led by a seriously top lad, went into see them and maybe get something sorted. They started to give it the large and it looked for a moment that is was going to go but the landlord must have called in the Old Bill as they landed on us in force. Just as well really because there were only half a dozen of us and we would have probably been battered. After the match, we all went straight back to the pub as we knew their vans were parked at the back. To give the Derby lads their due, they were outnumbered but they still broke away from their police escort and came towards us. There were one or two punches swapped but, before it really escalated, the police steamed in. The return meeting was due to be played just before Christmas but had been called off. We had planned to avoid the unwanted attention of the constabulary by slipping into Derby crammed into a 40 foot HGV but, in the end, we travelled to the rearranged fixture the following March in cars and mini-buses and, even though it was a Wednesday night, still had the better part of 200 lads there although not all together as one mob. By 6.30, around 100 or so of us were plotted up in a pub around a half a mile from the Baseball Ground. The clock was ticking yet there still had been no sign of the Derby firm. In the end, the anticipation got too much for us and we decided to make a move. We left the pub and, to our amazement, the police left us to our own devices. We seized the moment and made a quick get away, running through a park to a road running parallel to where we had come from just in case they had a change of mind. The road we now found ourselves in would soon become another name in the ever-growing history of the 6.57 Crew, Pear Tree Road. Without a policeman in sight and the glow of the floodlights in full view, we began to strut down the road knowing somewhere at the end would be Derby's firm. After a few minutes, we reached a small shopping area and, despite being so close to the football ground on a big match day, it was deserted. As we marched further down this road, everyone felt the expectancy then, all of a sudden, it happened and a chain of events would be unleashed and many people's lives would be changed forever.

A big looking guy with long dreadlocks walked out of a doorway and bumped into this mob of Pompey's finest. He shouted some abuse, some abuse was shouted back, next thing you know he was on the wrong end of a right hook. The doorway was the entrance to the Texas Goldmine, an Afro-Caribbean club where a lot of the black locals hung out only we didn't know that yet. Within seconds, the tension to take on Derby's firm was released on this club. Flares, bricks, For Sale signs, drainpipes, anything we could get our hands on was launched in the direction of the Texas Goldmine. The door was steamed and in we went but, within seconds, were on our way back out followed by many of the occupants carrying knives, baseball bats and pool cues. We had stirred up a right old hornets nest and it was serious. For over ten minutes, there were running battles up and down the street until the police arrived. At first, it was two scared looking officers in a panda car who sat inside in the middle as this conflict continued around them but, as more and more police arrived, the shout went up to get away before the arrests started. Once we had reached the ground, we could still hear the sirens blaring out from the direction we had just come from. The adrenaline was still pumping, 'Did you see so and so', 'What about when this happened' everyone talking in excited tones. By half time though the extent of the battle started to become clear. One of our mates was lying in hospital with stab wounds and another two being treated for head injuries. Meanwhile, the police were facing a riot. The first panda car that arrived had been turned over and burned out. A complete mistake had caused a ticking time bomb to go bang and now the Derbyshire police, along with colleagues from Nottinghamshire, were facing the backlash. We were inside the old Baseball Ground watching a thrilling 0-0 draw, oblivious to the events that were unfolding nearby. As far as we were concerned, it was nothing more than just another battle at football; the authorities though had other ideas. Before the wreckage had even been cleared, it was obvious someone would have to pay for this and it was pretty clear who it would be. By midnight, eighteen of the lads were nicked. They were joined the following morning by number 19, the lad who, having been stabbed, spent the night in hospital and was stood on Derby railway station waiting to catch the train home when he was pulled. One of those detained was taken back south, accused of serious offences in Hampshire and subsequently was never charged with the Derby riot. The morning after the disturbance, every national television and radio news bulletin carried the story. Douglas Herd, the then Home Secretary made a statement to the press and the House of Commons. The witch-hunt was about to begin.

Those that were left in the cells in Derby police station were held for the statutory 48 hours before a local magistrate granted a further 24 hours detention. During the questioning, the Derbyshire CID officers admitted that the lads were the most streetwise group that they had ever come across. No matter what they tried, they drew a blank. At one point, they wanted to set up ID parades; however in order for the parades to be legal, some 150 volunteers would have to be found. In the end, defence solicitors agreed to allow possible witnesses to view the Pompey lads while they sat in the interview rooms. Even this didn't go the way the police would have hoped, none of those being held was 100% positively identified with only two or three positive identifications out of a possible five being the best that the police could get. Some of them were not ID'd at all. The press had a field day as did some of the community leaders, some of whom claimed they had evidence that the whole attack was a set up and that National Front members from Derby and Portsmouth had joined forces in a pre-planned racist attack; even claiming that a few locals had been seen in the days before the riot taking photographs of the area. It was of course complete nonsense and besides, if there was such evidence, how come the only people arrested all came from the Portsmouth area?

The Derby 18 as they became known, were eventually released on the Saturday morning after each of them was charged with affray, a charge that, up until that time, none of the 6.57 Crew had faced. Even though eighteen had been charged, the investigation didn't end there. Derby police travelled south to take part in a series of dawn raids as well as visiting lads while they were at work. In all, a further forty people were questioned regarding the incidents in Pear Tree Road, four or five of which weren't even in Derby on the night in question. The case rumbled on for eight months, being adjourned three times. Eventually Derby Crown Court heard from the prosecution that, despite launching their most intensive investigation ever involving hundreds of man-hours, they had come up against a wall of silence. In the end, all eighteen were bound over to keep the peace for two years for the sum of £250 each. It was an unbelievable result seeing as they were each facing a sentence of between three and five years in prison. Each of the accused were delighted by the performance of their solicitor, Mr. Mann, from the Derby firm Brearly Mann & Co. Throughout the investigation and subsequent trial, he had not allowed the police to have their own way. It was thought by many that the whole thing was politically motivated and the police were under pressure to get the right result and so, speaking to the very relieved lads afterwards, they were grateful to Mr. Mann for their liberty.

Unfortunately, because of their bail conditions, none of the lads were able to see the exciting if nervous run in to the end of the season. The tabloid headline the morning after our promotion was 'Balls Up' a play on words seeing as Pompey manager was Alan Ball although it very nearly was a complete balls up. We went into the May Day bank holiday needing a draw from our match away to Crystal Palace. A single point would mean promotion. 10,000 plus Pompey fans crammed into Selhurst Park. Everything was going to plan as the minutes ticked away with the score 0-0 as the teams headed into injury time. Myself and a good mate, Pete B were sitting in the main stand among the Palace fans. We decided to make our way out of the ground in order to get onto the terrace area below so, when the final blew, we would be able to get onto the pitch in celebration. As we stepped onto the street, a roar went up. The South Londoners ruined our day by scoring the only goal. That meant, with only one game left to play, we needed Shrewsbury to do us a favour a couple of days later. By some miracle, the unthinkable happened as the Shrews, who needed the win to be assured of avoiding relegation, saw off the challenge of Oldham on our behalf. We were promoted to the top flight at last. We went into the final game of the season at home to Sheffield United with a chance of clinching the title. Unfortunately, some of the players who had formed a drinking club known as the Gremlins had been on the piss all week. Although we took an early lead, we had to be satisfied with runners up behind Derby County. For as long as I can remember, the Blades have been a bogey team to Pompey and usually manage to piss on our fireworks. This game was no different. They won 2 – 1 in a match that was held up time after time by pitch invasions. To be honest, the invasions started off as high spirits and basically to wind up the Old Bill. There had been several pitch invasions during the previous home game against Millwall. Then, during one, a massive mob headed towards the United fans stood on the Milton End. There was little chance of getting to the Sheffield. After all, they were behind a fence which was itself behind a moat added to which a line of police dogs kept the Pompey fans at bay. After the game, there was another invasion but this was in celebration. There was another half-hearted attempt to get at the Sheffield lads but everyone was more interested in celebrating promotion. As usual, the Blades Business Crew made a show that day and had a little victory outside the bookies in Milton Road before the match but sheer weight of numbers would of sent them home with a bit of a bloody nose had it of gone off after the match. In the BBC, Steve Cowens mentions that it was arranged for the 6.57 Crew and BBC to meet in Bournemouth that night. This may well have been one of those rumours that fly around. I have lost count of the number of times that Pompey were supposed to meet this team here or that team there. Nine times out of ten, it never happens. Bournemouth may only be an inch or so away from Portsmouth on a map but in reality it is 40 miles. I have never known a Pompey mob to travel there for a night out, a few go out there in a couple of the night clubs but only as individuals so I can't see anything being arranged there, especially seeing as the majority of us were out celebrating Pompey's promotion.

During the 1980's, the Blades had a very tidy firm and always used to show at Fratton Park so, as a consequence, we would always repay the compliment by taking a good mob up to their place knowing that things would be pretty hot. At one match, we took literally hundreds and really caught United on the hop and, although the Sheffield lads gave it a real go, there were just too many of us for them and we ended up turning them over big time. During one particularly nasty brawl that afternoon, fighting was temporarily suspended when a frail looking old lady happened by. One of the Pompey lads put his arm around her shoulder and guided here through the throng of people, both factions stood aside for her and as soon as she was safely away, battle commenced. At another match at Bramell Lane, Pompey needed the points to keep alive the slim hope of promotion. The blues were dreadful that day in a 0 – 0 draw, Mick Channon was given loads of stick by the Pompey fans chants of Scummer! Scummer! every time he touched the ball even though he was playing for us. A lot of Pompey fans thought that, as he was coming to the end of his career, he was just going through the motions for a good pay-day. Before the match, a few of us were sat on a grass bank. A mob of blades came around the corner and it looked as if it was about to go off big time but, before a punch was thrown, the two Portsmouth CID spotters were just feet away, nobody wanted to be the first in and be assured of an obvious nicking so began to back away. Soon the local plod were there in numbers and moved us into the ground. There comes a time in everybody's life that they say or do something that, no matter what great achievement they may have in the proceeding years, they will always be known for that one deed or sentence. One such moment must have come in the life of a Sheffield United fan, after a game at Fratton. As the Pompey fans approached the mob of around 40 Sheffield, he pushed his way to the front and defiantly shouted at the Pompey mob that was closing in on them 'We're Blades and we don't go nowhere'. This guy's defining moment had arrived. Forever he would be known to everyone at Bramall Lane as the guy who made the rallying cry at Fratton Park as the Blades battled with the 6.57 Crew. Unfortunately, his moment of destiny was lost forever unless of course he is remembered as the one who shouted 'Fuckin 'ell they're all around us, run!' which were the next words out of his mouth as the Sheffield mob scattered in all directions without a punch being thrown. This happened after the match where a United fan ran onto the pitch and poleaxed the linesman. There can't be a football fan around that hasn't wanted to do that at one time or another, most don't. This guy though ran along the touch-line and whack. The lino was out cold. The Sheffield fan wasn't what you would call a lad. He was wearing his replica kit and, as far as I am aware, had never been in trouble before. For some reason, he lost it but where he thought he would escape to afterwards, I don't know, but then again, if he had given his actions any thought, he would never of done it in the first place.

The promotion party lasted all summer as we waited for the fixtures to be published. A quick look saw that we were away to Oxford on the opening day, hardly an auspicious start but then the Football League computer spat out an interesting set of matches. Our first three home games of the season would be Chelsea, Southampton and West Ham with an away trip to Arsenal in there as well. You could almost hear the collective, Oh shit! That emanated from Portsmouth Central police station. The game at Oxford came and went without incident although we did get a taste of things to come on the pitch when we saw 5 goals go past Alan Knight. The following Tuesday saw the First Division One football match at Fratton Park for thirty plus years; the fact that it was against Chelsea just added to the occasion as far as the 6.57 were concerned. The Pompey versus Chelsea fixture had seen many disturbances in previous years; as far back as September 1975 saw serious fighting in Goldsmith Avenue after the match. In August 1978 Pompey played a pre-season friendly against Chelsea at Fratton Park. The game saw Chelsea fans try and take the Fratton End however the attempt was doomed to failure when hundreds of Pompey fans pitched into the battle by the fence between the Fratton End and the South enclosure. As the Chelsea fans were being run, the Pompey fans taunted them with chants of West Ham and West Ham's going to get you, a reference to the season before when pictures of the boys from the East End taking the Shed and running Chelsea across the pitch at Stamford Bridge were seen on national television. Twenty-seven fans were arrested. There was however tragedy later on when fans clashed on a train going towards Fareham. As the train pulled into Fareham station a sixteen-year-old Pompey fan fell onto the track where his leg was severed.

Warnings of what to expect were uttered by Judge Nathaniel Baker QC. At a ceremony at the Guildhall, hours before the first home game kicked off, he described Portsmouth as 'a city of violence', carrying on to comment 'What will happen now the football team is in the First Division, only time will tell'. He didn't have to wait long to find out.

Mobbing up in the usual haunts, we had, as expected, massive numbers out. We knew Chelsea would turn up and the events of when they had turned us over in 1984 were still fresh in many of our memories. Now though, we were three years older and wiser. There were one or two minor incidents before the match but it was after that the real fun and games started. A mob of Chelsea managed to get into Milton Road, however as they started to make their move, loads of us emptied from Dukes Bar. Chelsea stood their ground as, for a little while, it went mental. The air was filled the usual shouts as the battle raged back and forth. A little later on, it went off again with some Chelsea that were parked up in Glasgow Road. It took the police a while to restore order and, while both lots gave as good as they got, it was probably Pompey that just about shaded it on this occasion. The return game later that season saw 300 of us arrive at Stamford Bridge via Earl's Court undetected.

Both the police and the Headhunters alike were gutted that we had been able to walk around the area unhindered. After the game, with helicopters buzzing about overhead, we battered Chelsea down a side road near Brompton Park. An hour later though, the tables were turned when the Headhunters had us on our toes at the Embankment.

Although matches between Portsmouth and Chelsea have seen serious outbreaks of violence at Fratton Park, the level of disorder hasn't been the same at Stamford Bridge even though we have turned up there in numbers on several occasions. We even travelled to West London for a Full Members Cup tie catching Chelsea by surprise with the amount we took for what was basically a nothing game. Chelsea were backed off down the street after we had unloaded a skip and attacked them with the contents.

While the Chelsea game had been looked forward to by many, the game that everyone had been counting the days off to was the following Saturday. It had been three years since Pompey had played Southampton in the FA Cup and as many as eleven years since the sides had met in a league match. Early Saturday morning, members of the 6.57 Crew started to group together in various areas. First up were the Salisbury lads. They caught the train to Pompey via Scum, scouting as they went and picking up a few scalps along the way. Next up were the Fareham lads. Southampton to Portsmouth trains stop at Fareham which, although it is about half way between the two, has always been staunchly Portsmouth. They boarded the train that a few of the Scummers were on and terrorised them and so it went on, different train, different mob. Every stop meant more fear and humiliation for the Scummers. Although it had been sometime since the sides had played one another, some of the boys kept the rivalry going with little trips west such as the Bank holiday trip to Southampton common when it was known that their mob would be there. We turned up and the locals couldn't believe it. Before the end of the day, fourteen Pompey lads were arrested, nine in the city and further five after police stopped a Portsmouth bound bus on the M27 motorway. Unfortunately, the Scummers were true to form. Instead of accepting things as they were, a couple of them turned out in court and gave evidence against those who had been arrested, resulting in jail terms for some and heavy fines for the others.

By lunchtime, we had massive mobs in place around the various pubs. By 1 o'clock, word began to filter around that it was kicking off on Fratton Bridge but, by the time most of us got there, the police had restored order. Talking to someone who was involved, it was pretty much nothing more than an over reaction from a twitchy police force anyway. The atmosphere around the area of the ground was like a pressure cooker, ready to explode and it was very clear that, once it did, there was no way that the police would be able to control it. An hour or so later, the vast majority of the Pompey mob were in the three pubs that are more or less next to each other by the junction of Priory Crescent and Milton Road. The Hampshire constabulary had over 450 officers on duty and, for the first time ever at a football match, were using their Optica spotter plane in order to spot where mobs were gathering. A couple of guys came running into the Milton Arms and announced that the Scummers were coming down Goldsmith Avenue. Within seconds, the pub emptied as did the other two pubs who obviously sensed that this was it. We pushed our way through the police line as if they weren't there and ran down Priory Crescent. As this was happening, the first of the Scum mob had met up with a small group of Pompey fans and went into them. During the attack, one of the Portsmouth supporters was badly slashed. Just seconds later, the Pompey mob appeared around the bend of the road, unfortunately too late to save the Pompey fan from horrific injuries. The entire width of the road was packed as hundreds of us stampeded down the road. An ear splitting roar went up as we brushed aside the flimsy line of police trying to hold us back. Suddenly, the Scummers didn't feel quite so brave; they scattered in all directions, some into the park where they received a dreadful beating. Some tried to hide behind the police. Others ran back to Fratton train station and got the next train home. I know this to be true as I have since spoken to one of them that did just that, his excuse being that after they had been split up, he was with two others and surrounded by hundreds of home fans. They took the odd punch and kick and ran back towards the station with the intention of regrouping and maybe getting an escort back to the ground. After finding refuge by the station, a policeman apparently thinking they were Pompey supporters tried to move them on. They said that they were Saints fans but, instead of getting a sympathetic hearing, were told 'Well you shouldn't have come then, should you?'. They decided that it just wasn't worth dying for and got back on the train.

The slashing lit the fuse, setting off a chain reaction of events that would take the police long into Saturday night to quell. As the poor unfortunate Pompey fan was being loaded into the ambulance, his face cut to ribbons, a top lad from Leigh Park jumped up on the bonnet of a parked car.

'Look at this poor bastard' he shouted 'That's how brave these Scummers are, that's one of our own in that ambulance. Are we going to let these bastards walk into our town and do things like this?'

Another massive roar went up and, although the police attempted to push the crowd back, they had lost control. The mob surged down Carisbrooke Road towards the away supporter's turnstiles. There used to be a shop on the corner there and a group of the Inside Crew were huddled outside. Most of this group were already sporting battle wounds and looked like they had already had enough for one day and had run up the white flag; it was only half past two. The mob saw this group and headed straight for them. The look on their faces said it all, sheer terror. Within seconds, a group of 20 blokes had vanished and in its place were individual acts of brutality taking place. The police fought to gain control of the situation. As Alsatians were tearing lumps out of anyone who got too close, you could see that one or two of the policemen were fogged in 'red mist' (the police jargon for lost control of themselves) and were wildly punching and lashing out with their truncheons as the whole situation descended into chaos. Eventually the police managed to push us down Alverstone Road and a calm hung over the area as everyone, mob and police alike, seemed to take a breather.

The match itself passed without incident. Once the game finished, everyone left the ground and tried to make our way to the away fans exit. At one point, some of the lads on the North Terrace managed to climb over the fence next to the Milton End before they got anywhere near the Saints fans, however the police, with batons drawn, managed to force them back. Another group of blues fans had got into Specks Lane directly behind the Milton End and started throwing bricks at the fans that were penned in, unable to neither take cover nor retaliate. The police chased the gang off with dogs and blocked off the alleyway as well as Alverstone Road, forcing Pompey fans to go to the main Milton Road. What was going on here was almost surreal. Everybody seemed in their own little world, concerned only with what they were doing. Cars with Southampton FC stickers on the windows were being vandalised and little pockets of violence were flaring up. As I walked around the bend near the Renault car showrooms, there was this lad and a copper having a stand up fight. Both of them seemed oblivious to the presence of anyone one else around them. The strange thing was people just walked past them taking no notice whatsoever as if it were the most natural thing in the world. From what I can remember, I think the policeman was just edging it on points as I walked on leaving them to it.

A large mob now charged down the street attempting to get down Alverstone Road to the away fans exit. As the police tried to stop them, the Pompey mob emptied a load of bricks and other stuff from the front garden of one of the houses. At one point, a bedstead was thrown at a dog handler, injuring not only the dog but also the policeman who was taken to hospital with a suspected broken leg. Similar to the cup game a couple of years earlier, a large crowd began to gather in Goldsmith Avenue. As the police tried to clear a safe passage for the Saints fans to start their journey home, the disorderly mob, probably in excess of 1,000, splintered into the back streets where mini riots were taking place. As well as coming under a hail of missiles, flares were fired at the ill prepared police lines. By now, things were getting out of control. While half ran down Frensham Road, a tree lined residential area, in an attempt to double back towards the ground, the other half were being continually pushed down Goldsmith Avenue. In Frensham Road, garden walls were pushed down and a vicious assault was unleashed on the pursuing police. Meanwhile, the mob in Goldsmith Avenue had reached Fratton Bridge where an uneasy stand off was being played out. The Hampshire Constabulary had come under a lot of criticism from the business community after the FA Cup game in 1984 for allowing so much damage to be caused in Fratton Road. Now they were caught between a similar event happening again and keeping the Pompey fans far enough away from Fratton station. As this was going on, the mob that had broken off and were battling the police in Frensham Road had now reached Devonshire Avenue, a long wide road that runs parallel with Goldsmith Avenue. Here, they continued in their efforts to get towards Fratton Park with a view to cutting back down one of the side streets which would have brought them back out more or less to where the Scummers would be leaving the confines and safety of the ground. Obviously, this was the last thing that the police would want so began to force them down the side streets on the south side of the road. The result of this was more running battles and more damage to property.

After the best part of an hour, the police considered that it was safe enough to escort the Southampton fans to Fratton station although this was the signal for hundreds more Pompey hooligans that, up until now, had kept a low profile, to come running through Prince Albert Road and Milton Park in an attempt to attack the escort. It took the police around forty minutes to escort the fans from the ground to Fratton station, a journey of around half a mile, such was the job they had to keep the attacking Pompey mobs at bay. By now, myself and Pete had made our way to his car and were driving around to see what was happening. We reached Fawcett Road and saw a group of around twenty Pompey walking along. Behind the group were two police vans and a line of coppers. Suddenly, without warning, the police charged the group of fans who scattered. The police seemed to pick out one fan in particular who was a well-known face. Four of them got hold of him and literally started to beat him up. As they punched and kicked him, myself and Pete voiced our protest. Pete had a camera with him and tried to take a photograph of the assault that was taking place, however another policeman stood in front of him. We voiced our concerns to this particular constable but he replied that we didn't know what this group had been up to previously and that the guy deserved it.

We were all looking forward to going to The Dell later on in the season but the police made sure that there was not to be a repeat of the trouble. The game was played on a Sunday with a 12 o'clock kick-off. A good firm of us got off the train, a couple of stops before the main station. We were trying our best to get in unnoticed of course but it never had the desired effect. A passing police car quickly latched onto us and called in reinforcements. Despite there being absolutely no trouble, there had been no damage caused and we were the only ones around so there was certainly no one for us to fight with, everyone was arrested, well over 100. One particular tabloid newspaper wrongly stated that the arrests followed fighting at the station but then, why let a simple thing like the facts get in the way of a good story. We were arrested under one of those 'because we can' laws that every football fan knows exist. The cells in the Southampton City bridewell were full to bursting point as more and more Pompey fans were arrested, either as they got off the train or pulled off the motorway. Every single one of us was released without charge after the match. Had this been any other type of event, MP's, newspapers and those rounded up would have been screaming about civil liberties but, as it was football fans, it was bollocks to them. For the record, Pompey won the match 2 – 0, small consolation when we were eventually relegated at the end of the season.

It was a gloriously hot sunny August Bank holiday Monday when West Ham rode into town. The famous Inter City Firm were, without doubt, the number one firm in the country at the time. While Millwall were a nasty and vicious bunch and Chelsea a top firm who could turn out in large numbers, neither seemed to have the style or swagger that the ICF had. West Ham seemed to have an air about them that said, 'We are top dogs and we know it'. As expected, the ICF arrived that day with a very impressive mob, yet we were determined to show that we were worthy of our own growing reputation around the football grounds up and down England; this was truly a hooligan's top of the table clash. However, like a lot of big clashes, this one didn't live up to its billing. The beleaguered Hampshire police force that had been through the mill a little over the past week was determined not to mess about today. Just after 1 o'clock, there were a few small clashes although in the opening exchanges on the corner of Goldsmith Avenue and Priory Crescent, a few of the lads lost a bit of respect for the ICF. In fairness, looking at the guy, he was more likely to have been an 'Under 5' with his shaggy mullet-like permed hair, gold chain, wearing the latest designer number came bouncing towards some of us with a dozen or so mates, it looked like game on. One of the lads, Paul, who I have a massive amount of respect for, stepped forward and smacked him straight in the mouth. The West Ham fan picked himself up off of the floor and, instead of steaming in, went straight over to a police van and started to point out various lads. Fortunately, we all managed to slip away. There was only one major clash that day and West Ham got the better of it running us through Milton Park which is a large park near to the ground. It was men against boys as the ICF all seemed to be about ten years older than most of us. After the match, the police battled with both sets of fans in order to keep them apart, something they managed with great success. This was the day that police dog handler PC Yates and his dog Ajax, arrested 20 or so West Ham fans in one go after they tried to break away from the police escort back to the train station. By and large, the police won the battle that day although, when the two mobs did get together for a very limited time before the game, it was West Ham that came out on top. Later on though, we did have a moral if not actual victory in the return game at Upton Park. We took a massive mob to the capital, all of us keen to test our mettle against the mighty ICF. We got the tube as far as Canning Town where we got off and spent a little time in a pub, tucked up out of the way. From there, we walked to Upton Park, brazenly walking down the main road, in and out of the West Ham pubs as if we'd had been given the freedom of the City. Not a punch was thrown and whether the West Ham boys liked it or not, Pompey had taken a liberty and it went unopposed.

The first three games at Fratton Park that season saw 252 arrests, with thousands of pounds worth of damage and many injuries to fans and police alike. While it was a season to forget on the pitch, off it was more memorable for one reason or another. Having heard stories about the Gooners and the mob that they were supposed to have, when we went up there we made a point of making sure we had a good turn out. They had arrived at Fratton Park with most of their well known faces for the friendly a few years before but, by the time we travelled to Highbury, maybe most of them had left the football scene because, despite trying to find them, there was no sign of any Arsenal lads around North London at all.

On the pitch, Pompey were torn apart. At the West One pub in Piccadilly later that night, the question everyone was asking was 'What was the final score?' As most of the guys, seeing the lack of opposition from our Arsenal counterparts, had started to leave as the goals went flooding past an overwhelmed Alan Knight. Most had seen 4 - 0, some had seen 5 - 0 and a few had seen 6 - 0 which was in fact the eventual score-line. That night, during a great night out in the West End, myself and two others (its okay, lads I won't name you!) pulled some Swedish girls who were on holiday over here. While this has nothing to do with this book, I just love to remember the occasion! While we were doing our bit for Anglo-Swedish relations, some of the lads bumped into the elusive Arsenal mob. They asked them where they had been all day. The Gooners merely answered that they had been drinking out of the way. Our mates were happy to let it be but soon the Gooners were bouncing around the road being lairy. Needing no second invite, the 6.57 lads went into them. One of the boys passed a skip; he reached in and pulled out an umbrella. Unfortunately only the handle came out, not that it seemed to bother our man. He waded straight in. What the Gooners must have thought when this lunatic armed only with a brolly handle, steamed into them, God only knows. As for the rest of the Pompey lads, it was all they could do to hold each other up from laughing too much.

The season was a long hard slog for the Pompey team and, by the time May came around, Pompey, as we had all feared at the start of the campaign, had been relegated long before the last game but at least we would have one last hurrah with a trip to Manchester United. The Red Army hadn't travelled to Fratton and the Cockney Reds had found themselves simply outclassed after the game as they were quickly dispatched in Goldsmith Avenue. We had a feeling that things would be a bit different at Old Trafford so, with anticipation, we made a point of putting on a bit of a show. With no police escort, around three hundred of us tried hard to find some entertainment before the match but the whole day was summed up when, during the game, the United stood next to us started singing 'Where's your famous 6.57 Crew?'. We just turned towards them, waved and took a bow, all the time thinking 'walking around looking for you lot most of the day'. Meanwhile, ten lads from Fareham took the opportunity to make their presence felt, steaming in to a few manc's in the seats. After the game, there was another non-event as we spent ages on another fruitless search for the Red Army but it just wasn't to be. Maybe they thought that we wouldn't bother with the trip given there was nothing to play for. We would bump into the Manchester United Red Army eventually but we would all be on international duty during the summer.

6

THERE'LL ALWAYS BE AN ENGLAND

After establishing ourselves among the top firms in the country, we were looking around for a new challenge. Up to now, only a few lads had travelled watching England. Most of us had only seen the national team at Wembley. The next step was always going to be following them away from home. It wasn't long before the opportunity arose in the shape of a trip across Hadrian's Wall, an occasion not to be missed. For years, Scottish supporters had made a bi-annual pilgrimage to Wembley for the Home International match. To the annoyance of many English, the invasion of the Tartan Army went largely unopposed. The last straw for many was when the Jocks invaded the pitch and caused untold damage to the home of football. It's funny how I hear various Scottish celebrities and even footballers claiming to be part of the vandalism that day as if it gives them some sort of kudos. The damage was dismissed as over enthusiastic celebrations following the Scots win. I wonder, had it been the English on the rampage, if it would have been written off so lightly. English lads rarely, if ever, went north of the border when the fixture was played at Hampden although that was to change come the Casual era. From small beginnings in 1985 to total role reversal years later when the English mobs began to rule the roost.

We left Portsmouth & Southsea train station around teatime on Friday, twenty five of us at that time although we knew more would be leaving later. Once in London, we made our way to Euston for our connecting train only to be met by a group of Chelsea Headhunters roughly in the same numbers as ourselves. The Chelsea boys were a bit pissed off as they had just been done by the ICF, some of who were also still about. A stand-off developed during which one of our lads walked towards them, took off his cricket hat to reveal his freshly shaven head, saying 'I'm Pompey, who wants it?'. At this point, a well-known West Ham face sucker punched one of the Chelsea number which brought the police running over, defusing the situation. The majority of our lot decided to wait for the rest of Pompey's travelling mob who would be a couple of hours behind while the rest of us elected to stick to our original travel plans and continued our journey north. With the benefit of hindsight, we would have been better off catching the later train, ours broke down in Stevenage, and didn't get going again for another four hours, and this was only the start of a nightmare weekend travelling on the trains up and down the country. Eventually we were on our way again, and on arriving in Newcastle we were shocked to see so many wearing kilts, Geordies supporting Scotland! Their excuse being that they lived closer to Scotland than they did London, we countered that we lived spitting distance from Cherbourg but we don't support France. We did however get chatting to a few like-minded Newcastle lads and swapped stories of recent encounters with each other. At the time, we were more than happy to mix with fans of other clubs but one.

One of our old campaigners explained - 'Keep yourselves to yourselves because it only causes grief. You always get some idiot who will start saying, we done you in nineteen whatever and it ends up with ill feeling. Therefore fraternising should be kept at a minimum until you get to know lads from other clubs and you know you can trust them.'

From then on, while we mixed with others during trips and were never interested in some of north versus south stuff that went on from time to time, we did make a point of always doing our own thing and if others were okay with us we would always be fine with them, if not then so be it.

We eventually reached Edinburgh. The best part of fourteen hours after leaving Pompey, we, almost immediately, began to hear stories that Hibs and West Ham had been busy, another connecting train whisked us to Glasgow. The station was already very busy with Scottish supporters and you could sense the hatred from them. The atmosphere was unlike anything that I had experienced up to that point, as they spat at us. They weren't that interested in having it, they literally spat out their hatred. After grabbing a bite of breakfast, we set off on a long walk towards Hampden to see if we could find the rest of our lot. There were not many England fans present that day, maybe as little as 1,500 which apparently was the most that had travelled there before now. We entered the ground and were in the section directly next to the tunnel. One of our lads, George, decided to sit on the bench with the players, joining in with the national anthem and, at half time, helping to tread down the divots. It would have been even more funny had we not been under a constant barrage of flags with Bannock Burn on them, thrown by spotty teenagers. We hung our Portsmouth Union Flag on the fence facing the Rangers end of the ground only for a chorus of 'What the fucking hell is that?' to echo around the stadium. The game itself didn't live up to the hype but, shortly after Scotland had taken the lead, there was the first sign of action on the terraces when fighting broke out in the open end of the ground. There were a few surges and open spaces developed, a sure sign it's kicking off as more England lads grouped together. The police quickly moved in and ejected the English invaders, frog marching them around the pitch. As the rest of the ground booed, we gave them a standing ovation. They were brought into the section we were in. We noticed that as well as the Aston Villa lads (who we would get to recognise at many future England games), there were our lot. Apparently they had got onto the terrace together and stood unnoticed among the Jocks. It was clear that they were English when they didn't celebrate the goal so one of the Villa lads took a cross of St. George flag out of his jacket which had the effect you would think in the middle of thousands of pissed up Scots.

Once the game came to an end, we were marched to the nearby station and put on a train to Glasgow. Halfway through the journey, it was apparent that it was going off a few carriages further down from us. The train came to a sudden stop in the middle of a large council estate. Someone had clearly pulled the communication cord. Unknown to us, we were in the middle of the infamous Gorbels and the Jocks on the train were calling for help from the locals. On hearing the screams and shouts from the carriages, the driver had abandoned his train and gone to a track-side phone to summon help. We could hear Scots shouting that a couple of them had been stabbed a couple of carriages away, allegedly it was by some 'Boro fans. The train was so packed it was impossible to move from one carriage to another so we stuck our heads out of the window to try and see what was going on only to see locals pouring off the estate and descending on the train. It was like a scene from a western movie as the Indians attack the train. In our particular carriage were good Birmingham and Everton lads. Inter-club rivalries were forgotten. We were English together and were like sitting ducks. Fortunately, the train jerked into motion and got us out of it. The next station we rolled into was lined with riot police. Everyone was taken off the train and questioned which took ages; yet another connecting train was going to be missed. When we finally got to Glasgow Central, we stopped to make sure that we were altogether and then we encountered our only proper mob of Scots all day. They surrounded us but didn't steam in. There were a few verbal exchanges and one or two spat at us. Nice people the Scottish. They informed us that we had met the Aberdeen Soccer Casuals; we can't say we were all that impressed to be honest.

As we had missed our train back to London, but we decided that, as we'd had enough of Scotland, we would just catch the next one south and boarded one to Preston, settling in the first class compartment. While discussing the game, we discovered we had a journalist in the seats opposite us. He had been covering the match for one of the national papers and was complaining that he had to travel straight back to London, then on to Brussels to report on the European Cup Final between Liverpool and Juventus. We had barely left Glasgow when an English fan from one of the Manchester clubs was stomping up and down the train, mustering support to fight some Jocks in the buffet car. We saw him walk one way down the train and, seconds later, come charging back with a toilet seat in his hand back towards the buffet. It went off in the space between the carriages and, within minutes, we pulled into Motherwell where more police boarded the train. During the fight, someone had received a fairly serious head injury after he'd been hit with a bottle. Another four-hour delay! A quick drink in Preston and on to London.

After what seemed like an eternity, we reached Euston where we crossed paths with a group of Liverpool lads in their late twenties, a lot older than us. They were on their way to Belgium for a 'rob' and to witness a game that would change most peoples view of football hooliganism forever. We were nearly home. A quick stop at Casey Jones on Waterloo station to buy as much food as we could before the final leg of our marathon journey. I finally arrived home, tired and smelly around 1 o'clock Sunday afternoon.

Another milestone had been passed, my first England away game. It was like nothing that I'd experienced before. It was a new level of being a hooligan with a pride, passion and hatred I had not seen before. The Jocks, to be honest, did not seem that interested in fighting unless provoked. They just wanted us to know how much they hated us by verbal abuse and spitting. For the first time, the England mob had travelled north of the border in significant numbers and had done well. It was relatively small beginnings but there would no longer be a psychological barrier in taking it to the Scots. In the next fixtures at Hampden Park, more and more England Casuals would be making the trip with the 6.57 Crew being in the forefront.

Now that we had experienced what it was like following England away, we started making trips on a fairly regular basis. Some of the older lads had been England regulars for a while. One in particular is respected by all, not by just us in Pompey but also by many lads around the country. It was many of the original Pompey firm that had been involved when it kicked off in Switzerland in 1981 and it was a few of the same lot that had made the journey to Mexico for the world cup in 1986. They flew to America and hired a car for a month, driving south across the Rio Grande. Once in Mexico, they stopped in a few of the one-horse border towns. The locals were friendly and accommodating with many of them eager to learn English. Always happy to help, the lads gave them a few essential phrases such as 'Play up Pompey', 'Fuck the Scummers', etc which must have come in very handy when they were pulled up by the boarder patrol as they tried to enter the United States.

There was no trouble during the tournament until England met Argentina in the famous Azteca Stadium in Mexico City. Of course this game is most famous for 'that goal'. I know most of the football world revere Diego Maradona as one of the greatest ever footballers but, as far as I'm concerned, he will always be a cheating Eddie Large look alike! With the Falkland's war still fresh in the memories of everyone, it was pretty obvious that the Argentineans who heavily outnumbered the English supporters would be looking to take a few liberties. Inside the ground, there were a few isolated incidents but it was on the streets outside where most of the action took place with the small band of Pompey lads right in the thick of things. One of ours spotted a particular Argie dishing out a few sly slaps so, after wading in with a few digs of his own, the Argie was quickly put on his back. It was now that things quickly went wrong for our man though. The Argentine hooligan turned out to be an under cover Mexican policeman and, very soon, his colleagues were dragging our hero towards the cells where an extended stay looked to be a racing certainty. After a while, the English fans that had been arrested were visited by an official from the British Embassy. Notoriously, these officials have been regarded of as much use as a chocolate tea pot to football supporters detained abroad. This one though was of an altogether different breed. He made it pretty clear that with a back hander of around five hundred Pesos to the guards, even a suspected murderer could buy his freedom. It was quickly worked out that 500 Pesos was about twenty quid, cheap at half the price. Less than an hour later, they were toasting their freedom! It was with stories like this filling our heads that in 1988 we travelled to the Continent for the European Championships held in Germany.

Someone at the Football Association came up with the idea of a 30-day Euro railcard. 30 days wasn't a coincidence as they had organised a pre-tournament warm up game in Switzerland. Well, seeing as they had gone to all that trouble, it would have been rude not to take them up on their offer. Thirty of us boarded a cross channel ferry from Portsmouth to Le Havre before boarding trains to take us across the continent. Part of the group was made up of the 'Old Vic' football team who played in one of the local Sunday leagues including the player manager Chas. The 'Old Vic' lads were all top drawer 6.57 Crew, none of whom were very far from the front regardless of the opposition. The journey to Switzerland was an eventful one. Somehow, one of our group managed to get into 6 fights in 48 hours, first of all rowing with a French taxi driver at six in the morning through to head butting a Swiss skinhead in Zurich, thus causing a major battle between England fans and more Swiss skins who were wearing flight jackets, Union Jack T-shirts as well as the obligatory Dr. Martin boots.

Come match day we met up with Lewisham, an old school member of the ICF. Lewisham who had a bit of a soft spot for Pompey after he'd had an enjoyable day out at Barnsley with us. Lewisham and Chas decided that it would be a good idea to go into business for themselves. First of all, they pinched half the official match programmes, then stood outside the turnstiles selling them off at half price before investing most of their ill-gotten gain in local schnapps. It was then on to Germany for England's opening game of the championships against Ireland. Our little firm arrived in Stuttgart the day before the game; some of them had a walk around the town to see what was going on. The city centre was fairly quiet but they did spot a clothes shop with various designer labels in the window including Stone Island. At the time Stone Island was much sought after and only available in the most exclusive outlets, not the wannabe hooligan cliché that it is today. Seeing this as an ideal opportunity to earn a bit of extra spending money, the windows were soon going through and the contents emptied only to find some nice shirts but none of the Stone Island that were the original targets.

After the game there was serious trouble outside the stadium, not with the Irish but with the Germans who, as expected, were waiting for us to come out. One of our top lads came to the fore, leading the thirty of us, along with the rest of the English firm, through a tunnel in the shopping centre opposite the train station and into a barrage of flares and fireworks. The Germans were okay throwing things at us from long range but weren't interested when it came to close-quarters combat. The few that stood got battered. The riot police soon waded in and split up the English although we all managed to stay together. It was here that we came across the Red Army. They were so arrogant and, unlike the majority of other English lads, they made no attempt to mix in, keeping themselves very much to themselves. While nothing happened between us on this occasion, we would bump into them on a couple more occasions before our summer holidays were over.

The next stop on the European tour was Düsseldorf for the match against the Dutch. Being on the European mainland, we wondered whether the much talked-about Dutch firm would be in evidence. This, along with the fact that 12 months before many Pompey lads had been involved in vicious fighting with German supporters when England had played in the same stadium, meant our numbers had now swelled to around fifty. On the morning of the game, one German ticket tout learnt a valuable lesson in life; not to wave your tickets in the air when the 'Old Vic' football team is about. They relieved him of his tickets and made off before he knew what was happening. Just about every firm in the country were represented there. Outside the stadium, we came across a good mob of Yids, all game-looking lads but friendly towards us and happy to chat. On the pitch, England were appalling with Gullit and Van Basten taking the piss out of our defence, running out 3-1 winners. We were lucky it was only three. Once more, the Dutch hoolies were nowhere to be seen. I have no idea why Holland are considered to have one of the worse followings seeing as their hooligans which, in the past, been very evident in club matches are hardly ever about during internationals.

As previously, the Germans were out in force and, like in Stuttgart before, it was the Pompey mob that took the battle to the Krauts. The Germans were gathered in two corners by the station but, before they knew what was happening, we were steaming into them from behind. Along with us were three lads from Oldham, one from West Brom and a Geordie. The Germans once more had little stomach for it, backing off until the riot police turned up. Photographs of the battle were printed on the front pages of most of the national papers; one broadsheet in particular had a large photograph of the Pompey lad who had led everyone in. As we were being rounded up by the police, we once again bumped into the Red Army. This was becoming a habit. We asked why they hadn't joined in. They made the excuse that they were being held back by the riot police. We were still buzzing and looked for ways at getting at the Germans again. It was at this point we met up with a few of West Ham ICF, a mix of older heads and Under 5's. Among their number was Lewisham. Pleasantries were exchanged. There were now only about forty of us in total but we said to the West Ham lads that we were going to go into the Germans again. They tried to advise us not to saying the odds were too stacked against us but we were having none of it and steamed in again. Give the ICF lads their due, it might have been the 6.57 that started it but they were straight in and, true to their reputation, were all quality guys. What a day. We were behind enemy lines with little choice but to go on the offensive and had come away more or less unscathed.

So it was on to Frankfurt with a minor detour to Munich where a few of us managed to get into the Olympic Stadium and had a kick-about on the pitch. Chas saw this as ideal training for his team. The game against Russia saw England limp out of Euro '88. Off the field, the German authorities were taking no chances swamping the area with riot police, water cannon, the lot. The only trouble was by the main train station where five Pompey lads and a couple of Chelsea had a brief row with a mob of crazy Hamburg hooligans. The championship may have been over for England but it wasn't the end of our European tour. Taking advantage of the still valid travel cards, quite a few English lads including 40 of the Red Army boys who we had run into while in Germany went on to Lloret de Mar on the Spanish Costa. It was in Spain where the verbal would finally lead to physical confrontation.

Once again, we met up with Lewisham. The year before, West Ham and Manchester United had battled it out on a cross-channel ferry. Although United had the numbers onboard, it was West Ham that had come out on top. Seeing Lewisham in a nightclub, United obviously thought it would now be ideal for a bit of retribution, attacking him and us with glasses and CS gas, forcing us to run out of the club. The following night however, the attack came back to haunt some of the Manc's. We were out looking for them and came across a few of the ringleaders; vengeance was indeed sweet. Many of us spent 15 years having little respect for Manchester United and their Red Army but, in January 2003, twenty of us were sat in a pub just up the road from Trafford Park, prior to a lunchtime kick-off for a 3rd Round FA Cup match, when 100 or so old school Manc's came bowling in, clearly looking for Pompey fans. They could of taken liberties but we managed to walk away unscathed as, apart from a few verbal threats, they gave us a pass, so many of us had a renewed respect for them.

Many of us had got the bug for following England. Making as many trips as possible, we visited places such as Israel where it kicked off quite badly inside a night-club when Bish got the biggest black I've ever seen, as well as the more usual countries across Europe. With the fall of the Berlin Wall at the end of 1989 however, came the opportunity to go to many of the former Eastern Block countries. While some lads had followed England to some of these places before, there was always a lot of red tape involved getting visas so most didn't bother. Come 1991 though, England were due to play Poland who we always seemed to be drawn with in the various qualifiers. This particular game was played in Poznan. I was expecting it to be a grey drab place and, although the city in western Poland is an important industrial area, it does have a beautiful cobbled square with bars and cafes in. The night before the game, a few of us and some lads from Oldham who, as always with England trips, had a few boys there were engaged in a right royal battle with Polish skinheads in the doorway of a bar. The skins were armed with all manner of horticultural artefacts, probably dating back from the days of the horse and cart. It was a brilliant buzz walking back triumphantly up to the rest of the English lads who had elected to remain in the safety of the bar.

While making our way back from the ground, it became clear that there, among the English ranks, was a mob of Southampton, probably around thirty or so of them. A bit later on, one of our lot was standing on the station alone when he was approached and head butted. It was the Scummers looking for an easy victory. A raiding party was quickly mustered, only ten of us, but, what the hell, we couldn't let them do that to our mate and get away with it. They soon came bouncing out to the front where we were. They had more in Poland than they pulled out for a home match most weeks. As soon as they realised that the numbers suited them, they started making all sorts of threats.

After a short slanging match, it kicked off. We made a desperate stand by the doors and managed to hold them off although we weren't unhappy when the Polish riot cops steamed in, belting everyone with their batons. A little bruised, we retired to a nearby bar and sank a few cold ones. We stayed there a while but, as the evening wore on, there were a couple more fights with the local skinheads. One was started by a young Sunderland supporter. Through the day, he had been at bit of a nuisance, bugging everyone by keep asking daft questions about the 6.57 Crew whom, for some reason, he seemed to idolise. During the sporadic fighting, one of our mates was set upon by the riot cops. He was kicked and beaten all the way to their van before being thrown, head first, into it. He ended up being locked up in a military prison along with a few Chelsea fans as well as a few of the very game Oldham boys. Our guy was so pissed however that he spent the majority of his time in custody laughing at the police every time they tried to question him. In the end, probably because they were fed up with him more than anything else, he was moved to a mental hospital until he had sobered up enough to be deported.

Recently, it's the Turks who have become enemy number one for a lot of English fans. This has mainly come-about since the murder of two Leeds United fans in Istanbul. Turkey though has always been a bit of a nasty place for football fans to travel to as we found out in Izmir, Turkey's third largest city. Ten of us flew to Istanbul while a few of the others travelled via Dalaman. We had decided the best way to get around would be to hire a van and drive down to the Aegean Sea, a distance of about 565 kilometres but, at least, we would be able to do our own thing. When we were hiring the van, we were told that driving at night was extremely dangerous and should only be done in an emergency. Unfortunately, this is exactly what we had planned to do; spend the day taking in the sights and having a few beers then head down to Kusadasi or Bodrum. Istanbul was an interesting place to visit, walking through the streets that crusaders once marched. At one point, there was a dancing bear on a leash, something you don't see every day. Once we had visited some of the tourist attractions, we settled in The Sultan Bar where we met up with a couple of the Oldham lads we had become friends with. The thing about this bar was, before we could finish our drinks, the owner would bring over the next round. So, by the time we got out of there, we were all fairly merry to say the least. We stocked up on more beer, wine and potent raki for the long journey ahead and set off. The bloke at the hire place wasn't just trying to scare us with warnings about night driving. You really do take your life into your hands over there. If a lorry was overtaking another, they would simply drive straight at us and expect us to get out of the way. Several times during the trip, I woke up to find us bouncing over the gravel while our driver took evasive action avoiding another lunatic juggernaut.

The first night in Kusadasi was fairly quiet but it wasn't to last. The next night, things started to go haywire. After spending the evening drinking and chatting with the locals, all pleasant stuff, we made our way back to the hotel when the wheels came off. We were strung out, walking along the road, and didn't notice that a few Turks had got together. One of the snidey bastards ran up behind Budgie and cracked him over the head with a bottle. Most of us didn't see it happen but he soon had blood flowing from the wound. Comically, he seemed more concerned about his shirt getting ruined than the damage to his head. Running up to any likely looking Turk, shouting something about a Chipie shirt and crack! Obviously we woke up a bit now, got our drunken act together and waded in to help out. Little one-on-one scuffles were breaking out all over with the Turks as eager as we were to have it. Just as things were starting to hot up, the police arrived. This would usually be the signal for things to calm down but I distinctly remember hearing the words 'Do you lot want it as well then?' as soon as they got out of their vans. Before long, most of us had been nicked and I must admit that I was beginning to think that things were starting to take a major turn for the worse. I certainly didn't fancy the prospects of seeing the inside of a Turkish prison; after all, we have all seen 'Midnight Express'. Somehow we managed to negotiate our way back out. Maybe the sight of Budgie covered in claret helped. Either way, we managed to get back to our accommodation without any further mishaps.

In a small place like Kusadasi, news travels fast so we decided to make ourselves scarce and head over to Izmir for the under-21 match later that day. I volunteered to give Pete a break and take over the driving for a little while. Driving in Turkey at any time is an experience. I don't think they have any concept of lane discipline, indicators are null and void simply replaced by the horn which you beep to tell everyone else that you no longer intend to drive in a straight line. Although we had been on the lash since leaving England, this particular day I hadn't touched a drop to drink. It didn't make any odds though. Something happened and I somehow switched off for five seconds. As I sailed on, oblivious to the bus that had stopped to pick up passengers, everyone in the van shouted at once but it was too late. I swerved hard to avoid the collision but clattered into the back and side of it. We carried on for a further fifty yards as I tried to regain control of our van before we eventually ground to a halt. We got out to survey the damage. The door had a dirty great gash in it and the wing mirror and door handle were gone, melted into the bodywork of the bus. We debated as to whether we should stay and face the music or get out of there quick. We looked up the road to see the bus driver charging towards us. We piled into the van and decided to make our escape. Pete took the wheel and slammed the vehicle into first gear. Meanwhile, the irate bus driver had reached the van and opened the door. We kangarooed down the road while Pete tried to steer with one hand and push the Turk away with the other. It was a scene of pure chaos as the battered van lurched one way then the other while we were being thrown around inside. The bus driver gamely held on, his legs going ten to the dozen. Eventually Pete shouted 'Will someone please smack him'. Someone lent across the front and landed one right on his chin sending him tumbling. We sped off, waving out of the back window. We thought it was best to get out of town and decided to give the under-21's a miss, the games weren't usually up to much anyway.

On the day of the big game, we drove back to Izmir although, for some reason, I wasn't allowed to drive anymore. We parked up on some waste ground near the Ataturk Stadium and went to look for a place for a pre-match aperitif. Most of the area was occupied by garages and looked a complete shit-hole but we spotted a small bar on the corner of the road and it looked as good a place as any for a few quiet shants. We saw a few other England fans around but, as we got nearer, we could see that all the windows in the bar had been smashed. This didn't bode well for our quiet drink. We got talking to the other English lads and were told that the Turks had turned up earlier and had done the windows. They were pretty sure it wouldn't be long before they returned. We ordered our drinks and waited for the attack. Sure enough, the Turks were back and they were mob handed with their numbers growing all the time as blokes from the garages joined them. Looking at them, it didn't look as if they were there to enquire how we were enjoying our holiday so we steamed out of the bar as they started lobbing all sorts at us. It wasn't long before we were forced back inside under a barrage of rocks, bolts and bottles. Back inside the bar, we returned fire with a crate of empties that we managed to liberate as well as most of the furniture. During the mayhem, Pete walked outside with his beer looking completely unperturbed as ensuing bedlam was developing around him. He looked more concerned at spilling his pint than he did of any of the flying debris hitting him. With us were a game group of Sheffield United fans and a few others from different teams but the majority of the England fans had it away on their toes. The only police in attendance was a solitary traffic cop who seemed to think that blowing his whistle loudly would stop everyone in their tracks. Before long, the Turks began to get the upper hand and it became every man for himself. Getting run is horrible but there was no choice for anyone that day. We tried to keep our little group together as, all around us, people were getting felled in the onslaught. Unfortunately this included Budgie who wasn't having the greatest trip. He received a nasty looking stab wound and was bleeding heavily again. Luckily for him, a local woman took him to the nearest hospital to get treatment.

We were getting run around the back streets of Izmir and it was one hell of a dodgy place to get caught alone but, by the time we reached the main road again, we seemed to have given our pursuers the slip. By now we had all been split up. The three lads I was with managed to flag down a passing taxi and made our way to the city centre where, after a bit, we met up with the rest of our lot. There were a lot more English lads in a bar and, this being the pre-mobile age, they were completely oblivious to the earlier trouble. We kept together as mob and made our way back to the stadium. There was an air of hostility all around the area of the ground as there were rarely any visiting fans to Turkey and the press over there had been hyping up the visit of English hooligans for weeks. All those with tickets managed to get in without too many problems but around 100 of us didn't have them so were held outside. There were two representatives of the Football Association outside the stadium; the woman was doing her best to help everyone get inside while her colleague, a Derek Dougan look-alike, couldn't give a toss. Eventually, we got inside and spent ninety minutes watching an awful game being pelted by all manner of things by the Turkish supporters. The police and army did very little to stop them and, if any English tried to retaliate, they were met by a whack with a truncheon or rifle butt. Somehow, despite his injuries, Budgie rejoined us in the ground and he insisted on hanging up his Pompey flag which, by now, was covered with his own blood. The head honcho of the watching police shook his head in disbelief while Budgie dodged missiles as he tied the flag to the fence. Another of the 6.57 lads ended up going to the same hospital after being struck on the head by something; he had six stitches put in which looked like they had been done by Stevie Wonder. I could have done a better job with a needle and thread than whatever doctor had done that work.

At half time we joined up with a group of London boys who supported various teams in the capital. We'd had enough of the one sided pelting and the lack of action by the police to stop it. If they were going to do nothing, we would stop it ourselves. Before we had a chance to launch our assault on the Turkish fans next to us, the police waded into us - funny how they weren't so aggressive with their own lot. Somehow though, there was one lone loon who I think was an Arsenal fan who popped up in the middle of the adjacent section. He wasn't exactly in disguise with a Union Jack draped around his shoulders but the police managed to cart him off though before he could do any damage to either the Turks or himself. After the game, we were held inside for a while and we got ourselves sorted out a mob of around 100 lads from different clubs. As soon as the gates were opened, we went bouncing out into the street. Outside we could see the Turks mobbed up on the other side of the road, giving it the usual shit. We'd had enough of these wankers by now so leapt over the barrier in the middle of the road and we went straight into them. They had been throwing stuff at us all day and were keen to smash us up when the numbers suited them but now, even though there were still more of them, when it came to being up close and personal, they didn't fancy it at all. As soon as we got stuck into them, the Turks were soon legging it up the road. The Turkish police were a different matter however and soon it was the familiar scene of foreign police cracking English skulls. As always abroad, they aren't too bothered about public enquiries and they didn't give a fuck who they laid out with their batons; yet more injuries from a nightmare trip. We got back to our van with a few other lads in tow. We headed back to Kusadasi and didn't mind giving a couple of our countrymen a lift.

When we arrived, we tried to get into a bar that was already heaving with English lads but the owner was having none of it. Everyone seemed a little on edge so it may have already kicked off. We set off to try and find somewhere else to get a drink and soon bumped into a mob of locals on the prowl. We didn't need a second invite and steamed straight into them. I remember running past a lone copper, lashing out with his truncheon, hoping rather than expecting everyone to stop. We just ran around him and smashed into his countrymen. The Turkish mob ran off and we were soon rounded up and basically told to fuck off out of town.

We eventually landed in Bodrum pretty late into the night but found a bar that was happy to stay open all the time we were buying drinks so we stayed there until six or seven in the morning. The place ran out of beer so we were sat knocking back sparkling wine for breakfast. The day was spent relaxing in the sun, recuperating from the day before. I really thought that we had seen the last of the aggro and that evening would be uneventful. I was wrong! There were a fair few English lads in Bodrum which was a far nicer place than Kusadasi and, that night, a lot of us found ourselves in a bar with a DJ playing a lot of well known tunes. Inside the bar was a healthy mix of Turks and English and, on the whole, the atmosphere was relaxed although spirits were high. The DJ started playing New Order's World In Motion and things got a little out of hand. Somehow, a glass frame with the Turkish flag in it was knocked off the wall and smashed. Apparently doing anything to the Turkish flag is the worst crime you can commit over there and the place went bonkers! It went off and the bar got smashed to bits. The fighting went on for ages. Afterwards, as word about the flag spread, it seemed to bring every male in Bodrum onto the streets, vowing vengeance. Every street corner seemed to have a fight taking place on it. During the evening's entertainment, a mate of ours got arrested and spent the night in the local nick with a few other English. The following morning, we went down to bail him out but they were all appearing in court immediately. It looked as if it would get interesting at the court house as there were a fair few locals hanging about and feelings were still running high about the flag incident. Luckily, all the lads, including a Villa fan we knew from previous England encounters, got let out with a variety of fines. We gave two of the Villa lads a lift back to Istanbul. Pete drove pretty much non-stop for fourteen hours to get them back in time for their flight.

When my Grandfather was just fifteen, he lied about his age and joined the Hampshire Regiment to fight in World War One. He fought on the beaches of Gallipoli and was taken prisoner during a raid on the Turkish positions. Along with a few others, he managed to escape being badly bayoneted in the process. He hated the Turks until the day he died. Once I eventually reached home, I was met by my Dad holding a newspaper carrying lurid and wild stories about the trouble. Of course, all the blame was laid squarely at the feet of the England fans. He asked me if I had been involved. I gave him a smile and told that I was just carrying on an old family tradition.

With the World Cup being held in France in 1998, everyone held their breath hoping we would qualify. On the face of it, Italy looked to be our toughest test in Group 2 and this is exactly how it turned out to be. But for a defeat of the Italians at Wembley, we would have breezed through to the finals because of two shock 0-0 draws for Italy away to Georgia and Poland. There was everything to play for in the final match in Rome. Put simply, a draw and we could get our French phrase books out. Thousands of England fans made the trip more in hope rather than expectation and, as usual, we were there in numbers. It was arranged to meet up at 6pm on the Saturday evening prior to the game but just getting into Italy was going to be an effort alone. The flight carrying some of the more well known faces in the 6.57 Crew landed. Instead of being taken straight to the main terminal, the aeroplane taxied to an out of the way spot of the airport where it was surrounded by armoured cars and water cannons. Welcome to Italy, lads. Following stringent passport checks, everyone was allowed on their way. After a Friday night on the piss at the hotel where Nick Hancock of 'They Think Its All Over' fame was kept awake all night by the drunken activities of the lads, Saturday morning was spent having a leisurely stroll around the Spanish steps and giving the credit cards a bashing in the Armani shops. As the day wore on, it was agreed to meet at a bar around the corner from our hotel but, with such a major police presence in the city centre, we instead moved on half a mile or so down the road to a major roundabout. After a few phone calls were made, there was soon a mob of 200 made up from all sorts of clubs including some Welsh lads from Newport - what was that all about? As old friendships were renewed and beers drank, word spread that it had gone off earlier in the day with Oxford and Oldham boys, being led by one of the Oldham lads that we had met in Germany all those years before. As with the majority of England away games, there was a lot of small firms hanging around and, as more beer flowed, so the 'Here We Go' brigade of England shirt wearers got more vocal thus attracting the unwanted attentions of the local police who are always itching for an excuse to break open a few English heads with their batons. Never being ones who followed the crowd, we got ourselves together and started to make a move. About fifty Pompey lads, plus maybe a hundred more English, made up of smaller groups of lots of different teams. As always, the police kept their attentions on the singing scarfers who they perceived to be a threat. We walked for about an hour with a few stops at various bars. As we got closer to the ground, a taxi pulled up and out got the insignificant figure of the self proclaimed 'England's number one' Paul Dodd from Carlisle. He was sent on his way being told in no uncertain ways he was not wanted by us. As with all publicity seekers, he would have only brought unnecessary focus on us from both the police and press who seemed to be about in equal numbers. We got to the first checkpoint by the ground. The police began to split us up. We were down to just forty, all of us Pompey. Then, once we got through the second security check, there were only 10 of us approaching the turnstiles. We waited by some barriers to see if we could see any of the others, most of whom had been directed towards the English section of the ground. We noticed a group of Italians coming towards us, a few more English joined us but we were still heavily outnumbered. As the Italians came towards us, they pulled off their belts and started swinging them about but, as we went towards them, they scattered so maybe all those jokes about the bravery of Italians are true. The Roma Ultras may not have been up for a fight but the police certainly were. They ignored their fellow countrymen, despite them being the instigators, and charged into us. Inside the ground, the treatment dished out by the Italian police was seen by millions of television viewers as they indiscriminately beat English supporters with batons throughout the game. Fortunately, the ten of us were not in the England area of the ground but stood on our seats behind the dugouts as, on the pitch, the team played out a 0-0 draw - good enough to see us through to France. While the rest of the fans were kept behind for nearly three hours after the final whistle, we just walked out of the ground and into a very dark Roman night. The walk back to the hotel took nearly two hours and, at one time during the journey, we thought it was about to come on top for us as we were followed for about ten minutes by Italians on scooters. As we turned a large bend, we came face to face with a mob of Ultras, massively outnumbering us. With little choice, we kept going. To our amazement, the locals did nothing. Maybe it was our bravado or maybe we were given a pass; either way we somehow got through. In all the years of running around with the 6.57 Crew, this was without doubt one of the scariest and there was a huge sigh of relief when we got back to the hotel.

Before starting the journey home the following morning, we went to get some breakfast by the main train station. As we were about to take our seats in the café, we noticed 3 Scummers taking the piss out of a Pompey scarfer. They had hold of his flag with Pompey written across it and were threatening all sorts. They had a sudden change of heart however when we charged over to help him out; they begged for mercy. Instead of giving them the slapping they deserved, we just gave them the same treatment that they had given the Pompey scarfer when the odds were in their favour.

Eventually we were in the air on our way back home, planning our trip to France and the World Cup the following summer when Darren marched into the Business Class section of the plane, sporting a three inch gash in his head courtesy of the Italian police. There he confronted MP Tony Banks who, at the time, was Sports Minister and gave him a graphical account of the actions of the police and asking him what the Government intended to do about it. To his credit, Banks listened to what he had to say and, just as Darren was about to leave, the MP asked what team do you support? When the reply was 'Portsmouth', the late MP for West Ham simply smiled and said 'Pompey, I might have known'.

Whenever England reach the finals of a major championship, it seems the whole country suddenly believes what the tabloids are writing and are convinced we are going to win the tournament. France '98, again expectations were raised beyond what realistically could be achieved by the team. Many travelling to the first game against Tunisia genuinely thought that England would lift the World Cup. For many of us however, that wasn't what immediately concerned us. Despite warnings of violence, FIFA, in their wisdom, had decided to stage the game in Marseille, the second largest city in France and home to the largest Arab population in the country. There is also a direct ferry route from the city to Tunis. Arriving in the town, it was clear that the world's media had also descended on the place but, for every sports reporter there to cover the match, there was probably four wandering the streets looking for stories of their own. By Sunday afternoon, twenty four hours before the kick-off, many English fans were involved in running battles with the locals and police. As always, the police ignored most of what the indigenous population were up to and targeted the English which, in turn, increased the ferocity of the battle. We watched on from afar in a couple of side street bars, about forty of us in total. Rumours were spreading that various newspaper and television people had been offering money to English lads to kick-off throwing chairs and what have you so they could record the events. I have witnessed this first hand in the past and, unfortunately, there always seems to be some idiot who takes the bait. Come the day of the match, we were up early and made our way towards the ground. The atmosphere in Marseille was tense. As the temperature rose, so did our numbers. Around fifty of our lot had made their way to near the Velodrome stadium. It was still only 11 o'clock but gossip was doing the rounds about what had happened during the night. Some of us made our way into the ground while others moved towards the beach and the giant screen that had been set up there to show the match. England's 2-0 win was over shadowed by events that happened at the giant screen. I wasn't there but, by all accounts, the scenes there were those that have been seen many times by anyone regular at England away matches. Apparently, shortly after Alan Shearer had made it one nil, the English support which, on the whole, was made up of families enjoying the sunshine, came under a hail of bottles and other missiles. Obviously they were forced to flee, a signal for the French CRS riot police to charge in. Rather than force the Tunisian/French mob back, the riot police once more turned on the English, hitting and arresting anyone who got close. Under attack from all quarters, many lads put a protective wall between the families and the riot police, not forgetting that behind the police, the locals continued to throw whatever they could at the English supporters, totally unhindered by the police. It was clear that whoever was in charge of the policing had made up their mind that it was open season on anyone English. In order to protect themselves as much as anything, the English lads started taking the law into their own hands, charging forward, forcing both police and locals to give ground and allow those who wanted to get away a bit of breathing space. Of course, back home this wasn't the story that made the newspapers. As always, the trouble was blamed solely on the English supporters. No change there then.

For many of us, watching England play has never been the greatest experience although we wouldn't have missed it for the world. The national team has never reached the heights that some of the overpaid players maybe should have. We have had many great individuals over the years but they have never seemed to have put it together as a team. Of course, some of the tournaments we can consider ourselves a little unlucky with and then there has been the nightmare of penalty shoot-outs. Just the phrase alone is enough to send a chill down the spine of the average English football fan. It would be wrong to say it's been all bad. We have seen the odd decent performance but one match will forever stand out in the memory. Ninety minutes of sheer brilliance that almost wiped out every nightmare trip and every missed penalty. A trip that would go down in history. One where, in years to come, fans would be proud to say, 'I was there'. For once with England, it was the events on the field that would make the headlines around the world and the picture of the scoreboard that night is indelibly printed onto the memory of every English football fan - Deutschland 1 England 5.

The night before the big match, we made the Lowenbrau beer hall our home; it was clear from the start that this trip was going to be a party and not a repeat of 1988 although many of the same faces were in attendance. Back then, we were ready and looking for it to off; now though, it was all about friendships forged over many years watching football as well as experiencing different countries and culture along with whatever other delights were on offer. As the beer flowed, all of the old songs from the 1970's started to ring around the place, 'Drink the drink the drink to David Kemp', 'Tip toe through the Fratton End' and many more. Some of the fellas moved on to the Beatles bar for a Birthday drink with one of the old lads who now lives in Munich. A crazy night which ended up with the Germans being upstaged with chants of big fish, little fish, Cardboard box, with the big man from Emsworth performing the actions with his shoe, balanced on his head. The following day, while many nursed hangovers, close to 100 Pompey lads from across the generations met up and, once more, the beer flowed, stories were told and songs sung.

However, old habits tend to die hard. It was agreed to lose the attentions of the police by not taking the obvious train to the Olympic Stadium. In what must have been a first in the history of the 6.57 Crew, we all managed to stay together and got on the subway which took us to the opposite side of the arena to where the 15000 English fans were gathering, a walk of a couple of miles. Outside the station, there were very few police on duty although a handful did begin to follow us as we began to walk towards the arena. It was clear though that, should we bump into a mob of Germans, there was little those police would be able to do about it. In the end, the walk passed without incident. We took our places in the ground and watched a miracle unfold. It doesn't get much better than that, watching England put five past the Germans in deepest Bavaria. Afterwards, the Germans slipped away unnoticed as we celebrated. Perhaps they had seen enough for one night. The weekend passed by peacefully although we did do our very best to drink the Lowenbrau beer hall dry in celebration.

The triumph in Germany was a distant memory when we travelled to Slovakia for a key Euro 2004 qualifying match. Being somewhere else to visit, it had been decided sometime earlier that many of us would travel. Thirty old school growlers made up the Dads Army advance party. We left on the Friday, flying via Zurich to Vienna. The weather was both cold and very wet as half of us spent the evening hopping from bar to bar, drinking Jagermeister and the local brew while the others elected to stay in the hotel bar. We bumped into a few lads from Burnley and QPR who we had a chat and more beer with. All in all, it was a pretty quiet night. Unbeknown to us, two hours away in downtown Bratislava, other England fans were extending pleasantries with the local Mafia. All the clubs and bars were paying the mobsters protection money. Around one in the morning, a group of English were leaving a bar when an argument over an alleged unpaid bill turned violent; one fan was shot while another was badly beaten up. The whole trip turned from being one that was a jolly-up in the western tip of the old eastern block to a potential time bomb. Using our mobiles, we could easily keep tabs on where everyone was and make arrangements to meet up on Saturday afternoon. Ten of the Milton lads were flying out from Luton on a chartered flight in the morning while we left Vienna in a fleet of taxis, meeting up at 2pm in the old part of town. By mid afternoon, there were around seventy of us, congregated in the former Soviet Union 2000 miles away from Portsea Island. Andy T, well known for a banner and his camera, put up a sign reading '6.57 HQ' as we settled in before making our way to the ground. A sign of the times was when ten of the former 'Old Vic' crew left early as they had arranged a hospitality package. Meanwhile, the rest of us marched en-masse through the centre of the town. No hangers-on amongst this group and, while not looking for it, we knew it would take something pretty good to shift us. Once at the ground, we found a welcoming committee not made up of either the local loons or the gangsters but police commando units. They were all in riot gear with their faces masked with balaclavas. It was clear straight away that this was going to be another Rome. Fifteen minutes before halftime, all the forecasts came true as the riot police indiscriminately smashed into the English support. Despite the pictures being broadcast around the world, FIFA did nothing although the Slovakian FA were fined for the racist abuse dished out to the black English players. Some of the Pompey lads did get attention from the Slovak Mafia though. During the national anthems being sung, the 'Old Vic' lads were singled out by a group of smartly dressed meat heads who had obviously been to the Leeds Service Crew finishing school. They spoke very little English but they knew how to indicate a knife across the throat. The 'Old Vic' lads did, however, manage to get away unscathed and meet up with the rest of us later that evening.

Before we went out to Portugal for the European championships, one of the firm, Hoppy, decided that the time was right to tie the knot. Bored of the usual stag night trips to Amsterdam or Prague, it was decided his traditional last night of freedom should be in Tallinn. Although it was the last thing on the minds of all those that flew out, yet another city was added to the catalogue of places that has seen the 6.57 Crew doing what it does best. It was a quiet start to the weekend, arriving late on Friday night and watching Millwall get beaten in a pretty boring FA Cup final. Things got livelier as the day went on so, by the time we reached a night-club in the early hours of Sunday morning, most were fairly wrecked. It was probably this more than anything else why we soon found ourselves battling with off-duty members of the Russian army. At one stage, the place resembled the OK Corral. Ten Pompey slugging it out while one of the crazy Russians, spinning around in the centre of the dance floor, was trying to deliver karate kicks. He must have regretted it in the morning after he was met with a barrage of glasses, stools and well placed quality punches. The locals were stunned by the intensity of the fighting and, some time later once the security had cleared the soldiers out leaving us inside, the bouncers commented that they had never seen anything like it. A small bunch of lads who were all more like middle aged men, totally outnumbered but fearless, had not only held their own but driven these trained military men back. Tallinn could now be added to the list of places who had witnessed first hand those who follow Pompey are no easy pushover even for the 'real' Red Army.

It was a far less eventful trip to Portugal. Most of us made base camp in and around the Estoril area of Lisbon. The biggest firm we had out there was probably for the Croatia game when there was fifty drinking around the port area. The look on the faces of two Scummers was a picture. They came drunkenly down the road, their Union jack draped around their shoulders, singing 'When the Saints go marching in'. They sobered up instantly when they turned the corner and came face to face with us, all outside a bar, our large 6.57 Crew flag proudly flying. As usual, we declined to take a liberty.

That's not our style, regardless of who the opposition is. On the whole, the tournament passed off peacefully apart from a few plastic chair throwers around the holiday resort areas. It showed how far things have changed when England fans went on to be named the best of the championships for their fanatical support and good behaviour. Nowadays thousands follow the three lions wherever they play, it wasn't always that way. The biggest difference with the travelling England support now is that most of it is made up with families, men, women and children in their replica shirts and funny wigs, keen to try the local cuisine and shake the hands of the indigenous population.

7

EVERYTHING ENDS WITH AN E

It is fairly well known that the whole 'casual' scene started with Liverpool playing in European competition every season with their supporters sussing out the clothes shops in France and Italy before helping themselves to the stock. Suddenly the scallies were seen on the terraces back home in an array of sports and casual clothes. Outside of Liverpool, it was Tottenham fans that were the first to catch on to the new trend and, with trips to the continent themselves, began to put their own London slant on the scally look. It wasn't long for other fans to start to copy this look and Pompey fans took to the new casual appearance with relish. The word casual never took off in Portsmouth, preferring to be known as Dressers. It made no difference. At first, it was Pringle and Lyle & Scott jumpers that were all the rage, alongside the all time favourite Lacoste polo shirt. The shop on the Southsea golf course has probably never been so busy as this was the only place in the city that sold them although they also found themselves having to beef up security, pretty sharpish as well. It didn't take long for a shop in the city centre to take notice of what was happening - Hellrazors in Charlotte Street. The shop would open early on a Saturday morning, its shelves stocked with Lois jeans and cords of just about every colour and shade imaginable. They would be busy all morning with people getting ready for football in the afternoon. At one point, the fad was to wear them either frayed along the bottom or with small splits. For a small fee, Hellrazors would even do these alterations. The Milton End corner of the North Terrace, our preferred place to stand at the time, became a rainbow of colours. Diamond Pringle's of every imaginable shade as well as Sergio Tacchini, Fila BJ tracksuit tops and Ellesse among the favourites. It would be funny watching lads checking one another out, talking about various clothes, everyone needing to be one step ahead of everyone else. Some sports shops cottoned on, but, on the whole, there was still a drought of good clothes outlets in Portsmouth. This lead to shopping expeditions to London, Harrods was always a good place to start but other shops were sought out. Nick Naks in Soho was one where labels, not available in the city, were sought out but there you sometimes ran the risk of taxing. Groups would hang about near the shop and pick off lone shoppers, stealing their newly acquired garments. Other shops across London were found but, if it had better than average stock, its whereabouts was kept a closely guarded secret. A particular favourite of mine was La Pel in New Kent Road. It wasn't uncommon for lads, me included, to catch an early morning train to Waterloo so that they were in London as the shops were opening, do a bit of shopping and be back at Fratton Park wearing our newly purchased items before kick-off. The whole idea of the casual movement was originality where lads would go out of their way to find a piece of clothing that nobody else would have. Now though, it seems everyone of the 'new casuals' wants to look the same, wearing their clone island. We would go out of our way to get something different although it didn't always go to plan. One of the lads spent a fortune flying to Rome and stocking up on different clothes and you have to remember that this was long before Easy Jet came along with cheap and frequent flights. He was feeling pretty pleased with himself when parading in the Milton Arms until someone else walked in with same jumper that they had bought in the West End that very morning. There was a time when the old deerstalker hats were popular but, from what I can recall, the only place where good quality ones could be got was the gentleman's outfitters, Dunn & Co. These were accessorised by black push button umbrellas. I did a roaring trade with these as I used to do a bit of work for a bloke from London who used to work the markets. He got a case of brollies and I knocked them out to the lads. People were always replacing their old ones because, while they are great when you get caught out in the rain, they weren't really built for smashing over someone's suede. You can imagine somewhere 'Well, I don't really know officer, it happened so fast. One minute we were walking along, the next we were getting bashed up by the Sherlock Holmes appreciation society'.

The other thing was back in the early days of the casuals, it was so fast paced, a label could be 'in' and 'out' again in a matter of weeks. Soon, the sports look evolved towards a more casual look with Giorgio Armani being the most wanted label. With the GA eagle sewn on the arm over Farah trousers became the look on the Fratton Park terraces. Labels came and went with Gee 2, Marco Polo, Ciao, C17 and Chipie all having their moment on the terrace catwalk. I would regularly visit Hellrazors where its owners, Andy and Ian, would claim we've just had such and such a line in and we thought about you. In reality, they knew I was a sucker and I would buy it. Mind you, they did always give me nice discounts so fair play to them.

Away games soon became an opportunity to shop as well as football. A match in Bournemouth saw a mob of Pompey fans go through one shop like a plague of locusts as the shelves and racks were stripped bare of all ranges of jumpers and tops, Those who weren't there at the time were soon picking up a 'bargain' at Dean Court. Some labels that were massive elsewhere in the country never took off in Portsmouth. In the mid 1980's, West Ham were into Burberry for instance, some wearing the long cream coloured rain coats which made them look like a mob of flashers, bouncing down the road. Other clubs jumped on the Burberry bandwagon but not Pompey. Another such label was Kappa which was seen as a 'Man City' label along with those bloody awful sky blue Patrick jackets although I did have a pale green Kappa jumper myself. OK, I'm not proud, we all make mistakes. Mind you, bad dress sense did save one Aston Villa fan from taking a slap after a match at Fratton. The Off Licence local, to where I used to live, was owned by a family of Villa fans. When Pompey played Villa in the league cup, their grown up son took the precaution of wearing a grey 'Portsmouth England' (written in the 'Lonsdale' style) T-shirt under his jumper. As he left the game with other away fans, he was approached by a couple of Pompey fans that threatened him. He lifted his jumper to reveal the shirt and, in a deep Birmingham accent, said I'm a Pompey fan mate. The Pompey fans apologised and wandered off.

For every clotheshorse however, there is, of course, a fashion disaster and even wearing the right label doesn't always help. For instance, a lad who turned up one winters morning wearing a yellow duffle coat that Paddington Bear would have thought twice about before venturing from the house that morning, could only protest 'Yeah but its CP Company' when everyone rounded on him. Some lads though never caught on to the casual look. One particular guy from the Isle of Wight always turned up in his dungarees although most declined to take the piss out of his attire given the fact he was so game. On another occasion, a well-known 'older' lad arrived at Portsmouth & Southsea train station where everyone was meeting to board an evening train to Waterloo. While the vast majority were as usual turned out in the latest designer label, he had come straight from work. He stood there in hob nailed boots covered in brick dust shaking his head, 'Look at you lot, are we going to Millwall or Milan?' was all he could ask. The self-proclaimed 'top thug', Paul Scarret, who followed Nottingham Forest turned up outside the Milton Arms covered head to toe in army surplus camouflage combat gear. Nothing happened as there were only three Forrest lads but a few Pompey were taking the piss, shouting about it was a good job he was camouflaged and nobody could see him. No matter what you wear later on, one fashion disaster and it will haunt you forever. A lad named Nige from Grantham who met up with some of the lads and, like many inter club friendships, became great mates. Nige travelled to a lot of Pompey games, home and away and a few lads stayed up in Grantham on nights out on many occasions. Nige has never been allowed to forget a bright day-glow orange Ralph Lauren jacket he once turned up in. He looked like one of the stewards.

Although we weren't casuals by name, we were by everything else and were always on the lookout for a bit of fun. We were always happy to travel for it. On August Bank Holiday 1985, someone thought it would be a great idea to take the ferry over to the Isle of Wight for a day out; unfortunately 5,000 or so Mods and Scooter boys had the same idea. By mid afternoon, Ryde seafront looked like a Quadrophenia re-enactment. The only difference, of course, was that we were taking the place of the Rockers and, although we were massively outnumbered, we turned the tables on them as well although it should be said that the vast majority of the scooter boys were uninterested in trouble and were just looking for a good day out. The local police were less than impressed and, with the help from colleagues drafted in from the mainland, made over 80 arrests, quite a few of them 6.57 Crew.

Portsmouth has never really had a nationally renowned music scene but there has always been a healthy mix of bands playing in various venues in the area. In the early to mid 1980's, some bands such as 'Red Letter Day' and 'A Motion Industry' had decent local record sales and were playing to good-sized audiences but never ever looked like making much of an impact otherwise. One band did come along though and took things to a new level. Belting out tunes such as 'Ain't Home', 'Manta Ray' and what would become their theme tune 'Surfboard', Emptifish took the region by storm. At first the bands following was that of Psycho Billy's but, by 1985, gig after gig saw more and more casuals following them. It wasn't long before the band had been adopted by the 6.57 and, where Emptifish went, the 6.57 went and, where the 6.57 went, so usually did trouble. Around the same time as the trip to the Isle Of Wight, the local newspaper in the area held a 'battle of the bands' type event at the Rock Garden pavilion on Southsea seafront. While band member, Ian Sonic, readied himself for the gig he heard a bang on the window. As he opened it, around forty or so lads charged in, one at a time, to get out of paying. This was the band's first introduction to the 6.57 Crew. That night, there were about 900 people in the audience. As Emptifish took to the stage, they struck up the first chords of their opening number when an almighty fight erupted. The band did manage to belt out a couple of numbers but were soon forced off the stage. Now the Emptifish bandwagon had begun to roll, full speed and downhill! Most started following the band because one of the members was very good friends with one of the football lads who started to urge others to go and watch them and they, in turn, told others and so on. While those seriously into their music tutted at the antics of the band and its followers, band members George and Ian thought it was great because it gave the gigs more energy and there was an air of anarchy whenever they played. Not that things always went their way of course. After the band played another gig in the city, their fee was withheld to pay for damages including to one of the bouncers who'd had his glasses broken.

It was never a dull moment on the road with the band; they even left police in landlocked Reading scratching their heads as to how a six foot shark ended up in the middle of the road. The group were supporting The Meteors and were given a hollowed out Tope Shark by one of the lads who worked on the boats out of the camber. They took the shark with them onto the stage and were generally messing about with it but the stinking sea creature was making a bit of a mess so the management were soon telling them to get rid of it. At the start of the evening, the members of the Meteors had come across as arrogant arseholes so they thought it would be good fun to throw the shark on top of their tour bus. Obviously, as the bus left Reading, the shark fell off the roof and onto the road. The story made the national papers as did when they were booked to play in a Victorian pub in South London, Millwall country. The venue was an old building about eight storeys high with the gig to take place about half way up. They promptly gave the management their guest list, nearly forty names, all of them well known lads. The evenings entertainment started with nobody taking any notice of the other bands but, when Emptifish came on stage, the place erupted. However, it didn't take long for trouble to start. Soon the 6.57 lads were fighting with the door staff, most of whom were

Millwall Bushwhackers anyway. A canister of CS gas was let off. George tried his best to play on with his head out of the window, trying to get some air. It wasn't long until the police arrived and soon the venue was cleared, leaving the band and 'guest list' as the only ones left in the building. It was clear that the police were now waiting downstairs to arrest anyone from Portsmouth not connected with the band so upstairs the group's equipment was divided between all those left, couple of drum sticks here, a few guitar leads there and so on until Emptifish suddenly had as many roadies as the Rolling Stones on a world tour. The ruse didn't last long however. A short while down the road, the police pulled over the van to find one of the lads doing a drum solo, the constable waited for him to finish with the words, 'When you're ready Ringo' and promptly nicked the lot of them.

Despite their following, the band had begun to draw the attention of various record companies. They were invited to play a gig in London where a lot of the top A&R men would be in attendance. Unfortunately, disaster struck when, before the show, one of the members became ill and they were unable to play. A short while later, they did play at Basins in the Tricorn centre. The police were convinced that the gig would lead to a complete breakdown of civilisation as we knew it. The Tricorn was owned by a London property company and my Dad was head of their security. I was employed by them as well at the Tricorn so we were fairly confident that there would be no problems, at least not on the Tricorn anyway. On the whole, the night was peaceful but the police did flood the area with manpower. At one point, the Superintendent was on the ground floor when a thunder flash was thrown from the car park way above him. It went off about two feet from him, much to the delight of the watching constables who had to stifle their laughter. A short while later, the Superintendent got his own back by making the suggestion that the band would not be welcome to play in their home city. He pointed out to George who visited him in his office that, while he couldn't actually ban the group from playing, the police would simply make a visit to the premises and remind them when their licence was up. This was despite happily allowing bands such as King Kurt to play any time they wanted. King Kurt had a large punk following and they played at Basins three or four times a year. Every time they played there, it always kicked off resulting in a lot of damage to businesses in the shopping complex along with arrests and injuries. News of trouble rarely made the local paper and the Hampshire Constabulary never raised any objections to them visiting. But then the 6.57 Crew didn't follow

King Kurt. Such was the hysteria that surrounded Emptifish, you would think that the four horsemen of the apocalypse were riding into town. The band did manage to play one or two shows under assumed names such as 'The Manta Rays' but, due to pressure being put on by the authorities, venues just found them just too hot to handle and, before long, they were un-bookable. With nowhere to play, the record companies lost interest in them although the band was quick not to blame their following, pointing out that the trouble had been blown out of all proportion but soon they went their separate ways. Emptifish's moment in the spotlight had been brief but they had become the benchmark for all other Portsmouth bands. It is doubtful that any other Portsmouth local group has ever had either the potential or support that Emptifish had. Some years later, a benefit gig was arranged at the Wedgwood Rooms in Southsea, following the incident with the Coventry fans in Whitley Bay. The tickets sold out in under an hour, the fastest the venue has ever sold out and some fairly big names have played there in the past. While George needed a little persuading to do the show, after a few practice sessions, the mood started to come back again and, on the night, Emptifish for one night only rolled back the years showing what was and a little of what could have been.

Before the 6.57 Crew really began to take off in the early 1980's, there were several divisions within the Pompey ranks. While on a Saturday, most would join forces for the common cause, on the whole, people from various areas from the city and beyond would do their own thing. During the week, it wasn't unheard of for gangs from one part of the city to fight a gang from another part. The self styled Buckland Mafia had a long running feud with the Baffins gang and they would often clash. I can easily remember word going around my school that it had been arranged to take it to the Buckland lot on their own estate. That night, we all met up as arranged. It wasn't all school kids either. Ages ranged from early to late teens. There were well over a hundred of us. One of the lads who had arranged it even had a register and marked off all the names who said they would be there so he would know who had let him down. We walked to the estate and briefly it did go off although little damage was inflicted to either side. The local coppers were kept busy all night though. Not surprisingly, the guy with the register later went on to name the 6.57 Crew.

Portsmouth, like probably every other city in the country, has certain pubs and clubs that are for a while all the vogue. For us Friday nights always involved the Oliver Twist, a short walk from The Air Balloon. From there, it was usually on to Guildhall Walk and Ellie Jays. After a while, the Oliver Twist went out of favour and the 'in' pub became the Cambridge in Southsea. The Cambridge was always packed at the weekend with The Osborne and Ashby's also very popular. When it came to clubbing, it came down to a choice between Ritzy's and Fifth Avenue. Neither were the greatest clubs on the planet. There was also Peggy Sue's, an absolute dive of a place but at least you could wear jeans. It seems incredible now when door policies aren't so draconian but that was how it was during the eighties. Ritzy's was always popular but, before long, you would often see police advising the door staff who shouldn't really be allowed in. This led to many confrontations with the bouncers regarded as targets. Many of them were attacked and a couple badly beaten up as they left work.

During the non-match days throughout the Euro '88 trip to Germany, talk was about a new street culture taking hold in London. For many, the nights out in Portsmouth became a big bore and, as the Acid House movement started to appear with the added excitement of the illegal raves, more and more of the 6.57 Crew became involved. The 2nd summer of love came to many in Portsmouth via our ICF connection Lewisham who invited us to a rave party being held at Cricket-St-Thomas in Somerset. It ended up a crazy night. In between two full-on battles with glasses, chairs and punches being thrown, the new acid house music was thumping out of the sound system. This was something that the boys could really get into. The following week, Channel Four's music programme showed the party along with the 6.57 Crew having it off big time. Late August 1988 saw an excursion to a full-scale rave in the heartland of Millwall territory. The rave took place in the Downham Tavern, a large pub with an even larger back hall. The sounds and lasers were experienced for the first time by many of the lads. Only a few months earlier, the 50 or so Pompey present would have clashed with the many Millwall lads there and a full scale riot would have taken place but now, with everyone downing E's, violence was the last thing on anyone's mind. Some of the same crowd were to meet up again a few weeks later in Dagenham and another first for many of the 6.57 lads, a warehouse rave located in a container park. The door was being run by two of the top level West Ham lads, Swallow and Cass Pennant; football hooliganism had once more evolved and was at the forefront of the dance scene that was hitting the headlines. The dance floor was on the second floor and was hot and smoky but it didn't stop a couple of hundred loons dancing although the night was brought to a premature end when the police raided it. More raves were cropping up across the South, the majority of them attended by Pompey lads and most weekends the clubs in Portsmouth were forsaken in favour of bigger and better venues in London with Bonnies and The Wag being particular favourites. Before too long, many of those that had spent most Saturdays creating havoc across the country were now 'loved up'. Those of us not taken over by the musical phenomena and I was one of them, couldn't understand all this smiley faces bollocks. We still longed for Saturday afternoon tear-ups whereas the ravers looked at us with some sympathy as if we had missed the point and a good time along with it. While we planned a day out hundreds of miles from home, they were planning to spend Saturday in a drug induced state in a warehouse some place. The 6.57 Crew divided, with some very well known faces turning their backs on football forever. As usual, many of the national newspapers were outraged at this new craze that they didn't understand and lurid headlines screamed out about how every youngster would become a drug crazed, zombie if the music wasn't banned immediately. No different from Rock n' Roll in the 1950's. These were the same papers that had urged the authorities to take a tougher line with football hooligans. What those in the media failed to realise was that the era of the casuals rampaging around the terraces was coming to an end. The 6.57 Crew never really recovered. We would never be the same force again and neither would many of the other top firms as thousands of lads from across the country had found a new buzz. Many millions of pounds had been wasted on various police operations to smash the football firms with little or no success yet, almost overnight, the rave scene brought the war on the terraces to an end. Now the police were diverting their attention towards illegal and not so illegal raves. They couldn't have it both ways. Even then though, violence still occasionally reared its ugly head.

While most raves were giant love ins, one organised in a hundred acres forest in Boarhunt, near Portsmouth, turned into a riot when police moved in to shut it down. One police van was set alight as ravers went into police lines, led by some very recognisable faces. Once the rave scene died down a little, some of the lads did start drifting back to football but things had moved on. No longer did we or any other mob travel in our hundreds. There were rare occasions that this occurred but, on the whole, the curtain had been brought down on the casual era.

Fulham away just after we had bumped into the Chelsea mob.

Germany for Euro '88. A few of the Old Vic lads.
All of them top boys and game as they come.

Sheffield United at Fratton, 1987. The lads get a little over excited celebrating promotion.

Docker meeting the people on the election trail.

Flying the flag in Glasgow, 1987

The Jolly Boys Outing to Bournemouth, 1983

Eddie takes a well earned rest; all that life saving takes it out of you !

The lads at Waterloo, 1985. Docker smiling as usual.

Pompey World Cup HQ, Germany 2006

8
POLITICAL FOOTBALL

It is often said that sport and politics should never mix. Sometimes the fine line between the two becomes more than a little blurred. Whether this be the American led boycott of the Moscow Olympics in 1980 following the Soviet Union's invasion of Afghanistan or the Soviet led tit for tat move when Los Angeles hosted the games four year later. In the UK, we have seen the violent demonstrations when the anti apartheid movement protested against the South African rugby team being allowed to play here during the 1970's. On the whole, football in the United Kingdom has been largely unaffected by those wishing to make a political point if you exclude all those politicians that claim they support this or that team so as to get votes that is.

During the early seventies, the National Front did target football supporters to try and get a bit of a foothold. Most matches saw them selling 'Bulldog' and other such publications and, it has to be said, they had varying degrees of success from club to club. There was racism at grounds with black players given a torrid time, Fratton Park being no different where, like many other stadiums, bananas were thrown on the pitch and racist chants could sometimes be heard. It wasn't an organised thing and fortunately it wasn't something that was big at Portsmouth. To say the 6.57 Crew was a racist firm would be wide of the mark. It would be wrong to say that nobody held those views. It wasn't a wide spread thing and certainly not something that was widely discussed. I recall one day during the summer, some National Front/BNP supporters were selling their newspapers in Commercial Road. An argument started between them and one of the very popular black lads in the 6.57. When one of the Front members started trying to front him up, things turned nasty very quickly and the racist activists found themselves very much out of their depth.

After a friendly game away to Wycombe Wanderers where one of the lads had nicked a six foot square 'welcome' mate, which he thoughtfully placed in the doorway of every pub we visited, we were in Old Street in London when we were fronted up by a group of Red Action who were convinced we were BNP supporters. They made a big mistake. Had they simply left it alone, we would have gone on our way without any problems. As it was, they got the kicking of their lives.

During the 1987 general election, things took a new twist when the 6.57 Party unveiled their candidate for the Portsmouth South constituency; the legendary Martyn 'Docker' Hughes. Without doubt, 'Dockers' was a manifesto for the people. Duty free on the Gosport ferry, off course betting tax to be abolished and all magistrates to have served a prison sentence were among the vote winners. While some of the issues raised may not be seen as mainstream, it is interesting to note that, years later, New Labour actually abolished the off course betting tax and another of the 'policies', Portsmouth out of Hampshire, is also a reality as, at the time, Portsmouth was part of Hampshire County Council while now, it is a unitary authority able to make its own choices and decisions. Another, the demolition of the Tricorn Centre, finally happened during 2005. So maybe it wasn't such an oddball campaign after all and could actually be seen as years ahead of its time.

During the launch of the manifesto, Docker said that he thought he would appeal to the young voters and, quite prophetically, SDP supporters. When the idea was put forward for Docker to stand in the election, the cause was taken up with some real relish. Slogans such as 'Dancing Brave says Vote Docker' appeared around town, a testimony to his love of horse racing. During the election campaign, Martyn was plagued with obscene and pest phone calls at all hours of the night. The calls were made by those, let's say, more left of central who, believing everything they read in the papers, decided very wrongly that, as Docker was running for the 6.57 Party, then he must therefore be a Nazi. One day much later, I was talking with a woman who works for Portsmouth City Council in the Community Services department, at an equal opportunities course. She sat there very proudly saying how she was one of those who had made the pest calls because the 6.57 Party was actually a cover for the BNP. I couldn't believe her ignorance especially the way she spoke to the course with what many believed was great authority on the subject. When I asked her how she had come by the connection between the 6.57 Crew and the British National Party, she simply stated that the National Front orchestrated football hooliganism during the mid 1970's in order to cause civil unrest among disaffected white youths, thus the link. What got me was, could you imagine the headlines had it been members of the 6.57 Crew who had made the calls to other candidates running in the election. After news of Docker running broke in the media, Pompey chairman John Deacon was at lengths to point out that the party had nothing to do with the club. He also showed how in touch with reality he was when he went on to say that the club had no hooligan following and hadn't had for over three years.

One evening, Docker and two friends were out spraying their slogans when they were spotted; as the police were summoned, they were tipped off. A voice shouted, 'The Old Bill's coming'. The three of them looked up into the deserted buildings of the Tricorn, wondering for a moment where the voice from the Gods had come from. They did, however, take to their heels. Docker was caught but received only a caution and I have often wondered when I have spoken to the guys in question whether they knew who it was that tipped them off as, until now, I have never told them that it was me.

The campaign caught the imagination of everyone. Like many a would be Member of Parliament on the election trail, Docker had his battle bus. An open top bus was hired for a tour of the city. Decked out in the party colours and fitted with loud speakers, the bus made its way through the city streets with Docker and others taking to the mike, chanting slogans. Also, there was a public meeting attended by around 150 lads held at Somerstown First school. Docker was concealed in a cupboard and then made a dramatic entrance by bursting onto the stage but only managed a few words before he was carried jubilantly around the hall by a load of the guys. I was unhappy that he was unable to give his keynote speech in which he had promised to cover such important issues as Scimitarra's chances of winning The Oaks. The local media though was very upset and couldn't understand how a bunch of uneducated thugs could keep within the complex election rules. Come the day of the election, Docker polled 455 votes, an outstanding result coming in at forth place. Unfortunately, the party lost its £500 deposit so the lads had to put their hands in their pockets for the post polling day piss up. The SDP Member of Parliament, Mike Hancock lost his seat by 205 votes. During a night of high tension which saw two re-counts, 8 lads were arrested by jittery police, on duty at the Guildhall, for various offences such as breach of the peace but all were released without charge.

Sadly in July 1992, Docker died. After his usual Saturday night out with the lads, Martyn had gone home and gone to bed. At some point during the night, he had an epileptic fit and passed away. The following day, his mother Betty went around to his flat and found him dead. News of Dockers death was met with both shock and genuine sadness. I wouldn't be so presumptuous to say that I was a good friend of Docker; I wasn't although I did know him. He did have many friends, all of whom remember him very fondly and won't have a word said against him. Docker Hughes was one of those people that, if you met him, you liked him. Proof, if any was needed, was seen in the local paper for the next week or so. Literally, hundreds of messages were put in the personal columns. When the funeral came, 300 plus of Dockers friends walked solemnly behind the hearse to Milton Cemetery where he was laid to rest in sight of Fratton Park. There were so many there that the majority were unable to get into the chapel for the service. At the graveside, the vicar was great as he encouraged everyone to crowd in so as many as possible could hear what he was saying. He then deviated from the usual speech and talked about how those who were outside during the service must have felt like being locked out of the most important match of the season. Around the same time as Dockers death, Pompey played a pre-season friendly against Aston Villa at Fratton Park. During the game, Villa fans hung up a banner at the back of the Milton End saying RIP Docker Hughes. After the funeral, many of the lads went out for a drink. Typical of the police in Portsmouth, they couldn't help themselves. Everywhere we went, we were shadowed by vanloads of police officers. They must have had a very boring night as all they did was sit in a van watching us walk in and out of pubs. However, they must have had to justify their overtime because, the following night, the evening paper reported that some mourners had gone on the rampage. What this was, I have no knowledge. I can honestly say that I saw no trouble anywhere that night. Whether there was some sort of bother which was conveniently put down to the lads or the whole thing was made up, I don't know but it did tarnish the day a little and what his mother must of thought I don't know.

It was decided that a great way for the name of Martyn 'Docker' Hughes to always be remembered would be to hold an annual horse race, bearing his name at his favourite racecourse. So for the first time on 10th November 1992,

Fontwell race course in West Sussex became host to the Docker Hughes Handicap Chase with a winning prize of £2,196, the highest at the course that day. Knowing the type of man that Docker was, especially the way he liked a joke, it should have been no surprise to anyone when the aptly named Master Comedy left the rest of the field trailing in his wake, storming in first past the post. The nag that I backed is probably still making its way around. Dockers Mother looked proud when she handed over the silver plate to the winning owner. As a footnote, Docker proved he was looking down on his mum that day. She took one look at the race card and couldn't resist a flutter in the 3.40. Lasting Memory romped home, much to her delight. All these years later, the race is still going strong, a testimony to the high regard in which Docker is still held.

Over the years, there have been many characters among the ranks of the 6.57 Crew who, like Docker, for one reason or another stood out. Some of them are sadly no longer with us. Take Rob 'Fish' Porter who, as legend has it, stunned Portsmouth Magistrates when they asked him if he had anything to say on passing sentence for some misdemeanour or other. He simply replied.

'My name is Fish, I live in a dish, I haven't a dime, to pay the fine, so I'll do the time.'

Fish was one of the Air Balloon mob and one of the gamest about. Although he had a reputation for being fearless, I witnessed his sensible side as well. When we were run by Chelsea on Southsea seafront, someone said that we should have stood and had it with them, despite the overwhelming odds and all the steel that was flashing about. Fish calmly pointed out that there is a time and a place for suicide and this wasn't it. He died shortly after Docker and is laid to rest near him.

Rob Clark, aka Clarky, was well known by everyone across the city whether they went to football or not. He was one of the main faces during the 1980's and travelled far and wide following Pompey and England. When it kicked off, he was usually first into the fray and the last to leave it. He especially loved the action with the Scummers. After travelling back from one away game, a close friend of Clarky's was glassed in Southampton, scarring him for life. When Rob found out about the attack, he rounded up a couple of car loads and drove straight to their main pub, armed with a scaffold pole; he walked in and knocked their top man's teeth out. Everyone knew Rob's face, not least of all the local constabulary and he would never pass on an opportunity to wind them up. When he was on the run for six months, he would still go to away games dressed in an outrageous blond wig. One night, he was in a bar that was managed by his Mother when he noticed two plainclothes officers, obviously waiting for him to appear. He told the barman to wait five minutes while he slipped away and then to take over a bottle of champagne with a note saying, 'With compliments, Rob Clark'. He then went to a nearby telephone box and called the police hotline, to tip them off that wanted man Rob Clark, had been spotted sipping champagne with two policemen at the Stage Door Club. Within minutes, the bar was raided but all they found was two coppers, drinking champagne with a note from Clarky.

Rob was a formidable character, a charmer, smooth dresser and a lady's man. He died, aged just 36, leaving his two children who were his world. Towards the end of 2004, another of the old lads from the 6.57 Crew sadly passed away. Bob Richardson was one of the 'Old Vic' mob which followed Pompey everywhere as well as many trips away with England. While never one of the most vociferous, he was certainly someone who could be counted on when the chips were down. An unassuming and all-round great bloke, he died the day before his 38th birthday following a long struggle with heart problems. Known for his bounce and broad smile, he was a man of many nicknames, 'Bouncing Bob', 'Young Bob', 'Boring Bob', 'Baseball Bat Bob' - this one followed the incident at the Texas Goldmine in Derby where he was one of those that needed hospital treatment but probably, most significantly, 'Brave Bob'. He was well respected by all and specifically held in high esteem by the 'Chi Teds' and 'Old Vic' mob.

The expression 'Top Boys' is banded about far too easily these days although, where these individuals are concerned, its use is truly justified and, with at least two of them, the term can be used in its most defined meaning. They will all be missed and everyone connected with the 6.57 Crew, hope that they rest in peace.

9

GO ON, HOP IT !

Manchester City have, over the years, gained themselves a bit of a reputation on the aggro front. They have been known by various names but seem to have settled on the 'Guvnors' for the time being. There have been a few run ins with them and Pompey, especially during the 1980's. The game that sticks out in my mind was in 1985 at Maine Road. Before we reached Manchester, we gave the police the slip by getting off the train in Stockport where four of us managed to find ourselves on our own. After a couple of quiet beers in an out of the way pub, we made our way back to the train and on to Manchester. Time was getting on so we jumped into a cab outside the station. I don't know if the cabby stitched us up deliberately but I have my suspicions, afterall, he did drop us off exactly where the City mob was on the prowl. The four of us walked towards the ground but it didn't take long for the manc's to cotton on to us. As we walked along, a 40 strong mob shadowed us from across the road. One of the lads I was with was Raffles. Now Raffles wasn't everyone's cup of tea but we always got on very well. He was as game as they come as well as not exactly playing with a full deck - a fairly dangerous combination. Raffles was seemingly fearless and would often go where angels fear to tread. At away games, he would often wander around on his own making no secret that he was Pompey, often trying to organise battles, usually successfully.

What we didn't know was that, during our break in the pub, the rest of the lads had taken it to the City firm and had backed them off time and again. Now they were looking for a little bit of payback. Raffles started to get a bit edgy as the City fans began to cross the road towards us. We knew roughly where the rest of the Pompey mob were and were trying to get as close as we could to them before it came on top for us. This plan soon went out of the window however when Raffles went steaming into the first of the City lads knocking him to the ground. It is at times like this when you have a morale dilemma, do you (a) wade in and help out your friend and get a hiding or do you (b) piss off and leave him to his own devices as he shouldn't have been so bloody stupid in the first place. The choice was very quickly taken out of our hands. Our friends from the North needed no second invite as they charged into us. I would like to say that the four of us stood back-to-back fighting off the hoards in a stand not seen since Roukes Drift. However, in truth, I didn't even get my hands up before I was unceremoniously sent sprawling to the ground. The kicks rained down on me for what seemed like an age. I had no idea where my mates were or even whether or not that they had buggered off and left me. For now though, my only thought was for self preservation. I did like just about everyone else in the same situation. I adopted the foetal position and waited for the beating to stop or to pass out. Suddenly, I became aware of a voice 'Fucking leave him, cut it out' he shouted. I didn't recognise the voice but frankly, I didn't care, it was salvation I thought. The City mob quickly backed away and I looked up to see a large black guy approaching me. Thoughts about 'fat and fire' quickly came to mind. The guy veered away from me and started to push away more City fans that were attacking another prone figure. The lads hadn't left me but were getting similar to myself. I knew this at the time but, in situations like this, you can't help but wonder. It soon became clear that this guy was one of their top boys. 'Come on mate, come with me,' he said looking down at me. The thought of this didn't exactly fill me with joy. By now, the four of us were back on our feet looking a little worse off, apart from Raffles who, typical of him, didn't have a mark on him. Our saviour was stood between us and the City mob. 'What are you lot doing?' he shouted at them; he continued 'What aim is there in you lot onto four, who do you think you are, Munich's?' With that, he marched us through the City lads. 'Your boys are in this stand' he said, walking us to the turnstiles. As I was about to go into the ground, I turned and thanked the guy, 'No problem' he replied, 'Forty onto four is out of order, see you after the game when you are with your mob' he smiled and walked away. I reached the safety of the main stand and found the rest of the Pompey lads; I sat my aching body down and looked at the blood down the front of my jumper. Another of the Pompey lads sat next to me. 'Have you seen their firm?' he asked. I just nodded.

During the match, it sparked off a couple of times so much so that we were eventually moved out of the seats by the police with about ten minutes of the game to play. We were walked around the pitch and put into the away terrace. Things weren't over yet though. As the final whistle blew, we moved as one towards the exit gate and, as we left the ground, the City boys were on the other side of the road. A great roar went up as the 6.57 rushed towards them. The Guvnors fled. Not a punch was thrown. I was gutted. I'd liked to have been given the chance to at least get a little bit of retribution in. The Manchester police were on the case immediately, rounded us up and frog marched us straight back to a load of double decker buses which took us straight back to the train station where we were tightly marshalled until we were on the train homewards.

Later on that same season, the City lads visited Fratton Park. There were one or two small scuffles around the ground after the match but nothing serious. A while after the game, a few of us had had made our way to Fratton train station to see if there was anything going on there which there wasn't. While there, we noticed a City firm being escorted along Fratton Road, an unusual sight. We tagged along 'because you never know'. The City lads kept walking and walking. They hadn't come down on foot had they? After a while, they were escorted towards a housing estate some way off from Fratton Park. I think one of their lads must have had prior knowledge of the area as it wasn't the sort of place you stumble upon. There were two vans parked up right out of the way. Inexplicably, the police escorted them to the vans and then left them to their own devices. They got in and started to drive but, as they turned the corner, they came face to face with us. Although there were maybe fifteen or twenty of us who had tagged on to them, the City boys must have thought that there were more of us than there actually was as they nearly lost control of their vehicles as they tried to escape. In fact, one of them came close to taking out the traffic lights as they tore through them on red, leaving havoc in their wake.

The last time anything of note happened between the two sets of fans was at Fratton Park in the 98/99 season. After the game, some of the Pompey fans set up what became known as the Alverstone ambush whereby they noticed that the police never had anybody in Alverstone Road despite this being the very road that they always directed away fans down. The ambush had been successfully set a few times that season. Pompey would string out along the road milling around so, if it was looked down, you would not see a mob of lads hanging around looking for it. Sure enough, the City boys came walking down with the sort of bravado often seen at football matches; the walk of 'we're away and walking around with ease, come on then if you want it'. The clash was brief as few of the Manchester lot really wanted to know and they were soon sent scurrying for safety. As the Pompey boys started to make their way towards the pub, job done, they noticed one of the City lot coming back towards them. At first, it was thought that they were going to have a go back but soon it became clear what was happening.

'I've lost me shoe' he said. Everyone just laughed at him and started taking the piss. 'Come on lads, I'm going out on the town tonight and I've lost me shoe'. Surely he must have expected the reply of 'Well, you're going to look a bit of a cunt then mate' as the laughing Pompey boys wandered off, leaving him to look for it.

As the lads reached the packed pub, it was already shoulder-to-shoulder in the way that only a post match pub can. At Pompey, we have the attitude which is not exclusive to us but not wise to try in some parts of the country where, if a couple of the opposition lads come in the pub and keep themselves to themselves, then fair enough. (Note to any Scummers reading this, I can't guarantee this blind eye being turned to you). If, however, they start to mouth off then they should accept the consequences. Three City lads came into the pub and did exactly this. They were told in no uncertain terms that they ought to find somewhere else to have a drink; the atmosphere was hostile but not violent. Still they continued to gob off. I wanted to tap one of them on shoulder and ask 'Do the words General Custer mean anything to you?' One of them suddenly picked out Ernie, a black guy. Ernie was at the back of the bar and nowhere near the mouthy City fan and could not have got at him even if he wanted to. The City fan started to call Ernie various racist names. That seemed to be the spark. The three guys disappeared under a barrage of punches. The beating wasn't massive but the pub door was opened and they were tossed out onto the street. By now, a couple of the boys decided to walk on down to the next pub and have a drink there. As they reached the pub, they saw a little mob of City fans outside. This was a young firm, around fifteen or so in number and aged around 19 years of age. They had probably all known each other from their school days and had more than likely been having little victories up and down the country all year. This little mob had been spotted before the game giving it the large to a few a scarfers but now their little world was about to collapse around their ears. The City lads saw the Pompey fans approaching, only five or six of them (as I can vouch for the type of numbers City seem to like). There were a few more Pompey inside the pub, probably another half a dozen, however, unlike the City fans who literally were boys, the Pompey fans were men who had been doing this football lark since this lot were in the infants. As the Pompey approached them, one of the City fans grabbed a pint glass and held it front of him. 'Put down the glass then' said the Pompey fan; the City fan just stood there. The instruction was repeated a couple more times then the City fan, rather apologetically bent down and placed the glass on the floor. As he was about to straighten, a Pompey fan that had sneaked around the side of a transit van that the City fan was stood next to in the car park, levelled him with a great uppercut. More lads came steaming out of the pub and into the northerners who soon took to their heels. This was when their youth really paid off however as they were able to put some distance between them and their foe very quickly, leaving the far older Pompey panting for breath after only a few yards.

Raffles was a well known figure among all the 6.57 Crew lads during the 1980's although he wasn't always popular with some of the older fellas who, I think, resented the way he would often organise things with rival mobs. Regardless of whether they liked him or not, they all accepted that he was game as they come. On the opening day of the 1985/86, we were away to Hull City. We had taken a good mob up there. The group I was with had driven up in a van, planned by a great bloke known across the country through his England connections. The locals were out mob handed and were more than game for it. For a little while, they had the better of things. We were backed of a couple of times. Raffles though was having none of it and his actions were to turn the tide back in our favour. He grabbed a couple of milk bottles and steamed straight into the Hull firm, the rest of us following him into battle. The Hull lads seemed a bit taken aback by his actions and started to shy away which soon turned into a rout. Even those who weren't members of his fan club had to give him a begrudging nod of approval that day.

On the way back from Wolves once, myself and Raffles were on Birmingham's New Street station when we were approached by a couple of Aston Villa fans. 'Are you Pompey?' they asked. Straight away Raffles reared up 'Yeah we are. What of it? Do you want some?' The Villa lads were a little taken aback but then said that they were just about to have it with Leicester. Although not anything to do with us, Raffles was, as usual, happy to go along. We made our way down the escalator to see the Leicester mob just boarding their train. Raffles was off down the moving stairway. 'Come on then Leicester, lets go' he shouted. I don't know who were more surprised, Leicester or Villa although later Raffles did say that he was a little pissed off with the Villa mob that didn't seem to share his enthusiasm for the fray. The Villa/Leicester thing never came to anything as the police ushered the Baby Squad onto their train and us back up to the concourse. We chatted to the Villa lads for a while who were okay and we had a beer with them. I stayed in touch with one of the Villa lads, known to his mates as Snake. He came down to a few Pompey matches and I, in turn, went to the odd Villa game. One match in particular was a Villa home game against Birmingham. It came about when, coincidentally, my old friend Ian's brother was getting married in nearby Walsall. Pompey were due to play away to Stoke and I arranged to stay in Birmingham with my Villa supporting mate, then travel up to the Pompey game on the Saturday morning. As Ian was also travelling up for the wedding, we drove up together, meeting Snake at the Bull Ring. Snake took great delight in informing me that our game had been postponed because the Stoke City team had all gone down with flu but then invited me to the Aston Villa game. I of course accepted without knowing who they were playing. When I found out, I thought well what's the worst that could happen. It was with a little trepidation when I walked into the Crown and Cushion pub to be introduced to the Villa lads. Sprayed on the wall outside was the slogan, 'No Zulu zone'. The Villa fans were on the whole a good bunch with only one who got a little full of himself, going on about he had been done at Fratton Park. There wasn't a lot I could say to it although the tension was broken when another said that a few of them had been done that day. We also talked about the league cup match when we had gone to Villa Park and taken the piss, something that they all agreed Pompey had done that night. As the morning wore on, I started to notice a few faces outside the pub. I immediately sensed that these were Birmingham who had clearly not seen and taken any notice of the graffiti on the wall outside. More and more Zulu's started to gather. I had a sinking feeling inside. I was going to get battered at a game where, strictly speaking, I was a neutral. Villa steamed out of the pub and towards their rivals. Hang on a minute, maybe I was a little premature and Villa were going to be alright. No, actually I was correct as, seconds later, the Villa Youth as they called themselves at the time were sent scattering. Outside the pub, I kept myself to myself. I'd already lost the people I was with anyhow, such was the clamour for the Villa mob to escape and the Zulu's were now running the show. It didn't get any better for the Villa fans as they were bossed about by their neighbours all day, much to the annoyance of Snake when we went out for a few pints later that night.

Raffles was a real character. As he was out of work, he decided to set himself up as a painter and decorator. Unfortunately he couldn't drive. I remember a few times seeing him waiting at bus stops with his steps and paint kettles, etc. Another of his good traits was that he was always extremely loyal to his mates and would always be there when needed. One time, I was out on a Friday night and got involved in a fight with six or seven sailors. Suddenly a taxi pulled up and out jumped Raffles. He just happened to be going past with his long suffering girlfriend Penny. He stood next to me, not even asking what the fight was about. All he was worried about was one of his mates was in trouble. It seemed to me that Raffles had his demons that would eventually catch up with him. He moved up to London but soon got involved in an argument with a neighbour. One thing led to another and Raffles hit the guy with a hammer. Despite it being nothing to do with football, a big deal was made of Raffles' 6.57 Crew past although I know that he had genuinely moved to the capital in an attempt to get away from the football trouble. As he once said to me that, all the time he stayed in Portsmouth, he would never stop going. The case was heard at the Old Bailey and, after being found guilty of attempted murder, he was sentenced to ten years prison. Contrary to reports elsewhere, Raffles didn't commit suicide whilst in prison. We wrote to each other a fair bit and I visited him. After a while, the letters and visiting orders dried up and as he was moved from prison to prison and I lost contact with him. After he was released, he found himself living on the streets for a while which goes to show what a wonderful judicial system we have in this country. It is here that we have contrary opinions as to his whereabouts now. A couple of lads think that he is still living rough although I was told recently by a friend that he was talking to Raffles' brother and that he was now back in prison or rather psychiatric care after another violent incident in Gosport. Whatever he is doing I wish him well. Like I said, not everyone liked Raffles but I did. We got in to some scrapes together or, should I say, he got me into some. I remember he really appreciated it when myself and Pete who I was in the car with after the Scum game in 1987, gave evidence on his behalf after he was wrongly accused of kicking it off against Chelsea. The facts were the three of us were walking to the game and, while there had been some trouble outside the Shepherds Crook pub, it had finished before we arrived on the scene. Raffles was well known to police and was arrested for being in the wrong place at the wrong time. Although he was found guilty and sentenced to seven months, he was later released after an appeal. Like him or loath him, as far as I'm concerned Matthew 'Raffles' Ralls was always a class act.

10
NO ONE LIKES THEM, THEY DON'T CARE

Pompey's local rivals have always been Southampton. They will always be the team that we want to beat more than any other. Pompey fans will always have their traditional hatred for them but many of the lads have often been puzzled as to why many get themselves so worked up for games against them as they have rarely provided that much opposition.

There was however one team that were always happy to oblige and they came from the south London Docklands. On the terraces over the past 30 plus years, a rivalry has developed between Pompey and Millwall. The Bushwhackers have always said that the 6.57 Crew are one of the few firms from outside London that not only showed up their place mob handed but also went there with the intention of taking it to them. Between Pompey and Millwall, there is a mutual respect, if given grudgingly. We appreciated their fearsome reputation but we never feared it. For years and especially throughout the 1980's, the Pompey versus Millwall fixture was one that was almost guaranteed to turn to open warfare as both sides did their utmost to put one over on their foe. In a way, you've got to feel a bit sorry for Millwall fans. Such is their name built up over the better part of forty years at the very top of the hooligan tree, they are now a bit like Jessie James. They go riding into town and everyone wants to shoot them down. So much so that, no matter whom they play, the local faces come out to play in order to boast that they had tamed the mighty lions. Therefore, if you are Millwall you have choice, either go everywhere mob handed or go to some sleepy backwater and get slapped about. Added to this of course, the local constabulary go onto a war footing each and every away game that the South London boys go to on their travels. Of course, sometimes this is justified. Look at the matches at Manchester City or Cardiff in the past few seasons when the world and his dog knew that both mobs would be out in force and, when they played West Ham in a Division One fixture early in the 2003/04 season, over 800 police were on duty. Millwall have always given a special welcome to away supporters but, give them their due, there is no prejudice with them; they hate everyone. However, there are some supporters that they hate more than others.

Travelling to Cold Blow Lane was always a tense affair. It used to be that, when you visited some grounds, there was an atmosphere in the air that suggested that it may go off. At Millwall, it wasn't a question of may. Not that they have always had it all their own way despite what they may claim. Millwall are 'victims' of their own 'success'. Clubs with an up and coming firm, desperate to make a name for themselves, travel, if only to stand behind lines of policemen with dogs and horses, to tell all in sundry 'We went down to Millwall, they were nothing'.

Without doubt, during my time following Pompey, we have had more major clashes with Millwall than any other firm and we can both can shout about victories. In the late 1980's, things got so bad that, for a time, both sets of fans were banned from attending away games between the sides. Of course, being the fine upstanding citizens, both mobs paid full attention to this ban and stayed home watching Grandstand on the respective Saturday afternoons. Well, actually that's a lie, both lots turned up in numbers even though we knew we stood little chance of getting into the ground.

On one occasion, we got as far as New Cross but the Metropolitan police however had different ideas which ultimately led to it going off in a big way in and around Waterloo station. We had arrived in the Capital early and, but for a sheer bit of luck for the police, would have got to The Den undetected. The area around the Old Kent Road was alive with both Millwall lads and police alike however, we decided to stay well away and hope to catch them unawares. Instead, we went miles out of our way in the other direction on the tube and got within an ace of springing our surprise. After chopping and changing underground trains, we were waiting on the platform at Whitechapel. As the near empty train pulled in, two of the occupants stood out like a sore thumb. The two CID officers from Portsmouth stood open mouthed in the carriage; they later admitted that they had been racing around London in a desperate search for us. Now of course, the police were on top, despite trying to give them the slip again. Knowing the game was just about up, we made our way towards Millwall, hoping to bump into them somewhere along the way which we didn't. Plod allowed us to get as far as New Cross. We tried to get out of the station but they were having none of it. We were kept in a yard, surrounded by police with horses and dogs, while somebody somewhere made up their mind what they were going to do with us. There were a few Bushwhackers about so they knew we were here. After a while, someone made the decision to take us back to Waterloo. Once there, most of us managed to get away from the police. By now, the game had finished with a 4 – 0 victory for Pompey and the Bushwhackers were on their way to join us. The first clashes took place outside the Wellington pub. This though was a mere taster for what was to come. The police managed to force us down the road towards the grand main entrance of Waterloo Station. The problem for them was Millwall had doubled through the station and now came out of the large doors. Again the two firms fought on the steps of the station. Millwall began to back off as the fists and boots flew in. Shouts of 'stand' filled the air which is a sure sign that you have got the opposition on the move. The clash moved inside the station main concourse. Because of the enclosed area, the sounds of battle rang around the station as we went into them time and again. What worked in our favour was that the pretenders hardly ever used to go to places like Millwall so we had no passengers with us. The police were pressed hard, trying to keep us apart. Mini battles were sparking off all over the place as the police tried to separate the warring factions. During the mêlée, one of the Millwall lads received serious head injuries, leaving him in a coma from which, thankfully, he was later to make a full recovery. The Portsmouth bound train was held back and the transport police started to force lads onto it. The main bulk of our mob ran out of the entrance by the Shell Centre and towards the Embankment in an attempt to escape the law. We weren't there very long before it went off again outside Charing Cross. Again the police swooped on us and a couple of arrests were made while others were taken back to Waterloo. About fifty or so of us were left walking in the Strand when we were approached by around a dozen Millwall. A small scuffle broke out but the Millwall made no attempt to stand. They ran back up the road. A couple of the lads got a little too eager and went in pursuit of the fleeing Millwall. A few of the older heads tried to hold them back from the inevitable. Hundreds of Millwall came charging down the road. Everyone of them appeared to be tooled up. We took the sensible option and did the off. We had started off the day with about two hundred of us; we were now down to about thirty and, with Millwall out looking for blood with ten times that number, thought better of it to hang around in obvious places. There is a time and place for stupidity. We had had our fun and now was time to call it a day.

There was a fairly bizarre footnote attached to this game. There was a Pompey lad called 'John' who was part of the mob but, by no means, a 'top boy'. John was a mate with a Millwall lad which was fair enough until one morning when John woke up and decided that he was no longer a Pompey fan and that he would now be supporting Millwall. For reasons that will become clear shortly, I should point out at this stage that John still lived in Somerstown in Portsmouth. A guy known to all at Pompey called Shaft had managed to get a ticket for the match as his work took him to London often. He attended the game alone and was walking along when he passed a pub full of Millwall. John saw Shaft from the window and pointed him out to his new Millwall mates shouting 'He's Pompey'. The Millwall fans poured from the pub and chased Shaft up the street. Somehow he managed to get away unscathed. What made matters worse was Shaft and John, or Judas as he became known, had known each other for many years and were supposed to be mates. Nobody could have cared less that he had joined up with Millwall because he was no loss to us but now, in one stupid move, he became a marked man. John moved away and has not been seen for years yet, even now, the veins in Shafts neck bulge at the mere mention of the name.

Another Pompey/Millwall game that stands out for different reasons was at Fratton Park. I think that this was the match that Pompey won 5 - 1 although I may be wrong. After the match, a mob of Pompey hung around as usual but it became clear that this particular day there would be none of the usual post match shenanigans so, after a short while, people began to drift away to their usual watering holes. By 6.30, lads split into their smaller groups and began to head to wherever they were going that particular Saturday night. I had met up with a very good friend, Tony and the two of us sat in a near empty Milton Arms catching up with each other. The door opened and in strolled a dozen or so lads. They looked around the pub a little apprehensive at first but then came towards the two of us.

'Where's your firm Pompey?' they asked. The two of us looked at each other, a little perplexed. 'They could be anywhere,' replied Tony.

One of the lads continued. 'We're Millwall and we're right up for it' he said. Tony looked at the lad and commented that maybe he should have been around an hour and half ago. 'We've been in and out of all your pubs all day looking for you' said another.

The fact was we had been in the pub since the end of the match and they certainly hadn't been in that time. They then tried to name a few pubs as if to say we've done our homework and know all your boozers. However, they over cooked the pot when they said that they had been in the Talbot looking but there was nobody in there. Neither Tony nor I was very surprised they had failed to locate a mob in the Talbot due to the fact it had been closed for at least ten years and was now a women's refuge. It still looks like a pub from the outside and still has 'The Talbot' written into the brickwork. Their entire story lost credibility at that point although we thought better of it than to tell them. They left saying they would look elsewhere. I'm willing to bet they were soon looking in the buffet car of the very next Waterloo bound train.

Tony and I have been friends for years; he was even my best man. We travelled together to West Ham a few years ago for a mid week fixture. There were only around 40 or so 6.57 lads up there and, even then, we hadn't travelled as a mob but more in small groups and meeting up at Upton Park. Nobody was really expecting anything anyway. The hey day of the ICF was, by now, long gone. We took up our position on the away terrace. Just before half time, I went down and bought a tray full of teas. As I went towards the refreshment stand, I noticed some blokes I'd never seen before coming through the turnstiles but thought nothing of it. I rejoined the lads and handed around the drinks just as West Ham scored. Directly in front of us, about eight or nine lads jumped into the air and started celebrating the goal. They were those I'd just seen coming into the ground. Immediately behind us was a Pompey guy from the Isle of Wight. He was Pompey mad and as game as any one I have ever seen. Unfortunately, he was also in a bit of a time warp. Thinking we were back in the 1970's, he would kick it off any time, any place. I remember a game away to Millwall at the old Den. This particular day, he had been a one-man demolition machine, particularly in one pub where it had kicked off. Just as the game started, he walked into the Millwall stand on his own and sat there, bold as brass, without a care in the world;

nobody said a word to him. He didn't last long however. The police had been on the lookout for him over the pub incident and promptly arrested him. So, although he was seen as great to have around when the odds were stacked, he was also considered to be a little bit of a nightmare at times. This was about to become one of those times. He stretched his arms out wide and bundled down the steps of the terrace scooping up everyone in his path, us included. 'Come on Pompey, into 'em' he yelled. The teas went in the air, scolding everyone (what is it about tea at football grounds that makes it either lukewarm or boiling hot but never a happy medium in between?) Tony was pushed into the front as others piled in behind. Either as result of the initial push or voluntarily, the West Ham bravado was disappearing fast as they started to get a bit of a kicking. The police were slow to react. Maybe because things like this just don't happen in football grounds anymore (well, rarely anyway). Soon enough, the police took the West Ham fans to safety but, unfortunately, they arrested Tony, literally ripping the shirt off his back in the process. He was charged with threatening behaviour but fortunately the charges were later dropped.

You would think that Portsmouth and Millwall Football Clubs would do their level best to keep the fans well away from one another; however, before the 1977/78 season kicked off, a friendly was arranged at Fratton Park. It wasn't so friendly off the pitch with 21 fans arrested and another 21 ejected from the ground. There was fighting inside the ground and Millwall fans were attacked in Ruskin Road as they left the game.

One of the more bizarre decisions came later that same season when Millwall had their ground closed for the umpteenth time. They were ordered by the Football Association to play their home games at a neutral venue. I think this was after the time Millwall fans took exception to Ipswich dumping them out of the FA Cup but, in fairness, it could well be one of several times when the Football Association temporarily shut The Den. A few years ago, Millwall was the only place where you bought a season ticket which read 'to be confirmed' on every other page. A good example of this was when Pompey were due to visit The Den in 1967. The game nearly had to be postponed after referees and linesmen threatened to boycott all Millwall matches because of fears of being attacked after a game against Aston Villa when the referee was surrounded and knocked to the ground. Millwall were fined £1,000 and the boycott only averted when extra stewards and police were drafted in. Anyway, some bright spark somewhere decided it would be a good idea to play at Fratton Park despite Millwall and Pompey fans being at war with each other for years. Many saw it as the ultimate April fools joke as the game against Bristol Rovers was played on April 1st. Although little over 3000 people attended the match, the 150 police on duty were stretched all afternoon. This also included having to keep an eye on members of the Portsmouth branch of the Anti Nazi League who had made it known that, for some reason or other, they intended to 'confront' the Millwall fans. It was a strange atmosphere in Fratton Park that afternoon. Pompey fans took up their usual position in the Fratton End while Millwall were in the Milton End while the travelling supporters from Bristol were sandwiched in between on one of the side terraces. Long before the end of the match, Pompey fans left Fratton Park and took up position in Goldsmith Avenue. As the final whistle blew, Millwall fans stormed the gates at the Apsley Road entrance, smashing them down. Hundreds of Millwall and Portsmouth fans then fought running battles around the roads off Goldsmith Avenue. Eventually, police managed to get the Londoners on board their trains and only then did they allow the Bristol fans to leave the ground. The police had to begin the process all over again as the Pompey fans attacked the escort as it made its way to Fratton station.

Pompey fans made a surprise guest appearance when Millwall were away to Southampton; there was trouble in the Scum end with the Scummers getting backed off. The police rounded up the culprits, arresting some and escorting the rest to the away end, then stood there, bemused, when it kicked off in there as well. Of the twenty-eight arrested that afternoon, 15 were from Portsmouth.

In April 1981, the league match at Fratton Park was held up for around 10 minutes as Millwall fans in the Milton End fought with the police as they tried to invade the pitch. Meanwhile, at the other end of the ground, the police placed a line of dogs in front of the Fratton End to prevent the Pompey fans from getting onto the pitch. After the match, the London mob smashed down the same gates as they had after the game against Bristol Rovers and again fought with the police. There was fighting between the two sets of fans all along Goldsmith Avenue. The fighting also spilled into Haslemere Road where there were several house windows smashed. Before the match, there had been fighting in the City Arms after Millwall fans managed to avoid the police escort at Fratton train station and had carried on to Portsmouth & Southsea where a large mob of Pompey were waiting for them.

The following season, Pompey and Millwall were to meet four times ensuring that the hooligan element that followed both sides would keep each other busy as well as clock up the overtime for the Hampshire and Metropolitan police forces. Much to the police's dismay, the two sides were drawn in the FA Cup first round at Fratton Park. Despite having well over 200 police on duty for the match, they were still unable to prevent serious disorder taking place. Forty seven arrests were made as the two sets of rival fans yet again fought each other in Goldsmith Avenue leaving 7 police officers needing hospital treatment. The game itself was drawn 1 – 1. However, there was no repeat of the trouble at the replay in London the following Wednesday as a massive police operation kept on top of things, resulting in only a few isolated incidents with five arrests all night. The feud between the two sets of fans was by now getting so bad that Portsmouth City Council seriously considered taking legal action to prevent any matches between the two sides taking place in Portsmouth. The action came to nothing in the end. The sides were not to meet again that season until May and then we played twice within twelve days. The game at The Den was Millwall's last home match of the season. We took a massive mob to South London intent on putting on a show at our arch-rivals. During the game, we forced our way into the Millwall seats where for a while it went toe-to-toe until police managed to separate us. The Millwall fans were incensed by our cheek. Away fans aren't supposed to do things like this; they are supposed to stand meekly behind the police and fences, being thankful that the upholders of law and order were there to protect them.

After the match, Millwall fans invaded the pitch in an attempt to get at us. Two policemen were hurt as they tried to keep the fans apart. As always, that wasn't the end of the matter. Round two would be at Waterloo. Things there got so bad as 200 fans fought a running battle. For a while, the police were unable to cope so colleagues, returning to their stations after a pro IRA march in the central London, had to be diverted to help quell the violence. The very last match of the 1981/82 campaign saw Millwall visit Fratton Park. The fixture was moved to the Friday night in an attempt to avoid trouble. Portsmouth Football Club also issued vouchers at matches before the game. The idea basically was that, in order to get in to the Millwall game, you had to attend the match before. There was a 'no voucher, no entry' order in place. Millwall Football Club refused to issue their vouchers thus effectively banning their own fans from the game. Around ten minutes before kick-off, a mob of around 250 Millwall got off the train at Fratton. Immediately, they were rounded up by the police and put under escort to the ground. The police saw sense enough to put the Millwall lads in the ground regardless as to whether they wanted to go in or not, rather than let them roam the streets. There was a great photograph published in the local newspaper of the Millwall fans stood in the Milton End, surrounded by the police, with just about one copper for every Millwall fan. There was no trouble inside the ground that night but, in the streets afterwards, a massive Pompey mob fought with the police as we attempted to get at the Millwall fans being escorted to back to the train station. In all, there were 12 arrested of which 5 received custodial sentences.

The following season, the fixture at The Den was moved to a Sunday. Following our success the previous year, we once more took it to the home side. This time storming off London Bridge station and catching Millwall by complete surprise.

Before Millwall left their old ground at Cold Blow Lane to take up residence in their sparkling new stadium, we had one last chance to visit. As always, we turned up with enough numbers to make some impact and, as ever, they were more than happy to meet us head on. After making our way from Waterloo, we took up residence in the White Hart pub. It wasn't long before the Millwall mob came sniffing around. Just before 2 o'clock, they made their move, charging towards the pub. At first we responded in kind, steaming straight out of the pub and into them but we were soon forced onto the back foot. We were fighting all over the Old Kent Road with traffic bollards, glasses and all manner of other objects raining down. We regrouped and charged back into them but, once again, it was us who were forced to give ground. Police in full riot gear were quickly on the scene. They were obviously expecting something that day and were lying in wait, ready for when it did go off. More and more Millwall were arriving. Some of them getting off the bus carrying the shopping with their wives, leaving the old lady with the carrier bags and wading in. Things were on top for us. We had a very tidy mob, probably a couple of hundred yet we were still heavily outnumbered and, as usual, they were tooled up. Luckily, the Metropolitan Police were starting to get the upper hand, driving horses between the two mobs. Once the violence was quelled, we were escorted to the ground with moody mobs of Bushwhackers shadowing us all the way. Looking around, it seemed to be that everyone had claret on them. After the match, there was little trouble as the police kept us well away from the locals around the streets near the ground and, once at Waterloo, there was a massive police operation to keep the peace.

The previous match at Fratton Park, Millwall had turned up around 11am with about 100 or so lads. They made their way to the Navigators pub near to Portsmouth & Southsea train station. By pure coincidence, I had driven right through the middle of them. I had been driving to the shopping centre just as they were leaving the train station. I parked up and went to the Albany pub close by. There were already a few of our lads there and they too had seen the Millwall mob come off the station. We got a decent little mob together and contact was made with their lot. It was arranged that, at around 12.30, they would move across the road and into a quiet back street. At the same time, we would make our way into a parallel road on the other side of the railway tracks. We would walk to the top of that road, loop around and meet them somewhere in the middle. Soon after we left The Albany, some of the lads made a quick diversion raiding a skip at the local Quick Fit exhaust centre. One of the top boys stood on a wall and made a rallying cry and, with that, we made our way to the rendezvous; the Millwall mob however stayed in the pub. After a wasted and rather long walk, we got to the Navigators which was only 150 yards from the main Portsmouth police station. A few of the Millwall lads came out of the pub throwing glasses, one of which hit one of the Fareham boys as he ran into them, causing a nasty gash. Things were very quickly quelled by the police. We were forced away from the area while Millwall who were now beginning to spill out of the pub were held back until they were taken to the ground. Everything was peaceful during the game but there were running fights all the way down Goldsmith Avenue afterwards. During this, a Pompey lad tried to get at the Millwall mob while a police Alsatian was hanging from his leg. Later he was extremely pissed off while examining the rips in his designer jeans.

Pompey and Millwall were not to play each other for six seasons after the London club was relegated. Ironically, given the rivalry between the two clubs, Pompey played a part in their relegation by winning at Huddersfield while Millwall could only manage a draw against Ipswich. It was like we were never apart the first time we played them though; the game was switched to a Thursday night for live television. Given the game was a Thursday and the fact that many Pompey fans were keeping their heads down after the events against Coventry the previous September, the Pompey firm was not 'at full strength' although a number were still determined to make their presence felt.

The first trouble broke out when Millwall fans attacked the Windmill pub, a known Pompey pub when the blues are playing in London. Windows were smashed as the Millwall mob charged, tooled up to the eyeballs, as usual. The smaller Pompey mob retaliated by throwing bar stools and glasses as the fighting spilled out into the street. It was the shape of things to come. The game was played out in a hostile atmosphere so no surprises there then, after which the police held Pompey supporters in the ground for an hour. During this, scuffles broke out as some fans tried to force their way out of the stadium. Once they were allowed out, Millwall fans attempted to ambush the escort and more fighting broke out in Iderton Road as around 250 fans clashed. As we were being escorted away, we passed a car owned by one of the lads. He had made a mistake of leaving a Pompey sticker in the back window and the car had been trashed. One of the lads called out to him 'I hope you're in the AA'. He wasn't overly impressed by it all and, to make matters worse, while he cleaned up the mess with a dust pan and brush that he borrowed off some old girl, he had to do a runner when Millwall came steaming down the road again. Apparently, it was a very cold drive back down the A3 that night!

There was more trouble at Waterloo station as the two sets of fans had one last battle to round off the night. So the gauntlet had once again been thrown down, setting the scene for guerrilla warfare at Fratton Park when the two sides would meet in the return game. Looking across the Milton End from the South Stand, it took a moment to work out what was wrong with the Millwall crowd. It then clicked; there was no colour whatsoever. Usually there would be the away fans sporting their team shirt and scarves but today there was just a whole end of very surly looking geezers, each of them looking like they had stepped out of the Stone Island catalogue. Millwall had promised to turn out at Fratton Park and had not disappointed. Pompey were also out in numbers although these were somewhat diminished by more dawn raids only a week before, again in connection with trouble at Coventry. The timing of the raids was not thought to be a coincidence by anyone. Before the match, we had tried to meet up in a pub by the Guildhall but it didn't take long for the police who were thick on the ground (the Hampshire force being backed up by the British Transport Police who had drafted officers in from all over) to start making their presence felt. Meanwhile, a large mob of Millwall had made their way to the Castle Tavern, again shadowed by the boys in blue. Myself and Ernie were having a nose on one of the side streets behind the Lidl supermarket when we were faced with Millwall's mob, bouncing down the road. As we stood there, a car pulled up. The driver was a friend of Ernie's. He got out and asked what was going on. We simply pointed towards the oncoming mob. He then asked.

'Where's our firm?' We jokingly said
'You're looking at us, you up for it or what?' With that, he replied.
'Fuck that', jumped back in his car and wheel-spun away, leaving us still stood there. Wisely we made ourselves scarce before the Millwall lot got too close.

The game had been made a 12 o'clock kick-off by the police. As this Millwall group made its way down Goldsmith Avenue, there was a small scuffle with some Pompey who were waiting for their arrival. There were only a few blows exchanged and the fighting, such as it was, only lasted seconds before riot cops waded in and calmed things down. The Police put a cordon around the Pompey mob, not allowing them to go anywhere for over half an hour while Millwall were shepherded into the ground.

After the match, the police were always in total control. The major success of the plan was to only allow Pompey fans in the South Stand to leave from the one exit. Obviously, this meant the stand which was full was very slow to empty thus allowing the police time to prepare their lines. They also allowed the Millwall fans to leave the ground immediately; they did however put a cordon across Goldsmith Avenue to prevent them meeting face to face with their opposite number. At one point, the Millwall did manage to breach the police lines. Two of the lads stood watching them were very well known brothers; one of them went straight into the Bushwhackers on his own, quickly followed by his brother. They only managed to let a couple of shots fly when the Old Bill sorted things out. By now, a few of us had got together and were just ahead of the Millwall mob. All the time we were kept moving by the riot police usually with the help of a hefty thwack with a baton, not allowing anyone to stop until we were well past Fratton station. There, one of the lads made the silly mistake of saying to one of the brothers 'Fucking hell, when they broke through, I have no idea how I managed to get over that wall!' He had scrambled over an eight foot wall to get away from the Millwall charge. They have never spoken again to this day. While both sets of fans had enough numbers to cause serious mayhem, on the whole, while there were a couple of flash-points, the day passed peacefully due to the efforts of the police.

Pompey fans were again banned from Millwall during the 2002/03 season. The ban was part of the Metropolitan Police crack down on Millwall fans following the riot after Birmingham had dumped them out of the play-offs the previous season. The police operation that followed the disturbance meant The Bushwhackers would no longer be the major force they once were. It was 'suggested' to Millwall Football Club that, for certain games, it would be best for away fans not to attend. Earlier in the season, they had allowed Millwall fans to attend the fixture at Fratton Park. Not surprisingly the numbers of Millwall 'firm' were well down on what they once were. For this clash, there was probably less than fifty and the majority of these were youngsters, some of who probably had little idea of the history that this rivalry has. Maybe they didn't realise what they would be walking into as they swaggered down Goldsmith Avenue. With the police crackdown on them and serious prison sentences being handed out, many of the Millwall boys were keeping their heads down. What happened after the match came as a real surprise to most. The match finished with a Pompey win. That wasn't the surprise though. As the full house left the ground, the police opened the gates at the Milton End allowing the Millwall fans to leave and mix freely with the home supporters. In Goldsmith Avenue, the scene of so many battles between the two sides, the atmosphere was tense as both sides waited for the inevitable to happen. By the petrol station which is usually packed with police vans even for games which pose no threat of violence but, most strangely, on this day empty, a group of Millwall fans mobbed together. This was the signal for Pompey fans to attack from all directions. All around, Millwall fans were being picked off. It was interesting to see that many faces that had been involved in the fighting over the years wanted nothing to do with what was going on whereas others asked what would happen if it was the other way around at Millwall, there would be no remorse from the Millwall fans and what goes around comes around. Maybe they had a point but I still wondered how many of those dishing out slaps would have been happy to wade in if the numbers were more even.

After the Millwall fans had run the gauntlet back to Fratton Station, some Pompey supporters were asking if the lack of action by the police was a pay back to their colleagues in the Met, many of whom were injured during the Millwall versus Birmingham play-offs riot. Who knows? As some of the Pompey fans celebrated their victory, no matter how hollow, most of us saw it. There were a few of us who began to reminisce about how things used to be. The history between Pompey and Millwall stretches back to the late 1960's; there were times that Pompey fans came away from South London basking in the glow of victory and games at Fratton Park where Millwall were given a bloody nose. It has to be said however that, on the whole, it was Millwall that probably came out on top. We always made the effort when we played them home or away and so did they. Maybe it was because they had a bit of a ruthless streak; the south London boys were never shy when it came to using blades or other weapons while, on the whole, it wasn't really our style. As a result, they could get inside one or two peoples heads. The thing is though, at the end of the day, while we were good, I think they were just that little bit better. Another thing that seemed to make Millwall stand out from most of the other firms we were facing was that, whereas most of us were within ten years of age of one another, they seemed to span the generations; we would be having it with sixteen to fifty five year olds.

Millwall was always one of those places where football hooliganism was not so much frowned upon by the local community but thoroughly encouraged. The majority of the population appear to see the Bushwhackers as South London's own private militia defending their homes and way of life against invading armies every other Saturday. I have visited the Old Kent Road area many times in a boxing capacity either visiting friends or training at the Henry Cooper or Thomas A'Beckett. I was at the Henry Cooper one day with a friend and fellow pugilist from New York. He began to say that this area wasn't so tough and that various areas of the States were really tough. I suggested that he wander up and down whistling 'I'm forever blowing bubbles' when this lot are playing West Ham and that he probably won't find the natives so friendly. I must admit I know what he means though. I visited the world famous Kronk gym in Detroit; it is in the meanest area I have ever seen. No wonder it has produced many excellent World champions over the years. Maybe only the toughest survive making their way to and from the gym every day. I was certainly happy to get away from the area in one piece.

Being a self confessed boxing anorak, I've had the pleasure of watching the noble art across the world. A few funny stories with the lads do however come to mind. When Lloyd Honeyghan was World Welterweight Champion, he was defending his title against a well-rated American Gene 'Mad-dog' Hatcher. The fight was due to take place in a bullring in Marbella, Spain during August. I talked a few of the lads into going, pointing out that it would be great for a long weekend, a few beers in the hot Spanish sun, watch what promises to be a good fight and generally chill out. They took a bit of persuading and I think the cut-price ringside tickets helped. So we flew off to sunny Spain, only to land in monsoon type conditions. It was apparently the worst weather they'd had in that part of the Costa del Sol for 50 odd years. To make matters worse, because the fight was to take place in an open-air arena, the boxing was postponed for twenty-four hours. You can imagine how popular I was. Luckily the weather improved and so, on the Sunday night, the boxing went ahead. The chief support fight was Frank Bruno versus a guy called Reggie Gross. It was a terrible fight with Gross hanging on for dear life for eight rounds before the referee finally stopped it. Eventually, it was time for the main event and the lads had cheered up a bit by then so out come the two boxers, national anthems the lot. Seconds out, round one, ding ding bosh! Honeyghan has come out and floored the yank who somehow staggers to his feet. The referee waves them together, crash, bang, wallop; Lloyd is into him again and the fight is over, nineteen seconds including the count! By now, I'm being called every wanker under the sun but I tried to explain, that's boxing. They all had smiles on their faces later though when I managed to blag a few invites to the after fight party.

When Nigel Benn had his rematch with Chris Eubank at Old Trafford, like a fool I mentioned that I could get some VIP tickets. Tony B, Darren L, and one or two others asked if I could get them tickets to which I happily obliged. I didn't travel up with them as I had arranged to meet some friends from the boxing world. Anyway, I'm in the VIP reception, chatting to boxers from past and present, there are TV people the lot. Suddenly, the doors open, in walk my mates. They had been on the shant all day. First of all, they steam into the buffet and start abusing the waitresses. I am desperately trying to hide away so they don't see me but they do and shout across the room 'Oi, Bob'. One of the lads, Darren, starts engaging John Conteh in conversation; he asks Conteh who he thought would win. John starts talking about technique, style etc and then asks.

'Who do you think will win'?
'Nigel Benn' says our lad.
'Why's that?' asks Conteh.
'Because Eubank's a cunt' came the forthright answer.

In July 1985, Frank Bruno boxed Tim Witherspoon for the world title at Wembley Stadium. I had my usual ringside seat. While I was happily watching the under card, Jim McDonnell was defending his European Featherweight title. If my memory serves me right, it was going off outside as loads tried to storm the gates. Apparently they tried to force open the big double doors; some got in and made it as far as the ringside seats. Problem was, a lot of them were our lads. Of course, one or two see me and come over and start chatting. The stewards slung them out and tried to kick me out with them, despite the fact I had my ticket. Another Bruno fight where there was all sorts of trouble was the much hyped showdown at White Hart Lane against Joe Bugner. While Big Frank battered Aussie Joe as he was called by then to submission in eight one sided rounds, there were as many punches thrown in the stands. From what I have been told, there were many lads from various clubs there that night and old rivalries couldn't be put on hold. While this will be looked upon as double standards, I have always hated it when there has been trouble at boxing events. Maybe because, unlike football, those in the ring give there all in an extremely brutal sport and maybe because, deep down, many of those involved on the safe side of the ropes in a mass brawl are able to hide behind their mates whereas, in ring, there is nowhere to hide.

11
THE WHEELS ON THE BUS

It is very well documented that Pompey's firm was named after the time of the train they used to catch. On a number of occasions, the humble bus has been used as a Trojan Horse with mixed results it has to be said but the following anecdotes are examples of when the 6.57 Crew took to the road as opposed to the rails.

The bright red London double decker bus made its way through the leafy streets of suburban West London on a warm sunny Easter bank holiday. Pompey were away to Fulham and, after a morning of wandering around the West End, we started making our way to Craven Cottage. A short tube ride was followed by everybody getting on the bus. After a bit of banter with the conductor who decided it was far better to give up trying to get fares out of these bunch of Neanderthals, we were on our way. A short ride saw the bus pass a pub which, to the amazement of all on board, was packed inside and out with what was unmistakably a rival football firm.

'Who the fuck are they?'
'Fulham's mob!'
'Don't be a wanker, Fulham haven't got a mob! Not that size anyway!'
'What does it matter, STOP THE BUS!'

The bus driver refused to stop until there was a scream of 'Stop this fucking bus or we'll smash the bastard up'. On cue, the driver slammed on his brakes and opened his doors. Once on the street, our mob of about 40 went straight back in the direction of the pub. As we turned the corner, a mob of easily 50 were coming from the pub towards us, equally eager to do battle after obviously seeing the bus go by. This was no Fulham firm. This was their neighbours, Chelsea. Nobody was surprised. There has never been any love lost between us and, as they weren't playing that day, it was fairly clear to everyone that they would show up somewhere sooner or later. The ferocity of the battle seemed to take the Chelsea lot a bit by surprise; they had come out of the pub with glasses and pool cues but had thrown the glasses before getting in range. Undeterred by the barrage, we steamed straight in. Almost immediately, the Chelsea lads started to fall back. A moment of real comedy during the fight was when one of the brave Chelsea boys started hitting Pompey lads from behind with a pool cue. He ran up to one lad and bang, he hit him. Unfortunately for our London friend his aim and power were both astray and only managed to hit him across the shoulders with all the power of somebody brushing away a fly. The Pompey lad fronted him and it was at this moment that the cue wielders bottle went. He dropped the cue, turned and ran, unfortunately at full speed straight into a lamppost, knocking himself out cold. I bet, over the years, he has told the story that he was the only one of the Chelsea firm that stood against forty Pompey and that he was doing really well until someone caught him with a lucky punch from behind and all forty stuck the boot in. It wasn't long before the Chelsea had it away on their toes, leaving their unconscious mate to his own devices. They ran back into the pub that they had come from, holding the doors shut with us in hot pursuit. At this point, a garden wall was pushed down and the bricks began to rain down on the mock Tudor building. It wasn't long before all of the windows had been smashed but it was very clear that the Chelsea cowering inside had enough, the fight had gone out of them. Then a commotion was heard from above the crowd. A guy was leaning out of his flat window, throwing objects and shouting abuse. Nobody could make out what he was shouting. Maybe he worked nights and the fighting had woken him up. Still, he soon scurried back inside when two large stones flew up towards him, the first bouncing off of his window sill, the second smashing the window. During all of this, the first police started to arrive and, in the time honoured tradition, forty football hooligans tried to do their best to melt into the background with that 'It's nothing to do with me gov'nor' look on their faces. Talking to a couple of guys who had hung around, the Police seemed to be stood about trying to piece together how this quiet street had been turned momentarily into a battle zone but that's how it is with football sometimes; one moment, everything is normal then suddenly, without warning, a tornado comes smashing its way through then, almost as quickly as it starts, its all over.

The majority of our mob took up position in the paddock in front of the old stand. All the talk was of the fighting at the pub beforehand. Those that had missed it eagerly asking to be told all of the details. About ten minutes into the game, six or seven of the Chelsea lads that had been involved appeared on the terrace behind the goal where the Fulham fans were. The traditional hand gestures were given and it became clear that sometime the Chelsea mob would be back looking to even the score. The problem that the Chelsea boys were going to have was that, regardless of what numbers they mustered, we would have a lot more. This was a fairly big game for us as we were pushing for promotion so our support was in the thousands with a firm around 400. With five minutes to go in the game, the Chelsea lads disappeared. We had already sewn up the game on the pitch so many of us poured out onto Stevenage Road but could not see these Chelsea lads that had been giving it all afternoon, anywhere. We started to walk towards the away end when, on the junction of Greswell Street, we saw a mob of around forty Chelsea calling it on. We charged straight into them and, for a while, it went toe-to-toe. After a bit, we started to get on top and they began to back away before, for the second time that day, turning tail and running. There were one or two Chelsea who a taken a bit of a beating although we hadn't come away unscathed with one of our lot bleeding from a blow to the head from a hammer.

During the 1990's, Pompey played away to Barnet who, at the time, were a non-league side and yet to have their brief taste of professional football. The dreams of the FA Cup and the thoughts of a night on the beer in London drew a fair sized mob to Under Hill. Pompey managed to avoid a sizeable banana skin winning 5 – 1. During the game, one of the lads mentioned that he had been involved in a fight in a pub close by and that there were about thirty or so game lads there. It was decided to pay the pub a visit after the game; the police soon sussed that something was happening and rounded us up and escorted us onto the underground although the escort only lasted one stop so it wasn't long before everyone had made their way back onto the street and had boarded a bus back to Barnet. As the bus drew near the pub, a couple of the opposition were seen outside. We steamed off the bus and launched into the attack. The few stood outside made off like gazelles, completely taken by surprise. As we got within fifty feet of the pub, all hell let loose as those inside saw what was happening and unleashed a barrage of bottles and glasses. Even though we managed to get to the well-defended doorway, with so many people within such a confined space, neither side could inflict damage as the fists flew. It didn't take long for the boys in blue to return and escort us back onto the underground; this time however staying with us until central London. A rumour went around that the other mob was Tottenham but this has never been confirmed either way.

When we played Nottingham Forest away in the league cup, they were a top flight team whereas we of course were in the lower leagues. For reasons best known to others, it was decided to hire a Portsmouth City Council double decker bus to go to the game. Now those of you that use public transport in this country will know that buses aren't the most comfortable of vehicles to go on your weekly shopping trip, let alone a couple of hundred miles. So after a journey that took forever, the bus pulled up outside of the ground, only to be met by the finest that Nottinghamshire Constabulary could muster. The police would only let us off, one by one, and, to everybody's disbelief, for once the Old Bill had really done their home work as they had a photograph, home address and 'rap-sheet' for every single person on board.

The conversation went something like this;

'Hello Mr. Smith, welcome to Nottingham, it should be a good game this evening. Just one thing, we know who you are and where you live and should there be any bother tonight, we will be knocking on your front door tomorrow morning. Enjoy the match.'

Needless to say the night passed off quite peacefully. As a postscript, Dave the guy who organised the bus received a visit from the drivers and a few of his mates the following day. When they got the bus back to the depot, they had to spend long into the early hours cleaning it, such was the mess that we had left behind. They thought that they should get a bit of compensation and had brought their mates to make sure they got it.

Buses also played a part in the downfall of the Barnsley, Inter City Tykes. Now as everybody that is involved in football hooliganism knows, you can look down the fixtures on a Saturday and almost predict where it would be going off around the country that afternoon. However there are some less likely rivalries around the country, a game that both firms would be looking forward to all season. At Pompey as well as the obvious games, during the 1980's, we had two away games that we knew would be great battles. One was Grimsby Town where, after one match, two Pompey lads got split up from the rest of the firm and literally battled every step of the way back to the train station. When they got there, one of the Pompey boys found that he had lost his money somewhere along the way. The Grimsby lads seeing this had a whip-round so he wasn't out of pocket. Another fixture with a red ring around it was Barnsley. Neither of these sides ever came down to Fratton Park during the 'casual era' but would always give good reception when we went up there. As a consequence, when these games came around, everybody made the effort. As usual, we caught the 6.57 train to Waterloo. On reaching London, there was time for a quick bite of breakfast in the greasy spoon that used to be around the corner from Waterloo station and then on to Kings Cross to continue the journey to Yorkshire but not directly to Barnsley, instead to Doncaster. Once in Doncaster, we left the train station, made our way across the road and caught the local bus to Barnsley town centre. The short bus ride took us to right outside of the pub we knew that the Barnsley firm would be meeting in. It was around mid-day and the Inter City Tykes were starting to get edgy. They knew that we would be coming and were scanning the train station for our arrival. Suddenly, a great roar went up as we stormed across the road and into them. In the confusion, the Barnsley mob scattered in all directions. The battle hadn't been won; this was just the opening salvos but we had already got the upper hand. Barnsley regrouped at the bottom of a slight hill that eventually leads up to the pub. Time and again, the rival mobs charged into each other. The police tried to regain control but here you had two groups very much on a mission. Pompey were in town and doing the business and Barnsley were trying to regain face after being caught with their trousers down. The trouble continued most of the afternoon and, to be honest, Barnsley really did get a bloody nose. After the events that day in Yorkshire, a few Pompey lads were arrested. One of them was sentenced to three years after a couple of the Barnsley fans were cut up, one of the few times that knives were used by Pompey as, on the whole, they are frowned upon by the majority involved with the 6.57 Crew. It should be pointed out though, the person that was jailed was not the guilty party. Any other crime, it would have featured on a hard hitting exposé TV documentary but who wants to defend football fans? On another occasion, the game at Oakwell was one of the few in the country to survive the winter snow. As a result, the viewers of Match of the Day were not only treated to Noel Blake scoring for Pompey but also the sight of me, Raffles and a few others fighting with Barnsley fans in the goal mouth.

Before a match there in the mid 1990's, about a dozen of us were in this same pub where it used to kick off years before. A couple of hours before the game, playing pool and generally keeping ourselves to ourselves when a group of Barnsley lads came in and saw us. At the time, numbers were even. As we began to wait for the inevitable, they just waited. More and more coming into the pub until there were a good 40 or 50 of them. They were giving us the looks while we were steeling ourselves for their attack which now, given the numbers, we were certain would soon be coming. We had taken the precaution of staying by the pool table with the cues and balls handy. The Barnsley lads just stood there staring, trying to intimidate us while we continued drinking and playing pool, seemingly without a care in the world. By now, the time was getting on so it was decided to drink up and make a move towards the ground. We made a point of making sure we were all together and walked out of the pub through the Barnsley mob. As the last couple of us went through the door, one of the Northerners was heard to say, ' Aye, there they go, the 6.57'. They made no attempt to have a go maybe giving us a pass due to the numbers. After the game, around twenty of us went back to the pub but there were no Barnsley fans to be seen. We had a quick drink and jumped on the train. Myself and Tony went home via Sheffield where we had a two hour wait for a connecting train to London. We had a fruitless search for a pub near the station and ended up sitting back in the station buffet drinking expensive beer there. We were however better off than another group who took a more direct journey home. They ended up having a battle with a large number of Leeds fans from Doncaster in which one of the Fareham boys was glassed.

Another game in Barnsley that I remember was the time when there was a crowd of us in a pub drinking; a girl came round with a pint pot asking everyone for ten pence for the juke box. One of the lads put his hand in his pocket and fished out some change. He only had a fifty pence piece so he dropped that in glass. The girl went berserk and shouted at him calling him a flash Southern bastard flashing his money around and stomped off, leaving the lad somewhat bemused much to the merriment of the rest of us.

The most famous Pompey 'bus' story is a work of complete fiction, a made up story that hit the headlines across the country and was the backbone to a television documentary 'exposing' the Portsmouth 6.57 Crew. The documentary, on the whole, was made up of half-truths and non-truths. A couple of lads who were interviewed in silhouette said the usual things but the voice-over that said the cemetery near to Fratton Park is used to launch ambushes is total crap. I have never in my life known this to happen and trawling through newspaper archives going back to the mid 1960's, there was no mention of this anywhere. What is it with makers of programmes such as this that they can make up anything they want knowing that it won't be questioned by the public at large because they have been fed so much bullshit by the media about football fans over the years that the thin line between truth and fiction has all but been rubbed out. The documentary was filmed around a home match against Everton, not really the type of match that they would get any juicy footage so they had to make do with filming a few lads walking around the streets and a couple of police dog handlers hamming it up for the cameras giving a group of Pompey boys a hard time. One of the lads went to leave the pub but saw the television crew filming. Not wanting his ugly mug to appear in the programme, he pulled his scarf up high over his face and made his way to the ground. He looked just how the TV people wanted him to and they filmed all the way down the street. It didn't matter however as he was perfectly disguised. The afternoon after the programme was aired, he got fed up with every person who walked into the Milton Arms saying 'Alright Pete, saw you on the telly last night'.

The driver of a coach made up a story and the authorities happily embellished it; the facts are that the whole thing was complete bollocks. Pompey were away to Liverpool during our brief stay in the old First Division and even the most optimistic of us knew that the team at least was on for a hiding. The same day was the birthday of one of the 6.57 Crew lads. He had arranged a coach trip to take everyone on a piss-up in Blackpool. Most of the guys couldn't face seeing us get hammered at Anfield and, as the game was all ticket with those tickets being like gold dust, most decided to pass on the game. Some of us on the coach, about a dozen I would say, had tickets and wanted to see the game so we had a word with the organiser of the trip. The coach company had a strict 'no football matches' policy. Fair enough but, as this wasn't going to football, the organiser could see no reason why he couldn't ask the driver to make a slight diversion on the way, say Preston, so as to drop off those of us who wanted to go to the game in order to make our way to Liverpool and we would catch up with the others in Blackpool later. The coach driver seemed to be hesitant but agreed. After a stop at some services, we continued but noticed that a Police Land Rover was following the coach. In fact, the police of various forces followed us all the way to Preston railway station where we were met by more. Those of us who wanted to go to the game left, arranging to meet up with the others later in a certain pub on Blackpool seafront. We thought no more of it, got on the train and headed for Liverpool where, as predicted, we got stuffed by 3 or 4 – 0 if my memory serves me right. We then made our way by train to Blackpool; it was on the train that there was the only bit of bother all day. The dozen or so who were stupid enough to have given up on a day out on the piss in Blackpool, to go and witness the rubbish we just had, were sitting chatting when the train pulled into a small local station somewhere in deepest darkest Lancashire. Three Northern lads got out of their seats and made their way to the exit. As they passed us, without warning, one of them punched one of the lads in the side of the head with a shout of 'Come on then you Pompey bastards'. The three of them then ran to the exit doors; this is where things started to go very badly wrong for them. The train was a modern type where you push the button for the doors to open. The three lads were unable to grasp this fact and it wasn't long before the 12 of us took them up on their offer to 'Come on then'. The three of them had the shit kicked out of them and were dumped onto the platform. I was pleased to say that the guy who had started it all with the sly punch got the worst of it. Once we reached Blackpool, we made our way to the pub we said we would meet in. Sure enough, the others were there.

'How was the match?' they asked.
'Crap' we replied.
'How's Blackpool?' we asked.
'OK, the coach has gone home though' they replied.
'What do you mean the coach has gone home?' we shouted.

Apparently the driver had phoned the police at the services and told them that football hooligans had hijacked his coach. When they reached Blackpool under police guard, everybody was turned out and the coach returned to Portsmouth.

'So how the fuck are we going to get home?' we asked.
'Don't know, have a beer' they replied.

After a night on the town in Blackpool, we decided to head home. We made our way to the train station and caught a train to Manchester. Once there, we made our way to the London bound platform. We got to the platform to find police, a couple with dogs, waiting there. We just assumed that Manchester City or United were on their way in from an away game but, after a couple of minutes, a police sergeant and a couple of PC's approached us. 'Are you the 6.57 Crew?' asked the sergeant. We fell about laughing. He then went on to tell us that they had been warned that we had set fire to our coach and were trying to make our way home. Talk about Chinese whispers. When the London bound train arrived, we were ushered on even being told don't worry about tickets. Once in London, we were again met by a reception committee of police and were bundled onto the tube to Waterloo. Once there, we were put on the train to Portsmouth that had been especially held up for us. Now there's service for you. By the time we reached Portsmouth & Southsea train station and the inevitable police there, we wondered if the story had grown to us invading Poland and starting the Second World War. On the following Monday morning, the newspaper headlines screamed, 'Soccer thugs hijack coach' 'I thought I was going to die says driver'. The stories were pure fiction. Things got even better when, in the documentary, they interviewed the driver in silhouette, for his own safety of course where he made up this story of a military operation in which these thugs took over his coach. Apparently, we even had a rank structure and were calling each other General, Major, etc. It was pure fantasy on his part especially seeing, as for years, the 6.57 Crew has more gone on the lines of a 'socialist' policy where we have no leaders and everyone is equal. Of course, you have to take the a leaf out of George Orwell's Animal Farm and say that some are more equal than others.

Unlike other football firm's around the country, Pompey have never had a 'leader' as such. There have been those whose respect among the others has been such that most would listen but there has never been an individual who has taken charge. At times, this has led to our downfall with lads doing their own thing and, when we should have stayed together, have drifted off resulting in others being done.

12
IT'S A MOB AND THEY WANT IT !

Over the years, I have watched Pompey all over England. At one point, I had visited all ninety two league grounds. Now, as there is the promotion from the Conference, there are newer sides that I haven't been to. There are also of course the new stadiums that are springing up all over the place. During the 1980's, no matter where we went, there was a firm. Some of them were among the best in the country whereas others would only number a few. Everyone during the casual era wanted to be part of the football culture which resulted in spectacular punch ups in some unusual as well as obvious places.

Although they never had the same numbers as some of their neighbours, Huddersfield Town were still pretty game. A good mate of mine tells a story where, after a match at Leeds Road, he came out of the ground a little tipsy. He likes a drink although I would say that his brother has now taken the family tradition to another level. It went off and Pompey ran the Huddersfield mob. A little while later, my drunken friend was making his way to who knows where when he bumped into the Huddersfield mob. They took their opportunity for retribution. Being unable to run, mainly due to the fact he could barely walk, he tried to throw a couple of punches but was soon beaten to the ground and given what he describes as 'the mother of all beatings'.

Over the years, Pompey have been involved in two last day crunch matches away to Huddersfield. One of these was in 1985. We had to win and hope that Manchester City failed to do the same at home to Charlton. Thousands of blues fans made the trip north, so many in fact that we were given both ends of the ground and most of one side. There were one or two scuffles but Huddersfield knew that, despite being at home, the odds were massively stacked against them. Pompey were superb that day and won 2 - 0 but news soon filtered through that City had hammered Charlton and had gone up. We were of course gutted. As we stood in the ground, we got talking to a couple of policemen who mentioned that there was a fire at the Bradford City ground and there was a possibility that someone may have been killed. By the time our train reached London and on to a night out in the West End, the full horrors of the disaster at Bradford had begun to unfold. Although we were disappointed at failing to get promoted, what did it really matter?

By the mid 1990's, Pompey had become a struggling side. We went into the last day of the season needing to win at Huddersfield's McAlpine Stadium and hope that Ipswich could get a result at home to Millwall in order to keep our status as a First Division team. Everything went to plan. Pompey won 1 – 0 thanks to a Deon Burton goal while Millwall could only manage a 0 – 0 draw. After the match, Pompey fans flooded onto the pitch and Huddersfield's firm came on from the other end. At first, everything was good-natured but then a couple of them tried to be sly and whacked a couple of scarfers. We made a beeline for them and ran them back into the stands. Outside it went off again and, once more, we ran them. Only a big black lad stood his ground. He was game as they come but was let down by the rest of his boys.

The night before the game some of the 6.57 Crew elected to spend the night in Blackpool. There was a fairly violent row in a seafront pub with Sunderland fans celebrating their team's promotion. Some of the early arrivals found themselves in a large pub; only eight lads surrounded by literally hundreds of drunken Mackems, singing and making fools of themselves. During a lull in the singing, one of the boys jokingly sang out 'Play Up Pompey'. Within seconds, they came under a deluge of glasses. There was no way that they were going to get out of the pub through such a crowd so they tried to take refuge in one corner, punching and kicking any Sunderland fan that got too close while, all the time, under attack from flying glass. Amazingly, once the bouncers and police managed to restore order, they were able to walk away from the pub relatively unscathed. In the street, the lads were recognised once more and were chased by thirty or so Sunderland for about fifty yards, trading punches as they went. Turning the corner, they ran straight into three car loads of newly arrived 6.57 lads and, with the numbers evened up, a little took the fight back to the Sunderland mob. During the fighting, one of Pompey's number was punched very hard in the back. It wasn't until the following morning that he realised that he had, in fact, been stabbed although fortunately not as seriously as the cowardly attack could have been.

The Leeds Service Crew are another of the major firms that we clashed with on a few occasions. I have seen Leeds described as 'seat smashers' who would far rather smash things up than have a go. This is a sentiment that I have heard about them many times but I'd consider this unfair. Leeds often brought good mobs to Pompey during the eighties and we always made a point of returning the compliment. On one occasion, they stormed out of Fratton station and down Goldsmith Avenue, fighting all the way. The Service Crew were also one of the only firms during the casual era to have a proper go at the pub that we always used. They made a strong attack on the Milton Arms after one match but found the opposition a bit stiffer than they were expecting. They were soon put to flight but, instead of staying as a group, they splintered and one of the smaller groups were pursued down Meon Road where they took refuge in the Spar shop. As the Pompey mob laid siege to the shop, its windows were broken while they retaliated by lobbing cans of baked beans out of the broken glass. In more recent times, the two sides were drawn together in the FA Cup in successive seasons. Both clashes ended in violence. The first in 1998 was at Elland Road. Pompey took a big following to the game that ended in a shock 4 – 2 win for the blues. Before the game, we had run Leeds in a couple of pubs in the city centre and, after the game, Pompey mobbed up and again took it to Leeds not giving them any breathing space. Time and again, the 6.57 Crew gave it to Leeds outside the ground before the police got things under control.

The following season the two sides were again drawn in the competition, this time at Fratton Park. Leeds put the word around that they were coming down in numbers and were out for revenge following their poor showing at home. They were true to their word and did turn up in numbers but things didn't really go to plan for them though. They were sitting in a pub by Portsmouth Harbour train station when one of the main Pompey faces walked in. He looked around at the Leeds firm, shook his head and declared, 'Sorry lads, you haven't got enough'. With that, he walked out. Before the match there were one or two scuffles by the away turnstiles until around quarter to three when a Leeds mob of around 100 very game looking lads made their way down Goldsmith Avenue and into Frogmore Road. There were only about a dozen Pompey in the road and Leeds went straight into them. The Pompey lads did really well and, while they were backed off a little but on the whole stood their ground, more reinforcements charged up Carisbrooke Road and joined in the melee. Soon there were two large mobs going at it while the police struggled to separate them. The Leeds mob was pushed towards the turnstiles where again the two sets of fans clashed. Police dogs were tearing lumps out of people and, for a moment, it looked as if the police were about to lose control.

The police managed to move the Pompey mob back and peace was restored. The 6.57 lads made their way to a pub near the ground while the Leeds firm was put on a train away from the city. Without some of their top boys, what was left of the Leeds firm would have a tougher job on their hands but it didn't stop them giving it a good go. With only 10 or 15 minutes of the match left, the police did the strangest thing. There was a large Pompey mob in one of the pubs a short walk from the ground. Two police vans pulled up next to the pub. Now, surely the ideal thing for the police would have been to keep a presence at the pub and not let any large groups leave, but no, the police in their wisdom ordered the pub closed and ejected the mob onto the street. Obviously they headed straight for the ground and arrived at the cross roads by the Shepherds Crook pub just as the Leeds mob got there. Straight away, the two firms went to war, bottles and bricks went backwards and forwards as more and more joined the battle from both sides. It was during this fighting that the youngsters that were already making a name for themselves really came of age, turning the tide in Pompey's favour. This group of young guns were made up of mates who had mostly known each other from school days and went under the name of the Copnor North End Gas Squad. They had been hanging around mainly on the fringes of things for a couple of seasons but now would come their moment. As the opposing sides fought each other to a standstill, the youngsters doubled round a couple of back streets and, on the way, emptied a skip and pulled up half a dozen 'for sale' signs from outside a block of flats. They charged into the Leeds mob from the other side. Now, with Leeds having to fight on two fronts, their resistance began to crumble. As the battle raged, a builder's lorry drove through. A Pompey fan climbed on the back and picked up a shovel; waving it above his head he whacked a few Leeds as the lorry drove past them. The police went mental as did the local newspaper that launched a manhunt. At last, the police managed to regain control and put a cordon around the Leeds mob which made no attempt whatsoever to get away. Pompey however continued to try and get at them and the police repeatedly made baton charges to try and clear the streets. I remember seeing a young Leeds lad aged probably 18 or 19, standing on his own obviously wanting to get back to the safety of the Leeds mob behind the police cordon being taunted by a couple of the Pompey youngsters. The Leeds fan's face was as white as the shirts his team play in; clearly things had gone badly wrong for him as he saw first hand, probably for the first time, what it really means to come unstuck at football. Meanwhile at the Magpie pub in Fratton, another battle ensued although on a smaller scale. A couple of minibuses which had parked at the back of the pub had been spotted and a few of the Pompey lads were on a mission. A few windows were broken and the Leeds were run off up Fratton Road, leaving their transport at the mercy of the mob who, maybe surprisingly, didn't cause any damage to them but did hang around for a while to see if the occupants were going to attempt to come back. At first, they did but were quickly put to flight again. After a while, the Pompey fans got bored with the game of cat and mouse and began to drift away. The repercussions of this day were swift. Dawn raids pulled in around 15 or so lads including some of the youngsters. The court cases hung around for the best part of two years until they were finally dropped through lack of evidence. There was also the ludicrous remark by one police officer who, when asked if he could produce his pocket book, stood in the witness box and claimed that his dog had eaten it, sounding like an eleven year old schoolboy trying persuade his teacher he had a valid reason for not having his homework. The violence on this particular day was the worst seen at Fratton Park for many years and was probably in the memory of the police when the two sides met for the first time in the Premiership about five years later and the likely reason why the fixture was chosen as a dress rehearsal for the Pompey - Saints derby later on. For the first time ever at a football match in Hampshire, horses were drafted in from the Thames Valley force and, alongside dozens of colleagues in full riot gear, were used to keep order. The day passed off without incident.

Although we had found no action against Manchester United when we went there in '88', things were a little livelier when we played them in the league cup. We went up in a mini-bus and I felt we were lucky to get there at all. After we stopped in a little town on the way up, some of the lads helped themselves to some of the stock in the pub we stopped at. When they were caught by the landlord, they paid up which stopped him calling the local bobbies. I was driving and I don't think I had even locked the doors of the van when the rest of them were kicking off just outside the car park. The game that night was a cracker and we were unlucky not to win and, if it hadn't been for a bit of dodgy refereeing, probably would have. As it was, it ended 2- 2 with Paul Walsh running the United defence ragged. The replay the following week ended in a 1 - 0 defeat. We had it out with what I think were Cockney Reds before the game. To be honest, we absolutely battered them. One of the boys laid a United geezer out cold in a door way in Goldsmith Avenue. We were just far too much for them and ran them all over. After the match, we fought running battles, again in Goldsmith Avenue. This time it was a bit more even but our numbers were the deciding factor. The main event on Fratton Bridge went one way then the other before we eventually had them on the move. I had intended to meet Tony in the Froddington Arms but Fratton Road had a line of Police across stopping everyone who wanted to walk down it. I started to make my way down Lucknow Street where there was a minibus full of Man United fans parked up with the doors open. As I passed the van one of the United fans started to gob off. I ignored the guy after all, I'm not totally stupid. Besides, there were coppers everywhere itching to nick people so continued on my way. The mouthy one ran up and punched me from behind and the two of us started fighting but, within seconds, we were descended on by the boys in blue, albeit with florescent jackets. We were both informed that we were under arrest for affray. I was really pissed off with this twat; I mean, who kicks it off under the noses of the Old Bill? Before I could be loaded into the back of the waiting police van, I heard a voice. 'You can't arrest him,' it said. Both the copper and myself turned and saw an old guy aged about 80 years old. The old boy had just come out of the British Legion opposite. He repeated that I shouldn't be arrested. The officer asked him why and my knight in a flat cap explained that I was walking along, minding my own business when I was attacked. The copper asked if he was willing to make a statement to which he said he was going on to say that he had fought in the war and all these bloody yobbos should be in the army. Reluctantly the policeman was forced to release me. As I walked away, the old boy went with me with telling me all about his wartime exploits to which I was more than happy to listen to.

It's not just with the usual suspects where you can sometimes come unstuck; it's at the more quiet and unassuming grounds where you tend to let your guard down for just a minute that can, at times, be your undoing. We were away to Oxford one August when one such incident took place. After the match, myself and two others were split up from everyone else but thought nothing of it. As we walked towards the town centre, a mob of at least forty Oxford lads started to shadow us from across the road but it was clear that they were unsure what to do next. A couple of them started to cross the road towards us, giving it the big 'un when two police officers happened to come by on horse back. Having been in a similar situation like this at Manchester City, I really wasn't interested and was happy to see the cavalry come trotting down the road although they weren't at all concerned about our predicament. The faces of the Oxford lads were a picture however when one of the lads, Rob, grabbed hold of one of them and told him to fuck off back to the other side of the road. Fortunately, a vanload of Pompey lads came by which included my mate Tony who, seeing our dilemma, pulled over and started to empty out of the back. The Oxford mob disappeared off up the road while we climbed on board and got a lift to the station.

There are those that would consider the fans of Lincoln City as a bunch of fen land farmers but they can be a nasty bunch as small groups of Pompey fans found out one evening match up there. One incident saw two carloads ambushed at a set of traffic lights whereas, across town, a pub where Pompey fans were drinking was also attacked.

Wimbledon isn't usually the type of game that is worth a mention in this sort of book but one match at the old Plough Lane ground stands out for me. Before the game, it went off in a pub near the ground with a group of Millwall. The fighting was soon sorted out but tensions were running high. As a small group of us walked over the flyover, back towards the ground, a couple of Millwall guys walked towards us. They brushed by as we passed without saying a word. 200 yards further down the road, I looked down and saw a slash across my Sergio Tachinni ski jacket. I was really pissed off. That jacket cost me a small fortune. Mind you, I was glad that it was cold enough for me to wear to football that day even if it did go in the bin once I got home. It was during this game that I witnessed the most bizarre own goal ever. Just before half time, Wimbledon attacked and scored during which 'keeper Alan Knight took a slight knock. He was on the edge of the six yard box nursing his knee when Pompey kicked off. The ball was knocked back to Noel Blake who, in turn, played it back to Alan Knight who watched as it trickled past him to make it 2 - 0. In a cracking game that ended 3 - 2 to the Dons, their 'keeper Dave Beasent saved a penalty from Kevin Dillon. Just before the end of the game, Pompey fans began to invade the pitch. This must have really pissed off the Wimbledon officials as they had just spent £25,000 on fences to stop this happening. During the invasion, Beasent was punched by a Pompey fan but, to his credit, he didn't make a meal of it. Some players would have gone into their dying swan routine and afterwards he tried to play down the incident when interviewed.

Ironically, at the start of the 2001/02 season, Dave Beasent was brought in as emergency cover following the tragic death of Pompey's number one goalkeeper Aaron Flahaven in a car crash.

Another of what maybe considered one of the lesser London clubs would be Brentford. When Pompey played there in 1983, we attempted to take the home end but the opposition were a lot more game than had been expected as Spurs waded in to help their London cousins. Meanwhile, at the other end of the ground, the gates were forced open by Pompey fans trying to get in before the kick-off. During the second half, Brentford goalkeeper Paddy Roche was pelted with all manner of objects and, at one point, the game was held up while he received treatment after being struck. It made great copy for the tabloids the following day most of which used the headline 'Paddy Whacked'.

The games kept coming and maybe it was true Pompey could kick it off in an empty room. This time, it was the turn of Ipswich to be on the receiving end. After the game at Portman Road, there was a real toe-to-toe battle in the car park next to the main stand. Pompey had taken a fair sized mob and, to everyone's surprise, the Ipswich boys were really up for it. Their gameness wasn't a match for the 6.57 Crew this day. As a few of the Town lads started to drop, it was Ipswich who gave ground. First they began to back away as distress flares were fired. Eventually we ran them but not before the tractor boys had done their bit. Later on, it turned out that Ipswich had been reinforced by a few Chelsea lads as confirmed by one of them who was there when we got chatting at an England game.

A minibus load of Ipswich boys arrived at Fratton for a game towards the end of 1998/99 season. Outside the ground, they started to give it the big one until they saw a small firm of twenty or so Pompey bearing down on them. A few went and stood next to the police while the others scattered. Once most of us had been moved on, two of the Ipswich lads were seen trying to slip away. Some of us tagged on behind them, hoping that they would lead us to the others. After walking for a while, it became clear that either their mates had pissed off and left them to it or the Ipswich lads were hopelessly lost. One thing was very clear; they were shitting themselves and who could blame them. They must have thought that they were going to be set upon at any moment. We laid it on the line to a couple of eager young ones while others reassured the Ipswich lads. They were told that there was no way that anything was going to happen to them. They said they didn't have a clue where the minibus was parked. A couple of the lads tried to help find it while everyone else bid them goodbye. Ipswich's Norfolk neighbours didn't know just what to make of the Pompey mob. Most of us were supposed to travel to one game there by a coach organised by the Baffins lads but, for some reason, the coach failed to show up so instead we met up with lads from the surrounding areas and made the journey by train as usual. We would find out later that day the consequences of having to make the trip by rail but, for now, at least we were on our way. Although a large mob had travelled up to Carrow Road for the top of the table clash, around a dozen or so of us were split up from the rest of the Pompey lads. I think we had gone for a look around while the rest stayed in the pub and, by the time we got back, they had moved on. We weren't all that bothered, after all we were only in Norwich. We started to make our way towards the ground but, as we were walking by the river near to the stadium, we found ourselves surrounded by fifty or so home fans. Where they had been all day when we were in the town centre, I have no idea but maybe they sensed that we would be easier to pick off than if they tried to tackle the whole mob. Instead of being deterred, we went straight into them scattering the Norwich boys everywhere. Once they regained their composure, the Norwich firm regrouped and again surrounded us. We were now full of confidence seeing how easily we had put them to flight before and were really enjoying the attention. Again, instead of shying away, we started to entertain the would be attackers with a rendition of the Wham hit 'I'm your man'. I have absolutely no idea why. Before again scattering the Canaries once more, this happened all the way to the ground, we must have run them half a dozen times all the time asking the Norwich lads if they were getting bored of making themselves look complete pricks.

When we met up with the rest of the lads in the ground later, we were full of ourselves. It was typical of the 6.57 Crew in those days, regardless of the odds, we were game for anything. Most of our mob were sat in the seats along one side of the pitch so, as soon as the match ended, we were up and out of the ground straight away. We must have numbered somewhere in the range of 250 lads as we marched towards the town centre without a police presence to bother us. Just near the town, a roar went up as a mob of Norwich lads came bouncing down the road, lobbing bricks, bottles and other missiles at us. Taken by surprise, we were at first put onto the back foot but not for long. The moment they ran out of ammunition, it was they that started to back peddle as we surged forward and into them. By the time the first police vans began to screech to a halt, the Norwich fans had already fled. We were soon being escorted back to the station but thirty or so of us managed to evade the cordon in an effort to see what else may happen. We soon bumped into a similar number of Norwich lads who were game but outclassed. Again we were rounded up and, this time, the police were not taking any more chances. They frog marched us back to the station and stayed with us for half an hour until we were put on the next London bound train, around two hours after the match had ended. By this time, the rest of the lads were well on their way back to London. We would have to see if we could bump into them somewhere. Once at Liverpool Street, we went straight from the over ground concourse, down the escalators to the underground. While waiting for our tube train, we chatted about the day's events and the unexpected encounters we had found in Norwich. After a few minutes came the familiar rush of air and the rumble of a London underground train coming into the station. The doors opened and we began to board, simultaneously another much larger group exited the tube train. We looked at them and they us, each eyeing up the other, and both knowing the other was unmistakably a rival football firm. As the doors were closing, one of ours made the comment that is still laughed about today 'It's a mob and they want it'. It was as if trigger was pulled, shouts of ICF rang around the station as the other mob rushed back onto the train. We were facing all of West Ham's top boys probably ever and, with nowhere to go, fought back gamely. For a couple of minutes with our backs against the wall, the battle raged and, despite the odds being stacked against us, we came out of it with only a few bruises to show. We later found out that West Ham were on their way back from Liverpool and that they saw more action on that underground station than they had seen all day in Merseyside. We had shocked them by our willingness to face them even though we were totally outnumbered and that they had nothing but respect for us.

In the early to mid 1970's, Reading was one of those places regularly terrorised by the Pompey boot boys. When Reading visited Fratton Park in 1976, the Berkshire fans were attacked as they queued to get into the ground and, during the game, Pompey fans fought battles with the police, leaving one officer hospitalised and four others with minor injuries. In all 4 fans were arrested whereas another 88 were ejected from the ground. The worst incident between the two clubs came in March 1977 at the fixture at Reading's Elm Park. There was trouble before the match with Pompey fans attacking a couple of the pubs near the ground. As Pompey went 2 – 0 down, blues fans invaded the pitch and charged into the Reading end, scattering the local fans. During the attack, one Reading fan was cornered and brutally beaten. The fan, Leslie Cross, was left unconscious on the terraces with serious head injuries and was taken to hospital where doctors had to resuscitate him three times as they battled to save his life. Fortunately, he was to make a full recovery. After the match eventually finished, Pompey fans smashed down the gates at the Tilehurst Road end of the ground and rampaged down Wantage Road, smashing windows and over turning cars as they went. Hundreds of Pompey fans then chased the Reading fans along Oxford Road, causing hundreds of pounds worth of damage including destroying the furniture on display outside an antique shop. Police reinforcements were called in until there was a substantial fight outside the aptly named Battle hospital. Berkshire police launched the type of investigation into the violence that is commonplace today but, at the time, was unprecedented for football related trouble. Photo fit pictures of those said to be involved in the attack on Mr. Cross were published in the papers. In due course, four Pompey fans were jailed for four years each for the assault on Leslie Cross. At the time, this was seen as a colossal sentence for football associated violence. Several others of the 52 Portsmouth supporters arrested were given jail sentences for their part in the day's events. A campaign was started proclaiming the innocence of one of the Pompey fans jailed as part of the attack on Leslie Cross. Leaflets were handed out at home games and, at one match, campaigners ran on the pitch with banners stating he was innocent; their campaign came to nothing. The newspapers were horrified at the level of violence at this match, describing all those that took part in the day's events at Elm Park as animals. Rather than being shamed by this, one of the shops in Commercial Road did a roaring trade in T-shirts proclaiming 'I'm a Pompey Animal'.

In December 1978, the two clubs were drawn together in the second round of the FA Cup, a match due to be played at Fratton Park. As a direct result of the violence at Elm Park, the Reading supporters organised a mass boycott of the fixture. Reading Football Club were forced to cancel the special train and coaches that they had booked to take the expected 2000 fans to the match. In the end, they only sold 200 tickets.

Of late though, a trip to Elm Park or more recently the Madjeski Stadium is usually seen as a day out for a quiet drink and nothing else. This was until the last time the two teams played each other at the old Elm Park. At Fratton Park earlier in the season, a small group of Reading lads done an even smaller group of Pompey boys while the majority were either on their way home or in the pub. After the fight, the Reading lads wisely scurried off home before anything else could be made of it, obviously making the most of their triumph. Back in Portsmouth, nothing was really made of the events other than a 'Oh well, shit happens' attitude.

For some reason, the Reading 'firm' rate themselves very highly although, from what I can gather, a lot of them can't decide whether they follow Reading or Chelsea. The sad fact for them is that nobody else cares about them; well maybe Oxford do and possibly Swindon. Anyhow, things came to a head this particular season when a few of the Pompey lads had an altercation with a few of the Reading/Chelsea lads (is it Cheling or Readsea?) in a pub in London. Pompey were due to play away to the Royals a few weeks later so one of the Reading lads made a challenge.

'If you're brave enough to come to our place, we'll sort it out once and for all, Pompey'.

Now, on the south coast, we pride ourselves in our manners and would consider it rude to pass up such a gracious invitation. Word soon got around and, for the first time in years, Reading away became a 'must go' game. The morning of the game saw a massive mob get on the 9 o'clock train. By the time it had stopped at the various other outlying regions of the Portsmouth area such as Fareham, the train was packed with lunatics. As the train pulled into Reading, we got off in an orderly fashion and quickly made our way to a pre-arranged pub in some back streets and waited and waited. Contact was made with the Reading lads.

'We're here' said Pompey.
'We know' said Reading.
'What's the next move?' asked Pompey.
'Er, well, there's too many of you' replied Reading.
'You're at home, you prick' said Pompey.

Everyone thought they were trying to take the piss. Nobody said anything about strictly limited numbers. What did they think this was, West Side Story?

That was that. Reading had decided that they didn't want to play after all. We started to move from the pub in search of our own entertainment. The Berkshire police tried to pen us in. At one point using horses to hold us against a large department store. A few simply opened the shop doors, legged it through the store and out the other end into the shopping centre. There was a bit of a run around with the police but most of the lads were captured and escorted to the ground. Those of us who had avoided the escort searched around the town centre in a vain effort to find the mythical Reading firm but alas, like the Holy grail and the Golden fleece before it, it could not be found.

After the match, we again made our way back to the town centre where legend has it, the Reading crowd was found. Nobody is sure for certain for, although a group in the finest Stone Island could be seen locked in one pub, the only sort of confrontation that was had before the police horses and dogs pushed us back to the train station, was when one of the Reading lads opened the pub door, poked his head out, shouted 'Where were you at Fratton Park?' before slamming the door shut and locking it. You can picture the Reading lads in the pub nodding with agreement, saying yeah that showed them, they won't be back here again in a hurry. We just burst out laughing at him; we're here in your town now and taking the piss mate. Many of the lads made up for the disappointing show by the Reading fans on their way home. Stopping off in Winchester, they went to a known Scummer's pub and turned it and the occupants over.

Just a few miles from Reading is a firm of an altogether different quality. Bristol City were another team where we were virtually assured to find a row whenever we visited. One particular year, we went up there for the opening game of the season. Bristol being one of the very few places where we can catch a direct train to, we took fairly big numbers by rail, catching a train so we would be there well before lunchtime. On arrival at the main Bristol station, the awaiting police shepherded us into a large cage on the station so, naturally we thought, the day had come to a premature end. Oddly, once they had searched us and taken names, they allowed us to walk to a pub nearby. From there, we managed to shake the police altogether and made our way to another pub called The Bell near a large estate. The police either didn't care or were totally inept for allowing a hundred and fifty plus lads wander off. It was only a matter of time before the Bristol City firm found where we were. It probably helped that their top fellas were known to a few of ours from England games and calls were made in advance to let them know we would be coming. Before long, four or five City boys were stood outside the pub mouthing off. There was a rush towards the door but, before a punch was thrown, the five had wisely bolted. One of the lads that had made it onto the pavement was puzzled as to why so few had followed him out but, when he returned inside, he soon found out why. Another of our lot who had been standing by the door had attempted to throw a glass; unfortunately for the rest of us, it was still full of lager. One of the lads in particular had taken the full force and spent the rest of the day smelling of Stella.

Shortly after, Bristol turned up in full force. The local constabulary was in tow who put a ring around the pub. We made an attempt to get out of the pub via the fire escape but, after a bit of to-ing and fro-ing, we were escorted to the ground with the local mob shadowing while not trying to attack the escort. By the time we reached Ashton Gate, we were champing at the bit to get at the City mob. The police with truncheons drawn put a line across the road facing us, trying to encourage us unsuccessfully to enter the stadium. During this stand off, a few Bristol started to mouth off from behind the police ranks. It was frustrating as no doubt, if we tried anything, we'd soon be taking a trip to the cells. We were about to give up and go through the turnstiles when a hooded figure appeared among the Bristol mob. The guy went straight towards the mouthiest of the City lot and decked him with a single punch. By the time the police reacted to the commotion behind them, the guy had slipped back in with the rest of the Pompey lads. The home lot gestured to us to go into a particular set of seats. Around twenty of us managed to do so. Despite the invite, they seemed surprised that we had taken them up on their offer. Soon, punches were being swapped and a few plastic seats thrown.

Police and stewards soon bundled us out and onto the away terrace with the others. After the game, it kicked off again on the way back to the station but it was all quickly quelled. The following Monday, photos of the fighting in the seats were published in the newspapers which resulted in a few of the boys having their front doors being taken off their hinges.

Later on that season, City repaid the visit with one of their own to Fratton. Again, we knew that they would be on the way because of a few phone calls to confirm. One of our lot had a police scanner and we listened for confirmation that they were en-route; as a result, we gathered in the City Arms and awaited their arrival. Because we had the scanner, we knew that they didn't get off their train at Fratton so immediately went across the road to Portsmouth & Southsea station. The Bristol City Service Firm were shocked at the welcoming committee. A bin was thrown through the glass doors as we steamed into them. A few others had been waiting in the buffet on the station and they too steamed in. The City were trapped and took a bit of a slapping as they tried to run back onto the station concourse. It wasn't long before the police wadded in and arrests were soon being made. As a result, one of our lot got three months.

13
OUTSIDE INFLUENCES

The city of Portsmouth is predominantly made up of Portsea Island. Since the end of World War Two, the city has increased its urban sprawl northwards, the first houses of which were built as emergency buildings to house those bombed out during the blitz. Some of these temporary buildings are still standing. As you continue over Portsdown Hill, there are the smaller towns such as Waterlooville and, towards the west, Portchester and Fareham and east, Havant, Leigh Park, and Hayling Island which, whilst outside of the city, due to increased demand for housing in the region will no doubt before long become the outskirts of 'Greater Portsmouth'. Many of Portsmouth's estates, like countless across the country, are riddled with crime and the menace of drugs. With many bored youngsters hanging around, violence is never far away.

By the time of the early nineties, the vast majority of the Pompey firm was made up of those from out of town. As lads from across the area took over the reigns while their predecessors were busy raving or grafting but, long before then, many of those from off of the island were well established within the firm.

It is not just the immediate area that Portsmouth Football Club draws its support from. Large parts of West Sussex are staunch Pompey while most of north Hampshire and even as far up as Guildford and beyond can be considered as a Pompey stronghold. There is a group from the Yateley area that attend every match, home and away. There was talk in a couple of national papers that David Coupland, the right wing extremist who planted the nail bombs in London in 1999 who is from Yateley, was a member of the 6.57 Crew. This however is false. Although a few of the lads from the area knew Coupland either from school days or from being about town, they confirmed that he never went to football with them.

To the west of the country there is a large, blue coloured oasis home of a hardy band of Pompey fans from Salisbury and Devizes. Despite living closer to Bristol or even, heaven forbid, Southampton who draw a lot of supporters from the area, these lads are Pompey through and through; they attend every game, home and away and, in days gone by, were never far from the action. One Friday night before travelling on one of the Salisbury arranged coaches, it was one of several that was organised by the Salisbury lads, most probably to Glasgow for one of England's trips to the other side of Hadrian's wall, but can't be certain as they also organised coaches to Pompey away games as well. Regardless to which particular trip it was, a healthy mob of 6.57 Crew was in Wiltshire this particular night and a good piss up ensued. While in the town centre, a large group of guys came swaggering in to the pub, trying their very best to look mean and intimidating although they were neither. Given their manner and their style of dress i.e. badly, it was obvious that this lot were army squadies. It didn't take long for the atmosphere in the pub to change; before this lot had come in, there hadn't been a hint of trouble all night. One thing led to another and it went off big time. It turned out that these guys were from the Parachute Regiment; they were giving it 'Paras this, Paras that' but suddenly they were being attacked from all sides by street tough football hooligans who have no respect for reputations. The battle spilled out into the street. There were a few soldiers from other regiments about but they didn't get involved. By all accounts, they were quite pleased to see the Paras getting a bit of a kicking because of the superiority complex some members of the Parachute Regiment have over members of the army. Apparently, they would swan around wherever they were garrisoned, mob handed, bullying guys from other units. The police cordoned off the street and a few arrests were made while a couple of the soldiers were taken to hospital. Without doubt, the Parachute regiment are one of the best army units in the world, more than capable of taking on anything in the battlefield but this particular night, a few of them showed that some of them were unable to handle a few beers and came badly unstuck as a result.

The trip to Hampden Park was another eventful one. Once the coach finally got underway, we travelled through the night arriving in Glasgow early Saturday morning. The idea being that, after the game, our party would stop in Ayr before travelling back arriving home sometime Sunday morning. It wasn't long before it kicked off in the streets of Glasgow. At one point during the morning, a few lads from various other parts of the country including a few Leeds boys joined the Pompey mob. It kicked off outside a pub with a few sweaties; I am led to believe that they were Aberdeen fans. It was hard to tell because, regardless as to which team they followed, they were off faster than Alan Wells, the former jock sprinter, out of the starting blocks. As the Scots were chased down the street, the combined English mob took up the chant 'SIX FIVE SEVEN, SIX FIVE SEVEN'. After the match, we arrived back at the coach only to find it surrounded by police. The driver claimed that he was unaware that the coach was being used to ferry lads to the match despite the fact that, on the way up, there was a whip-round as a sweetener for him which netted him £100. All the belongings were off loaded and the coach disappeared into the distance, leaving everyone with the problem of making their own way home.

Another of the coaches that the Salisbury boys organised was to Carlisle in December 1986 which led to events that are still talked about in the Cumbria town today. Everybody on the coach, along with about twenty or so that had arrived by train, were wearing blazers and tie over an Aquascutum shirt which is something we used to do regularly in those days. By lunchtime, we were in a city centre pub. Being only a few days away from Christmas, spirits were high and not too much action was really expected from the day. As the beer continued to flow, a small group of us went off to a joke shop to buy silly party hats and streamers. It was that sort of day. While in the shop, some of the locals spotted us and, as we left, we were fronted up. The Carlisle mob probably thought it was going to be an easy victory but were soon in for a shock when the rest of the Pompey firm came pouring out of a pub. I don't suppose they expected such a large firm to travel that far. We ended up running the Carlisle mob through the town. At one point, a ginger haired Carlisle fan ran through British Home Stores with a Pompey lad in pursuit who shouted to a security guard 'Stop him'. The guard looked pleased with himself as he grabbed the fleeing lad but didn't know quite what to do next. The Pompey lad ran up and knocked down the prisoner with a single punch, turned to the guard and simply said 'Cheers mate' and sauntered out of the store.

As we moved towards the ground, it went off again. Again we had the upper hand. One of the lads grabbed a Christmas tree from off a market stall and led the charge while the woman stall owner was less than impressed, chasing him up the road in an attempt to regain possession of her tree. The lad in question, Eddie, is without doubt the King of the blaggers; he once got himself and several others into a major world championship boxing match in London by pretending that he was an ITV engineer there to cover the fight. He got the lads in who were holding a roll of cable by pretending to bollock them for being behind in their work. The security guard took pity on the 'workers' and ushered them in without checking their ID. He may be able to blag with the best of them but Eddie has a heart of gold. He is without doubt one of the fittest people I know. I bumped into him once and he said that he was bored so he decided to go on a ten mile run. One morning as he was running along Southsea seafront on his early morning jog, he heard cries coming from the sea. Two men had gone out fishing during the night and somehow their boat had turned over and they were left stranded clinging onto the upturned craft, literally fighting for their lives. Eddie heard the pleas for help and swam out to them; he got the first man to shore then swam out and got the second. Once he got them safely to dry land, he ran to a 'phone box and called the emergency services. While it has never bothered him in the slightest, he has never received any kind of official recognition for his bravery, added to which he had to endure cries of 'Save me Eddie, Save me' whenever he walked into the pub and was called 'Baywatch' by many for a while. At the start of the 2002/03 season, he struck a bet that he wouldn't have a hair cut until Pompey had secured promotion. As they raced towards the championship, his hair grew wilder but, once the title was clinched, rather than cash in on the bet, he decided he'd rather raise money for a children's cancer ward. At half time during Steve Claridge's testimonial match, he had his head shaved, raising £2,000.

Once we walked triumphantly to Brunton Park, one of the Carlisle stewards took one look at us dressed in blazers and let us into the ground thinking that we were part of the team although just how big a squad he thought Pompey had, I don't know. During the game, we were in the seats behind the Carlisle mob that we had been having fun with earlier in the day. Some of them looked a bit sorry for themselves and, although threats went back and forth, nothing happened inside the ground. After the match, those on the coach were rounded up and taken to it while those on the train made the walk back to the station. Stalked by the Carlisle mob that now fancied their chances due to the drop in numbers. It went off two or three times during the walk. Each time, Pompey stood their ground until the Police took them to the station. There was a wait for over an hour for a London bound train and the police were threatening to arrest anyone that tried to leave the station while a few Carlisle boys hung around outside.

Again, the following season we played away to Carlisle a few days before Christmas. This time, it was on a Sunday with a mid day kick-off. A minibus load of us made our way to the game, leaving on Saturday morning and having a night out in Blackpool. The trip up was relatively quiet but, on the outskirts of Blackpool, it was decided to stop at a pub to get changed into clothes for going out on the town. Once changed, there was time for a quick drink and off again. The minibus had got as far as Blackpool seafront when there was the familiar sight of flashing blue lights. The van was pulled over for a traffic offence which resulted with the driver being breathalysed, a test that he failed. The two coppers were okay explaining that he was only just over and were pretty confident that he would pass on the toximeter machine at the station. While one of the officers drove their prisoner to the station, the other drove the minibus as everyone else on the van would have melted the breath machine, let alone make the lights flash. As predicted, the toximeter showed that the driver wasn't over the limit and that he had only had the one at the quick stop, the two coppers showed him into the car park where the rest of us waited. Shouts of free the Portsmouth one were, by this time, starting to piss off their colleagues. The two officers chatted for a while and then suggested a couple of pubs that would be worth a visit. Ten minutes later, we were in the first suggested boozer, a lively chrome and plastic place with loud music blaring out. Even before the first pints could be sunk, it kicked off although nobody had a clue what had started it. One thing was for sure however that some of our mates were involved in a vicious fight with the bouncers. One of the bouncers fell to the floor and was getting a real kicking as the boys in blue turned up. The first police down the steps and into the bar were the guys that had pulled the van over. They grabbed hold of me and said.

'Get your mates together and fuck off before someone finds out we told you cunts to come in here.' We didn't need a second offer.

We eventually arrived in Carlisle around 10.30 the following morning. As we drove through the town centre, a couple of locals tried to large it but, as soon as the van pulled over, they were off, even before the back doors opened.

We parked up the van next to the ground and, as we stretched our legs, an old guy in a flat cap with a dog-end stuck to his bottom lip said 'Alright there lads, good journey? Games off'. The guy seemed to take great pleasure from this last bit of news. Apparently the river next to the ground had flooded in heavy rain and the fire brigade were pumping the water of the pitch. The brigade must of done a great job as the referee passed the pitch fit for play at 11.30. The match ended with a 1 – 0 win, Mick Channon scoring the only goal. The day out at football passed peacefully but, on the journey back south, a stop off was made in Stratford upon Avon. We went into a pub/ club and it must have been the place to go on a Sunday as it was jam packed. We started to play up, dancing on the tables and generally being a pain. The locals started to mass together and it was clear, it was about to go off big time. With the odds stacked against us, the word soon went around to make our way back to the van. As we left, one of the lads let off a CS gas spray. The van moved off and as we looked back, we could see the pub empty as the gas took its toll.

While sitting on a train returning from another away game (I have no idea where), one of the Salisbury lads entered our carriage looking a little worse for wear. A brief inquest soon established that he had been in an altercation with some 'Greasers' a few carriages up. The lads moved up and, sure enough, there were a load of ugly looking 'Greasers', all leather and dirty denims, a couple of them were big lumps. Fighting soon engulfed the carriage and the 'Greasers' were more than willing participants, giving as good as they got. There were cuts and bruises on both sides. The fighting went on for a little while and there were no innocent parties in the carriage. When the train pulled into the next station, the BTP boarded the train. Everyone quickly moved to various parts of the train in order to distance themselves from the fighting. However, a couple of the 'Greasers' walked up and down the platform pointing out a few of the Salisbury boys who were arrested.

The Salisbury lads have always been a real handy bunch. As a group of Wolves who tried to take a liberty with them found out. Returning from an away game with Crewe, about a dozen of them were drinking in a bar near Euston when around thirty Wolves came in. After a bit of a stand off, the black country mob steamed in. However, rather than cowering in the corner, they took the battle to them, forcing them out of the pub and even at one point running them into Euston station. Unfortunately though, numbers started to show and eventually they began to get picked off but they gave as good as they got and maybe more.

Although I am from the City of Portsmouth as opposed to the outskirts, for a while, I went to games with lads from other parts, either the guys from Fareham or Hayling Island. One of the Hayling lads I went with regularly was Mark T. He used to stand out from the rest early in the 1980's. When everyone else was starting to get into the designer clothing, Mark was wearing Punk gear. When I was going to games with my mate Ian, we used to see him all over the place and more likely in the front line. We used to meet up with him all the time despite neither of us knowing his name until we had no option but ask him. Up until that point, we had referred to him as the Hayling Punk. Before too long though, Mark toned down his image, explaining that being dressed different to everyone else made him stand out a little too much, especially to the police. I would occasionally have a night out in Hayling. One night, I had Raffles with me. We met up with the Hayling football lads and went to a few bars until, for some reason, it kicked off in one of them on the beach. Raffles, true to form, took things a little further when he CS gassed the place. Tongue in cheek, Mark said to me that I was welcome anytime but could I leave Raffles at home as Hayling used to be a nice quiet place and not really ready for the likes of him. After Ian stopped going to games, I used to travel to a lot of away games with the Hayling lads, all of them great blokes. Usually, this meant Mark driving. We were once on our way to Leeds when his car broke down on the motorway. A guy stopped and took us to the Leicester Forest service station. From there, we walked across loads of fields until we arrived somewhere on the outskirts of Leicester. We then caught a bus to Leicester train station and caught a train to Leeds. For all I know, the car could still be on the hard shoulder. Another game at Sheffield United, we were making our way in traffic after the match. We had a couple of extra passengers in the car as we were giving a lift to a couple of other lads whose car had broken down on the way up. I don't know what it was with the Hayling lads and cars. They had left it to get fixed and were taking them back to it. Unbeknown to us, one of the lads had been giving the verbal to the Blades throughout the game. As we sat in the traffic, around twenty blades walked by. They spotted our passenger and came straight for it. Mark put the car into gear, crossed the central reservation and managed to get us away before it came badly on top.

We used to go miles in Mark's car. Yet another long journey we made was to Middlesbrough. We only took about thirty lads to the game but all would be prepared to stand and have it should it come down to it. The match finished and, as we left the ground, the 'Boro lads were on the other side of a temporary metal barrier. Cheered on by Pompey's scarfers, we pushed the barrier aside and went straight in, taking both the police and 'Boro lads by surprise. Despite being outnumbered by at least 2 to 1, we were soon backing off 'Boro down the street. The police charged in and rounded everyone up and began to march us back to our cars.

Anyone who went to the old Ayresome Park will know that back-to-back houses and the streets all ran into each other, surrounded it, making it dangerous ground and ripe for an ambush. As our escort reached the end of the street, only the police were surprised that the 'Boro lads were waiting. It went off again and, once more, the police separated the sides and the escort continued. The very next corner, it happened again and the next and the next. Word soon got around that, as soon as the escort reached the next junction, rather than wait for the attack, it would be better to charge the 'Boro. The plan was successful and the 'Boro lads were backed off with hardly a punch being thrown but, once again, we were soon penned in by the local constabulary who were starting to lose their sense of humour. Suddenly a policeman on a horse who may have watched the film Lawrence of Arabia one to many times, came galloping into the crowd waving his long truncheon around like a sabre. At the time this was happening, there was neither any trouble happening nor was there any threat that it was about to go off again, most of the 'Boro lads having been moved on by the local constabulary. The copper on the horse brought his truncheon crashing down on Mark's head, splitting it wide open. Mark dropped immediately with blood gushing out of the wound as lads and policemen on foot rushed to his aid. Everyone went mad and, to give them credit, two particular policemen openly had a go at their colleague on horseback, disgusted at what they saw as over the top actions. An ambulance was called and Mark was dispatched to hospital where he was treated for a nasty injury. Years later, Pompey and Middlesbrough were drawn together in the FA Cup at Fratton Park. 'Boro brought a large following as usual and with it, a game firm. Before the match, some of them were served up a bit of a beating when it went off in the Milton Arms whereas, after the game, a mass brawl broke out outside the ground.

POMPEY FANS ON RAMPAGE

Soccer fans in Southsea pub brawl

PORTSMOUTH was today braced for its second taste of soccer savagery in eight days.

Two coach-loads of Newcastle fans, who arrived last night for today's Division II clash with Pompey at Fratton Park, were involved in a Southsea pub brawl that ended with three arrests and three people in hospital.

Hundreds more Geordies arrived early this morning in a fleet of 15 coaches. They were defying Government guidelines which say visiting fans should be kept out until two hours before kick-off.

Police kept a close watch on the fans' movements in the city today to prevent further trouble after the battles between Pompey and Saints fans at last Saturday's South Coast derby.

A Southsea police spokesman said the "advance party" arrived about 9.30 last night. "The trouble started in one of the pubs about an hour later," he said.

Three people were arrested on public order charges near the Coastguard Tavern, Clarendon Road — one from Newcastle and two from Portsmouth.

The fighting involved 20-30 men. Three Newcastle fans were taken to hospital for treatment to minor cuts.

Behave in the Lions' Den

By GRAHAM NICKLESS

THE Football Association will be keeping an eye on Millwall's first round Cup replay against Portsmouth at the Den tonight.

More than 1,000 Pompey fans are expected to make the trip and Millwall don't want a repetition of Saturday's ugly incidents at Fratton Park.

Three years ago Millwall were banned from playing Cup-ties at home for two years after a game against Ipswich ended in a crowd riot.

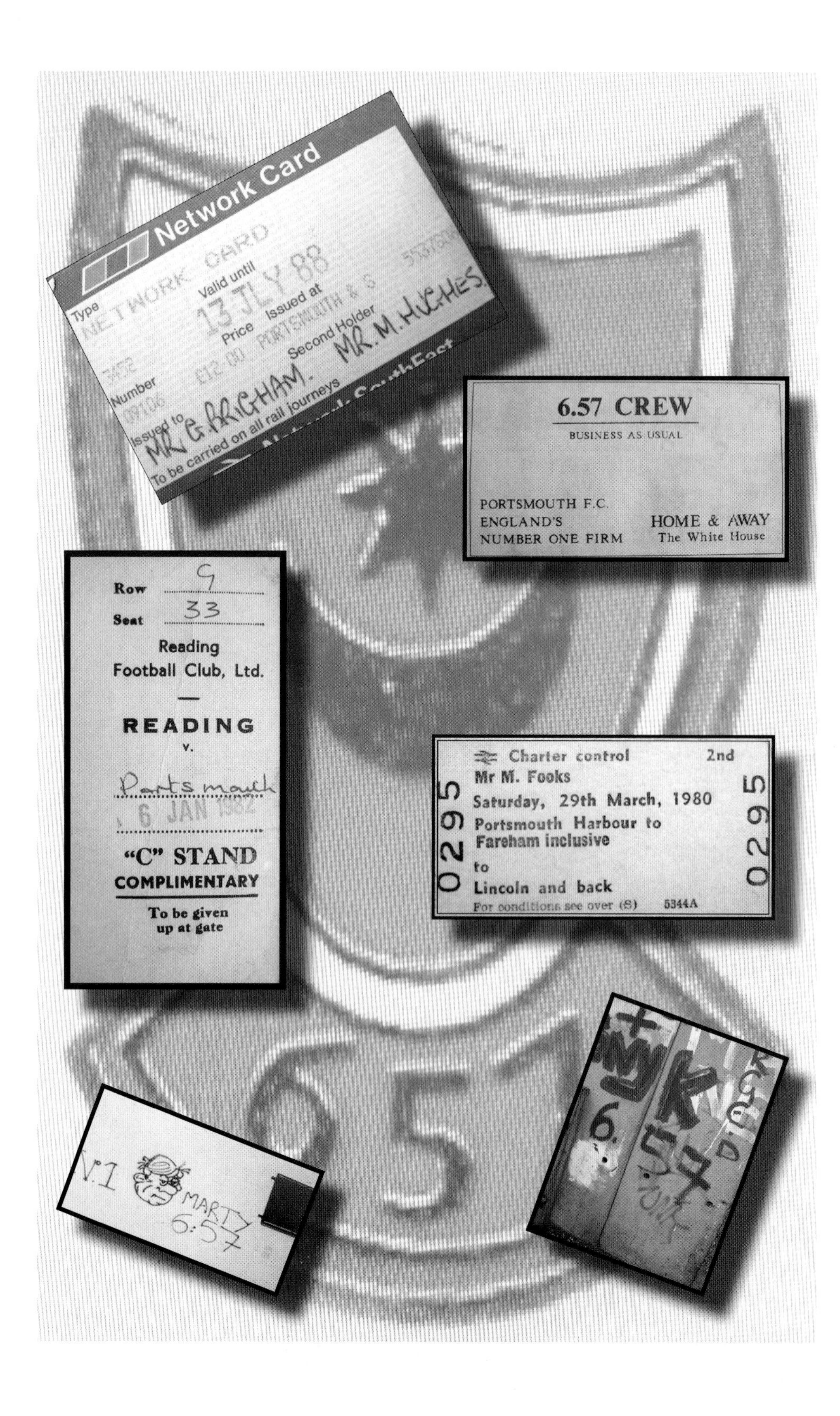
Network Card
Type
NETWORK CARD
Valid until
13 JLY 88
Price
£12.00
Issued at
PORTSMOUTH & S
Number
Second Holder
MR. M. HUGHES.
Issued to
MR G. BRIGHAM.
To be carried on all rail journeys
6.57 CREW
BUSINESS AS USUAL
PORTSMOUTH F.C.
ENGLAND'S
NUMBER ONE FIRM
HOME & AWAY
The White House
Row 9
Seat 33
Reading
Football Club, Ltd.
READING
v.
Portsmouth
6 JAN 1982
"C" STAND
COMPLIMENTARY
To be given
up at gate
Charter control
2nd
Mr M. Fooks
Saturday, 29th March, 1980
Portsmouth Harbour to
Fareham inclusive
to
Lincoln and back
For conditions see over (S)
5344A
0295
0295
V.I
MARTY
6:57
6.57

TOP OF THE COPS!

ALAN BALL'S Portsmouth top the League of Shame for arrests inside soccer grounds, *writes MARTIN SAMUEL.*

They added to the woe of being relegated to Division 2 under coach Ball with a tally of 282 arrests — an average of more than 14 per game.

Pompey chief executive Ron Jones said: "I don't wish to play down the figures — but a fair percentage were for offences other than hooliganism, such as swearing."

Chief Superintendant Bob Dawes, in charge of police at Fratton Park, said: "Swearing would lead to an ejection."

Horrific

He added: "Portsmouth's record is nothing to be proud of, but most of the arrests were in the first three matches against West Ham, Southampton and Chelsea.

"These games were horrific because Portsmouth's fans were looking to see what new blood they had to fight."

Chelsea were second in the table with 271 arrests while Luton, whose membership scheme is championed by Sports Minister Colin Moynihan, had just **ONE** arrest.

Moynihan revealed the police figures in the Commons yesterday.

● Last season's arrest tables for Divisions 1 and 2 are shown right.

THUG LEAGUE TABLES

Team	Gates	Arrest
Portsmouth	324,780	282
Chelsea	408,538	271
Southampton	290,617	208
Coventry	350,165	194
Arsenal	598,059	153
Newcastle	419,742	149
West Ham	396,473	149
Nottm For	384,648	130
Oxford	218,632	105
QPR	265,813	91
Sheff Wed	395,519	90
Derby Co	343,107	86
Tottenham	517,970	74
Wimbledon	159,691	49
Watford	291,464	43
Manchester U	783,099	38
Liverpool	791,977	33
Norwich	313,904	32
Everton	555,692	24
Charlton	173,629	14
Luton	161,884	1

Team	Gates	Arrest
Aston Villa	403,836	308
Bradford	285,509	197
Leeds	443,094	184
Bournemouth	168,757	149
West Brom	222,261	132
Huddersfield	150,334	126
Middlesbrough	321,219	110
Birmingham	188,722	101
Ipswich	258,037	99
Leicester	223,049	81
Blackburn	211,120	79
Crystal Pal	215,496	78
Shrewsbury	108,202	68
Swindon	209,800	67
Sheffield Utd	223,960	60
Stoke	211,234	57
Barnsley	168,339	55
Millwall	185,165	44
Hull	157,507	38
Manchester C	428,655	35
Plymouth	226,152	29
Reading	150,352	20
Oldham	147,995	19

POMPEY STAY AWAY

By IAN GIBB

SECOND DIVISION leaders Portsmouth have stepped in to avoid crowd trouble at Millwall on Saturday by warning their supporters: "Stay away."

Director Mrs Joan Deacon, wife of chairman John, said last night: "We have put up posters round the city asking fans not to travel."

Mrs Deacon added: "I can't understand why some of the Millwall and Portsmouth fans hate each other so much. I assume it's because they are from dockland areas and they are used to scrapping."

5/6/87

'Docker' gets carried away

MOST elections meetings are attended by the brigade of the party faithful, politely clapping their candidate.

"Docker" Hughes's first — and probably his last — public meeting was bound to be different.

For a start it was better attended. More than 120 people turned up at Somers Town First School for a meeting that was only arranged that morning, compared with 50 or 60 at some election meetings covered by The News.

By ALISON MOORE

The candidate was nowhere to be seen for the first ten minutes of the meeting, making a surprise appearance from a cupboard, in which he had been closeted for the previous half hour.

Docker — the 32-year-old candidate of the 6.57 party — managed about three words before his jubilant supporters carried him around the room on their shoulders, as if he had already swept into power.

Docker is a man of few words anyway, bu[t] his supporters tol[d] had hoped to make[...]note speech, outlining the reasons behind his support for Scimitarra in the Oaks.

The keynote speech never materialized as the meeting came to an abrupt end.

One person turned off the lights, a second set off a fire extinguisher, and the rest of us fled.

What are Docker's chances in the election? His supporters are certainly hopeful.

Agent George Brigham has pledged the party to give half of its £500 deposit to The News Scanner Appeal — provided they get the deposit back.

To retain the deposit, Docker needs five per cent. of the vote in Portsmouth South — 3,550 votes.

Somers Town is his stronghold — and he might just reach that target.

His supporters are young — not a person over 30 to be seen — and do not seem to be worried by his lack of economic policies.

The 6.57 party denies any National Front or Loyalist connections, but says it is making serious points while having a lot of fun.

It is calling for more facilities for youth in the city and Government support for racing, though the abolition of off course betting tax.

■ **TRIAL:** Sophisticated technology identifies hooligan caught hurling rocks

The ugly face of football violence

CCTV captures an image of football yob Paul Oldreive throwing concrete at the Stoke fans

by James Glover & Khushwant Sachdave
The News

THIS is the moment football hooligan Paul Oldreive was caught on camera hurling rocks at rival fans in a sickening act of match-day violence.

The damning CCTV evidence was crucial in getting violent Oldreive banned from every Portsmouth game in the country. Oldreive, 27, carried out the attack in November 2002 after Pompey – then in the first division – thrashed Stoke City 3-0 to continue their march to the Premiership.

Away fans had been shepherded to Fratton station because police feared violence would flare up between the two sets of fans.

But when the away supporters walked down the steps to the platform, Oldreive struck.

He stood in Selbourne Terrace, which runs alongside Fratton railway station, and hurled lumps of concrete at them as they waited for the train home.

Police trawling through hours of surveillance video came across footage of the incident almost a year later.

Oldreive, of Stane Street Close, Pulborough, West Sussex, denied the attack and tried to claim the yob on the video was not him.

But police used sophisticated face-mapping technology for the first time in a football hooligan case to prove beyond all doubt that he was the man.

Oldreive was convicted of one count of affray following a trial at Portsmouth Magistrates' Court.

And yesterday he was given a community punishment order and a three-year ban from football matches.

Terms of punishment given by court

PAUL Oldreive was handed a 160-hour community punishment order and told to pay £750 in costs.

But the main punishment was a three-year football ban forbidding him from going near Fratton Park for two hours before and after each home match.

The order also bans him from going to any city where Portsmouth or England are playing – again, for two hours before and after kick-off.

He is not allowed to go by train on Pompey and England match days, and must give up his passport five days before any England fixture abroad.

If he breaks the order he faces a possible jail sentence.

POMPEY FAN'S 'BRAINLESS VIOLENCE'

Terrace terror
4 Portsmouth fans are jailed

BOOTS AND BRACES are passe; today the well-dressed football fan swaggers through the recession in his expensive brand-named sportswear — Pringle sweaters and Nike trainers (useful for "doing a runner" when aggro looms). But the leopards have still not changed their spots.

My colleague Phil Shaw dropped into a pub by Waterloo station in London one Saturday morning and found it packed with nattily-attired Portsmouth supporters. When the barman briefly left his post, they raided the bar for cigars, crisps and spirits. Seconds later, bulges under their Tacchini tops, they left.

"Nice lads," said the barman, returning just in time to [illegible] them a good game. [illegible] well turned out."

Police say: We were powerless

A POLICE chief admitted yesterday that his men were powerless to do anything about the soccer fans who went on the rampage in Portsmouth after Southampton had snatched victory in Saturday's Cup-tie.

'We couldn't arrest the offenders because there were too many of them committing too many offences,' said Superintendent Tony Thompson who was one of the officers directing the 350-strong force in the biggest security operation ever staged at a match in the city.

'All we could do was try to disperse them,' he said. 'We have a hard-core here who are hell-bent on causing trouble. The law of the jungle takes over.'

There were 59 arrests and 36 people will appear in court this morning, charged with assault, criminal damage or threatening behaviour.

Referee Lester Shapter is reporting Portsmouth to the FA because Southampton's Mark Dennis and a linesman were struck by missiles during the game.

☐ THREE Swindon fans and six from Blackburn appear in court today after being arrested during fights outside the County Ground following the Wiltshire side's 2-1 Cup defeat. Ten other Blackburn fans face charges as a result of incidents in Cheltenham and Gloucester on Saturday night.

BRIAN SCOVELL

Portsmouth & Southsea

'Morons' are blasted

The man in charge of policing last night's testimonial match has fiercely criticised the yob element of Pompey's fans.

Superintendent Phil Scott said he was appalled by their behaviour during and after the match.

"These people responded to a friendly testimonial match with violence. They have got absolutely no concept of decent behaviour."

He said about 1,700 Southampton supporters at ... match were very well behaved ...

... fools were intent on attacking Southampton supporters and when their plans were thwarted, they turned on private property and the police. People can be thankful for the actions of a lot of brave officers."

Diane Boorah of Joan Barrell florists, Fratton Road, faces a repair bill running into hundreds of pounds after rampaging fans smashed three windows with bricks, a dustbin, and part of an armchair.

Edith Myall, aged 55, watched as one fan jumped on her car in Goldsmith Avenue.

"I have lived in this house for 24 years and this is the worst I have ever seen it. It was terrible. The police deserve medals," she said.

---

way, would be my dearest wish today. Sadly missed, Gary Legge and family

PORTER Robin (Fish). A good friend, sadly missed but never forgotten. RIP. Paul Harris and family

PORTER Rob. The news of your sudden death has been a heartbreaker for so many people. The only comfort we all have is that we know your life was cut short, but you will always be remembered for living every minute of every day to the full. You were what we call 'one of the boys.' You will be deeply missed by us all. 'Till we meet again Rob. Goodnight and God Bless. Deepest sympathy to his Mother Sonia. From Stephen and Mark Davis.

PORTER Robin (Fish). The face at Pompey Away, RIP. Barry Ze and George.

PORTER Robin. Fish, a sad loss of a good mate, peace after pain. From Eddie and George Kelly and families and Colleen and John Bee and family.

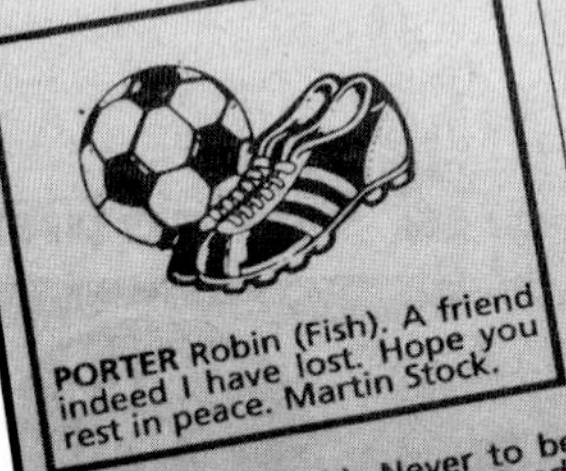

PORTER Robin (Fish). A friend indeed I have lost. Hope you rest in peace. Martin Stock.

PORTER Rob (Fish). Never to be forgotten, from your friends Stan, Jackie and Gary

mate. RIP. Soudi, Saidi, Hamdi, Riyami.

PORTER Rob (Fish) you will be sadly missed, God bless. Richie and Danny.

PORTER Rob. You told me of the pain you were in and selfish as it seems, we didn't want to let you go. Free from suffering, walk tall again Rob, the way I remember you, God bless Rob, Kathy X and Steve X. Deepest sympathy to Sonia, Caroline and daughter Jade

PORTER Robin (Fish), died Saturday July 23. Will be sadly missed and never forgotten. RIP mate. Gary S, Brian P and everyone else who knew you up at 'The Plover'.

PORTER Robin Mark. (My name is fish and I live in a dish). Fish, the town won't be the same without you mate, the Captain of the Air Balloon. Gone but will never be forgotten. God bless Fish. Martin and Denise Day, and Derek Chambers

PORTER Robin (Fish). It has all been said, wish I'd known you longer. Dennis Mac.

SOCCER / *Knives are confiscated outside ground*

Rival fans clash outside city centre pub

By SUE BOWEN
Sports Mail

Rival football fans went on the rampage outside a Portsmouth pub before today's division one game at Fratton Park.

Dozens of Pompey and Millwall fans clashed outside the Navigators Arms in Isambard Brunel Road.

One Pompey fan was injured by a flying bottle.

Officers from Portsmouth Central police station, within yards of the pub, raced to the scene and cordoned off the two sets of fans. Trouble broke out around 1pm, two hours before the match kicked off.

Scuffles broke out with fans arming themselves with bricks and bottles.

Police later confiscated knives found on supporters going into the ground.

A police spokesman said: "It was fortunate that officers were on hand to part the opposing groups of fans."

The pub was forced to close to stop further trouble. There were no arrests.

FLASHPOINT ● The Navigators pub in Isambard Brunel Road

Mark is another of those who, for varying reasons, stopped going to games long ago. Its strange how people you see week in week out and then disappear altogether. I haven't seen Mark for a few years now although a few of the original Hayling lads are still about supporting Pompey. If I didn't travel with the Hayling lads, I sometimes went away with a group from Fareham. One of them in particular was Paul Finnegan. We are still good mates today. Like myself, Paul is no longer active and hasn't been for some time. There were and still are some great lads from the Fareham area. During an FA Cup match between Bournemouth and Fareham Town, a few of the Fareham lads travelled to the match. They were rounded up by the local police who excitedly reported back to headquarters that they had rounded up the 6.57 Crew. To the hilarity of the others, one of them pointed out to the officers that they weren't the 6.57 Crew but the Fareham Urban Guerrillas. It was the first time any of the others had heard the name but it has been jokingly used by them ever since.

The surrounding areas have always provided some of the very best of the 6.57 Crew. Leigh Park, a sprawling council estate which was built to provide housing for some of those made homeless during the blitz, was to provide a lot of the original Pompey boot boys. Names such as 'Dog meat' Jones, would supply the front line with their coaches organised by Clive Limbrick leaving The Fox pub. It was the mob from The Fox that was at the forefront when Cardiff's Grange was taken in the 1970's. It was these people that many of us looked up to. 'Dog meat' is probably most famed for his chant 'Alouette'. In my very first 'proper' job when I left school, I found myself working in an ice cream factory. I was introduced to some of the other workers including the foreman, none other than 'Dog meat' himself. He took me under his wing and we spent most of that summer chatting about Pompey and he would regale me with 'war' stories from away games. Nobody from the management bothered him and the job, to be honest, was a doddle but, as summer began to fade away, the demand for ice cream lessened and my seasonal job came to a close. I wasn't bothered though. I had already found myself a place on a job training scheme and besides 'Dog meat' had also handed in his notice despite the pleas from the owner for him to change his mind. 'Dog meat', like many of the early faces, drifted away from the hoolie scene. I suppose, like those from my own football generation, the responsibilities that come with growing up far outweighed the crack of football.

A chapter about those lads from outside of the city who stood firm for the Pompey cause would not be complete without a mention of Addo, a lad from Grimsby. He was a serving matelot based in Portsmouth. He started going to games and got to know a few lads. Before long, he had established himself in the ranks and considered himself a Pompey fan.

14
THE LAUGHING POLICEMEN

In 1985, Portsmouth fans were among the very first in the country to have police officers attached to them. While other police forces had covert operations on various football hooligan gangs, many of which were to end in disaster after many trials collapsed due to unsafe evidence, in Portsmouth, the policing at matches was very much in your face. Two CID officers were appointed to shadow the 6.57 Crew wherever they went. Unlike other operations, these officers made no pretence about who they were. I remember a game at Luton in the FA cup when a Bedfordshire police officer tried to blend into the Portsmouth crowd. His cover didn't last long, especially when one of the lads asked him how long he had been in the police. He protested his 'innocence' claiming, 'I ain't a copper'. He was then asked why his coat kept on talking then as his radio could be clearly heard. Another such operation, possibly by the BTP, came on a train going to an away game. A guy dressed in his neatly pressed Brutus jeans, shirt and polished Dr. Martin shoes with a rolled up copy of the Daily Mail in his back pocket, sat next to a group of guys in the buffet car. His opening words were, 'Alright lads, where have we planned to have it today?' For the next hour, he was told all about the plan and that, although there were about eighty on the train, this was only a diversionary tactic and that the real mob, as he probably knew, was hiding in the back of two removal vans hired especially for the occasion. As a matter of fact, a removal van was used as transport to many games not long after. He was then 'reminded' not to forget that everyone was meeting in Trafalgar Square that night as there was an arranged battle with Millwall or possibly Chelsea or maybe both. I would have loved to have been in his boss's office the following Monday if the useless undercover officer had acted on the false information.

The idea of the two Portsmouth police officers to attend games was much in the same way that nowadays every club has a uniformed police liaison officer attached to them whose job it is to act as a spotter for the local force at away matches. DC's King and Hiscock seemed to be fairly good at their jobs but would also chat and have a bit of banter with a few of the lads, taking the piss a little, such as when we were run by West Ham in the park before their match in 1987. King asked 'What's up lads, they too good for you?' Which isn't to say that they wouldn't have arrested any wrong doer, given the chance. There was much mirth later when a Chief Superintendent John Harrison was reported in the press as being 'furious' that 'Police Magazine', the imaginatively titled magazine for police officers, had leaked details of this secret tactic used to wage war on football hooligans. Apparently he had written a report that somehow managed to be published by the magazine. Reading the highlights of the report, it contained the usual bollocks such as the 6.57 Crew having its origins in the National Front. It must be great being a senior officer because you can spout any old crap and speak seemingly with conviction even though you haven't a clue what you are talking about because the media lap it up. The Chief Super (probably retired now on a big fat pension) can sleep easy as everyone knew about his secret tactic long before Police Magazine blew the whistle.

Pompey played Tottenham in the league cup in 1986; the game at White Hart Lane was a 0 – 0 draw. The support Pompey took to north London that night was terrific. At least 10,000 fans packed into the ground. After the game, we received a bit of a battering at the hands of the Spurs Yid Army. We had gone mob handed yet, on the night, it was Tottenham that had a result. The replay at Fratton Park was also to end goal-less with very little happening off the pitch either. The two DC's approached a group of us at around 11 o'clock as we made our way home after the match. They struck up conversation asking if we had heard the result of the coin toss to determine where the second replay would be. We said we hadn't and they continued saying that the game would again be played at Fratton Park. We were pleased and said it would give us a chance of beating Spurs. Their reply astonished us.

'You don't want to play here, you want to play at White Hart Lane' they told us. When we queried why, they went on to say.

'Because if you play up there, you'll have it with Tottenham all night long, the

Met haven't got a clue but we've got it sewn up down here so you won't get a sniff'. With that, they bid us a goodnight with a 'See you boys, Saturday'.

Their words would come back and haunt them although, on the whole, they did seem to have things sewn up.

The Spurs firm had come to town by coach; they had made their way to the Travellers Rest in the Somerstown area of the city. They weren't in the pub for very long before a few passing 6.57 Crew boys noticed them. Word soon got around and a mob of Pompey snaked up Goldsmith Avenue away from the area near the ground and towards their unsuspecting foe. Once at the pub, one of the boys ran in and announced that they we're here. In seconds, chaos reigned, every window in the pub was smashed as those outside threw bricks. Meanwhile, the Spurs fans returned fire with the boozer's furniture, glasses and the usual ammunition associated with a pub brawl. Some of the Spurs lads gamely managed to get out of the pub but they were soon backed back into it as our onslaught threatened to overwhelm them. As the first police units began to arrive on the scene, Spurs lads again managed to get out of the pub but they were again set upon by the 6.57 Crew mob. Now the violence spread into the adjoining roads with damage to property in Baileys Road as, eventually, the police managed to get things under control. While some officers pursued us back up Goldsmith Avenue, their colleagues rounded up the Tottenham fans. When it came down to it, while the Spurs lads were very game, it has to be said that technically they were the innocent victims. The police didn't see it this way. Once the trouble died down, fifty-three Spurs fans were arrested. They were all ferried to Portsmouth Central Police Station. The scene of devastation was searched. Along with broken pool cues, various knives were found. The following day, the police paraded these weapons for the cameras. I have spoken with a Spurs lad who was at the Travellers that night. He claims that they were confident of getting a result but admitted that it really did come on top for them. Pompey and Spurs seemed to be fairly evenly matched off the field. At White Hart Lane, Pompey came off second best when, during a Division One game in the 1987/88 season, Spurs fans bouncing around in Seven Sisters Road, pointing to a carpet shop saying turn left there Pompey. We were going backwards from the moment we turned as Spurs poured into us. At Fratton, it was Spurs who seemed to come off second best.

One FA Cup tie that was ruined for us by Paul Gascoigne whose individual brilliance snatched victory from the jaws of defeat for Tottenham. During the game, Pompey fans charged from the North terrace and into the Spurs fans in the Milton end. There was more trouble after the game, again with Pompey having the upper hand. At the post match press conference, Pompey manager Frank Burrows commented that the Spurs boss Terry Venables had asked him whether or not they should go over to the trouble. Apparently he replied, OK you first. Years earlier at Fratton, Spurs had been run onto the pitch during a pre-season game after Pompey mob had got behind them in the Milton End and steamed in after Spurs scored.

After DC's King and Hiscock left their spotters job, several others replaced them over the years. None of them were as good as the originals as they all seemed to overestimate their importance. Many times over the years following Pompey, I have witnessed Police officers act in a way that, had it been a supporter, they would, without question, have been arrested and charged with various offences. Some policemen seem to think that they are above the law and can treat football fans any way that they please. One season at Brighton, police repeatedly baton charged Pompey fans and rode horses into us at Hove train station. There had been no disorder there, only a rush to get on trains. A few fans were hurt as police totally over-reacted.

We were on our way to Charlton one season. A fairly large mob left Waterloo station and made our way across Waterloo Bridge. As we did, police vans started to pull up in an attempt to escort us although where to I have no idea as it was still only around 11am. In an attempt to get away from the police, we ran down the steps and onto the Embankment below. Soon the police came screeching down the road, blues lights on, sirens blaring out. It didn't take long for us all to be rounded up and were told by an Inspector with a megaphone that we were being escorted to Charing Cross and, from there, taken to Charlton by train. As we were being escorted it became clear that the Inspector was prone to temper tantrums. As always, a few of the lads tried to escape the escort. As they did, they were brought back into line by the PCs but the Inspector started to hit people with his megaphone. Not surprisingly, what started as being quite peaceful gave way to raised tensions. Once at Charing Cross, we were taken to a side entrance that isn't there anymore and were told by the Inspector to queue on the right of the stairs that led to it. The Inspector was at the top of these stairs looking down and started screaming into his megaphone for the fans to stand on the right which they did. He continued to scream for everyone to get to the right and then launched into another attack with his megaphone, hitting out at anyone in the way. One of the constables pointed out that everyone was standing on the right and that, as he was looking down, he was possibly confused as we were on his left. We were taken to Charlton and, once there, were basically left to our own devices. Before the game, a large mob of us got onto the home terrace and ran the Charlton fans before being rounded up by the police and escorted around the pitch to a standing ovation from the Pompey scarfers.

After the match, there was little incident until fans reached London Bridge where our bad tempered Inspector was waiting. There was a bit of pushing and shoving and again he hit out with that bloody megaphone. This time however the Inspector was soon engulfed in fans who gave him a bit of a slap before he was rescued by colleagues. I am sure however that the constables took their time getting to him probably feeling like just about everyone else that he was asking for it.

Another jolly jape performed by those responsible for upholding the law was performed by the South Wales police. The boys in blue released a police dog into the back of a van in which some of us were travelling. Not surprisingly, the dog proceeded to savage the first person it clapped eyes on and he still has the scars to prove it. The incident happened after it had gone off at Cardiff. As soon as the police started arresting people, we jumped into the back of the van and pulled down the shutter. Not long after, a policeman banged on the side of the van and ordered us to get out, only to be greeted by barely muffled giggles. He banged on the side and repeated his order. Instead of getting out of the van or keeping quiet, one of the lads, Eddie, simply replied 'There's no one in here' which was greeted by roars of laughter. The comedy value obviously didn't translate well in the valleys as it was shortly after this that the Alsatian made its unwelcome appearance, sending all those inside tumbling out in a bid to escape the Hound of the Baskervilles. The police ordered us all to sit on the ground in a line with our hands on our heads. Obviously not learning from the van that Welsh policeman don't have a sense of humour, Eddie started singing that an all time wedding reception favourite by the Gap Band 'Oops! Upside side your head' and the boyo's were not at all impressed when the whole lot of us started, actions and all.

Now the police have the HOOF campaign, Hooligans Out Of Football, this campaign must be costing them thousands of pounds and is, by and large, a complete waste of money although, as an antidote, a friend of mine has produced some great POOF t-shirts. Everywhere you go, there are policemen with state of the art digital video cameras, filming, turning lads into movie stars as they walk into pubs or while they are standing chatting or better still while they are making their way to the match or even walking along the road with their kids. It must make riveting watching back at the nick. Nowadays, match day policing is way over the top at Fratton Park, fifteen to twenty years too late. While some games need to be heavily policed, most don't, however, if this was to be admitted, maybe the guy in charge of it would have to start working for a living. The camera coppers do however bite when you ask them if they are available for birthdays and weddings.

It is funny how things change in life. Towards the end of the 1997/98 season, Pompey and Stoke fans were involved in fighting at the Britannia Stadium where Stoke were kept on the back foot for most of the day. By the time the 2002/03 season came along, most of those who were serious players in the 6.57 Crew had given it up. Stoke's Naughty Forty were about the only team to come to Fratton with any serious intentions that season. A good mob of about 80-100 lads got as far as Havant where the police rounded them up. Unlike Leicester though, quite a few of the Stoke lads managed to give the police the slip and caught taxis into Portsmouth City centre. It wasn't long though before, once again, they were under the control of police in full riot gear. The Stoke lads were taken to the Raven pub which was surrounded by Robocop's. A good friend of mine, Ernie, had, over the years, become very friendly with Jasper, one of Stoke's very top lads and author of the book 'Naughty'. They had arranged to meet up for a drink. Ernie picked me up and we started to make our way to the Raven. Halfway there, our mobiles started to ring with lads saying a good mob of Pompey were on their way to The Raven. On arriving at the pub, we saw the police presence and weren't all that upset to be honest. Franticly, we started phoning around to put off the Pompey lads, explaining about the amount of police. We didn't want loads to be nicked when it could be avoided and also we didn't want Jasper to think we had set them up. Job done, we went to go in the pub but was stopped by the police. We tried to explain that there wasn't going to be any trouble as did Jasper. We then tried another way in, only to be threatened by another copper dressed in his Saturday best. We both looked at this guy and thought if only you knew we have just spent the last twenty minutes ensuring you don't have to earn your overtime today. Seeing that there was no way we were going to get into the pub, we gave up and joined the others in Fratton Road. Towards the end of the match, twenty or so of the Stoke lads managed to slip away from the ground and walked straight into a little firm of youngsters. The fighting, though vicious, was brief. Weight of numbers had the Stoke fans running back towards the safety of the ground but not before one of the youngsters had received a broken nose.

15
CAN'T RAIN ON OUR PARADE

Football supporters who have spent their entire football watching lives following a side that has spent all that time in the top flight, have no idea of some of the places that the rest of us have travelled to in order to support our teams. One of the things that keep us going through the rough times is the thought of a big day out, even those who can be considered 'also rans' in the Premiership. With play-offs and various cup competitions, the chance of going to Wembley or Cardiff has, over the years, increased massively, yet still Pompey have never managed to give us fans that big day out so the chances of actually watching our team play in Europe have always been thin until someone came up with the idea of the Anglo - Italian Cup. The ill-fated competition between English First division sides and their Italian counter parts hardly captured the imagination of the paying public. There were very disappointing crowds both in this country and Italy. Although I am sure that, had Pompey reached the final at Wembley, they would have taken massive amounts of support to the game. One game that has now passed into legend is the away match with Bari. It was the very first 'competitive' game played in Europe by Portsmouth Football Club and, as such, many Pompey fans decided to mark the occasion. Around this time there was a good scam in operation where very cheap rail tickets were around. Pompey were not the only mob that took advantage of the deal. I don't know if the guy that was sorting the tickets got greedy or whether it was the sheer volume of tickets that were being sold under the counter but British Rail investigators and British Transport Police were waiting for Pompey fans at Liverpool Street on their way to Ipswich. After this, the cheap tickets were consigned to history but not before the 6.57 Crew took full advantage of a trip to Italy. There have been plenty of scams involving tickets over the years. For years, the season tickets consisted of a single card that was simply shown to the turnstile operator. It was then just passed through the gate for someone else to use. I think the record stands at about 53 people into Fratton Park with the same ticket. One more fiddle came about when somebody noticed that, as people were entering the ground, the turnstile operators weren't tearing off the stubs on the tickets. For weeks, he got into the ground early and asked people if he could have their ticket, coming up with some excuse or other. He then slipped out of the ground and resold the tickets. Another lad was keen to work through his dinner hour which must have impressed his bosses at the printers where he was employed. He was actually knocking out forged tickets for the various games. When asked for tickets for a game against Middlesbrough, he admitted that he couldn't do tickets for that particular game as he couldn't spell Middlesbrough!

Armed with knocked off Inter Rail Tickets, we made our way to Bari in southern Italy, some stopping on the way to take in the AC Milan versus Inter Milan derby. If you are unsure of the way to Bari, then follow the trail of Union Jack stickers bearing the legend Portsmouth 6.57 Crew. One of the lads had his girlfriend sit up all night with him, writing out the stickers which he then plastered literally hundreds of them across Europe. Once we reached Bari, we made our way out of the train station but as we walked along, a group passed by on mopeds. This group then pulled up a little way ahead and got off their bikes and fanned out across the street and pavement. Like a red rag to a bull, we needed no other invitation and went straight towards the Italians who were dressed in Valentino and the like. As our mob got closer, it could be seen that the Bari lads were holding up little 'lollypop' sticks with Polizi written on them. After being searched, the police allowed us to go on our way although kept a careful eye on us. The trip never looked like turning violent. There were no Italians about looking for it and soon the trip developed into one big piss up and a group of English mucking about abroad. One poor local had the misfortune for his car to break down just outside one of the bars. He was happy when a few of the lads went to help push-start his motor but looked like he was about to burst into tears when they pushed him straight into the path of another car. They left the outraged Italian motorists, shouting at each other.

The match itself was something in nothing; we lost 3-0 inside the San Nicola stadium which holds 60000 but on this particular day we rattled around with a ridiculous crowd of just over 800! Mind you, that total included 250 Pompey fans. The travelling support wasn't lost on the famous La Gazzetta dello Sport newspaper who told of the magnificent English supporters. We then moved the party across the country, eventually settling in the English Bar in the beautiful coastal town of Sorrento and an eighteen hour party. We played another match in Italy in the same competition four weeks later. This time, nobody bothered with the game but I took advantage of the still valid rail card. I went to Ascoli to see us get beaten 2-1, although the real reason for the trip was to go to Berlin and see Henry Akinwande fight German Axel Schulz for the European Heavyweight title. That ended as a draw so not the greatest trip.

As Pompey stumbled towards financial meltdown, the receivers were brought in and fans began to realise that there was the very real chance that the club could fold altogether. There began to be a backlash against the perceived incompetence of Chairman Martin Gregory. There were protests by many of the Pompey fans; some were better thought out than others. One protest was held at the offices of Blue Star Garages, Gregory's company. The protest was held on a Saturday with the offices shut so you had the spectacle of a bunch of football fans shouting at an empty building! Whilst this particular protest fell a little flat, there could be no questioning the commitment of those that took part. Other protests were more symbolic such as the mock funeral cortege which walked down Goldsmith Avenue to Fratton Park before one home game. While all this was going on, a pre-season friendly match was organised away to Le Havre in northern France, just a ferry ride away for Pompey fans. The French had initially wanted to play the game at Fratton Park due to fears of English hooligans. The Pompey club officials persuaded them that their fears were misplaced and that everything would be fine. Doh! In the words of a mate of mine 'I knew it was going to be one of those days when I turned up at the ferry port at five in the morning only to see one of the lads cracking open his second bottle of champagne'.

Ten minutes into the game, around 100 Pompey fans ran onto the pitch chanting 'Gregory out'. The game was held up while police and stewards cleared the fans away. The game was restarted and, as the half time whistle blew, stood at one goal each. During half time, there was another invasion. This time, there was a sit down protest in the centre circle which, despite the efforts of officials, continued into when the match should have resumed. In the end Terry Clueless Fenwick who has the absurd cheek to describe himself as a football manager refused to take the Pompey team back onto the pitch for the second half even though the French team had already taken to the field. The game's abandonment led to the usual headlines whereas most couldn't see what all the fuss was. Back in town, Pompey fans settled in bars. Outside one such bar, three lads were approached by some French/ Arabs. In broken English, one asked 'You English football hooligans? You want to fight?' The three then proceeded to kick the living daylights out of the Arabs including, at one point, battering them with shoes taken off the rack outside of a shoe shop, all the while being cheered on by the lads in the bar opposite. Soon Le Plod turned up which led to one of those comic Benny Hill style chases around town. Fearing he was about to get caught, one of them took cover in a newsagents and, picking up a newspaper, pretended to read it despite the paper being upside down and, as stupid as that sounds, I swear it is true.

The journey home turned into piracy on the high seas. In mid channel, the duty free shops were robbed and one of the bars ransacked. Nobody was allowed off when we docked as police went through the ferry searching and arresting people.

A pre-season friendly at Fratton against Dutch side Feyenoord saw a big mob of Dutchmen arrive in the city. On the Friday night, they were involved in fighting with doormen in the town centre, the following day, a few youngsters went over towards the hotel where the Dutch fans were staying but were soon sent scurrying as they came flying out of the bar. By the afternoon, the temperatures were in the mid-nineties and, apart from some of the Dutch who still seemed to think that it was the 1980's not 2003, nobody was looking to kick it off. As some of us sat outside the Shepherds Crook, one of them came bouncing across the road sounding more like the Swedish chef from the Muppets 'We are the fotbol hooliguns, are you wanting too fight?' As most of us dissolved into laughter, the reply was 'Fuck off mate, its too hot'. The Feynoord fan wandered off to join his mates who were giving the police a hard time probably totally disillusioned with English football hooligans.

To be honest, it makes me angry when I hear the tired old lines that football hooligans aren't real fans or that they aren't interested in what happens on the pitch. They are as die-hard as any other fan; in a lot of cases, more so. Myself and other Pompey fans that, at time to time have become involved in disorder, love Portsmouth Football Club. I have travelled the length and breath of this country supporting my team and you need to remember that, while the pages of this book that contain images of violence, they are stories that have been condensed from my and others' memories over many years of following the club home and away, many hundreds of football matches. For every game that there has been trouble, there is easily twenty, probably more, that have passed without incident. Were these matches any less of a day out, of course not.

When my son, Lloyd, was born in February 1996, he was only a few hours old when I held him in my arms, a very proud Father. I stood looking out of the big windows in the St. Mary's Hospital maternity unit that overlooks Fratton Park. I stood there with the weak Winter sun shining down, looking at Fratton, its almost tumbledown appearance. I began talking to Lloyd like the scene out the Disney film, Lion King, telling him that one day he to would be going there, supporting the team that my Father had introduced me to. I went on to tell him that, while he would not always enjoy what was happening on the field of play, sometimes he would feel so frustrated that he would want to cry and maybe on some occasions he may actually shed the odd tear, something would keep pulling him back. A strange type of force field would always keep making him go back to the place where previous Saturdays there was so much sorrow and despair and yet one special occasion would more than make up for what had gone on before and, like an unfaithful lover who you just can't stand to be without, you will forgive her, knowing that she was sure to break your heart again. And the reason that this special place would have such a dramatic effect on him is because it is in his blood. I suddenly became a little self-conscious of the conversation I was having with my new-born son. I looked around me and saw that apart from my now my ex-wife who was sleeping off the exertions of the previous six or so hours labour, Lloyd and I were quite alone. I held him to the window and showed him Fratton Park then cuddled him in closer to me and, as I looked down at him, I could feel the slight burning feeling in my eyes as the tears built up. I thought to myself I don't know what the future holds for you but part of it is over there. I don't care what team you support and I mean real football fans here not the 'celebrity fan' who says I have supported so and so since I was a child yet the only games they have ever been to are those where somebody gave them free entry to their executive box. I mean the true fan, the ones who queue for hours in the pouring rain hoping beyond hope that the tickets won't have sold out by the time they get to the front. Or the fans that thinks nothing of travelling to the other end of the country on a Tuesday night to cheer on their team in a second round second leg Mickey Mouse cup game. No matter what your team is you don't get to choose. As a kid, I thought I supported Chelsea until that day I was taken to Fratton Park. A friend of mine, Tim, has never lived in Portsmouth. He is from the Midlands. He used to go to Nottingham Forest until the day they played Pompey; he has been a confirmed blue ever since. A couple of hundred mile trip for a home game is above and beyond the call of duty yet he is not unique. There are many fans of Pompey like this as there are of probably every club. True supporters of any club aren't created by media spin. They are born fans of their team. That is why Leyton Orient fans and those like them follow their side when they have far more glamorous clubs only a bus ride away. Some of these supporters liked to indulge themselves in trouble, others didn't but neither is any less of a fan than the other.

Over the years, Pompey fans have become famous for the ferocious support they give the team. Despite up until recently not having all that much to cheer about, gates have always been fairly healthy and, as was seen when Pompey topped the First Division for most of that championship winning season, it is all but guaranteed to be a sell out at The Park when times are good. When the blues were in the old Third and forth Division, clubs would love playing away at Pompey as, in those days, the away team received a percentage of the gate money so you can see that various chairmen of 'smaller' clubs loved coming to Fratton when there were nearly 25,000 against Bradford City or 21,000 versus Newport County, both Division Four games. Pompey are also a club that has always had big away support. Famously we once took the best part of 15,000 to Anfield in 1980 for a fourth round League Cup match. It was a midweek game, not a bad turn out when you see that the total crowd was 32,021. All day, the local Merseyside radio made appeals for the scouse fans to go to the match so their supporters wouldn't be outnumbered. The following night, the Liverpool Evening Echo was full of reports about Liverpool's win away. The game saw serious fighting in the streets after. Legend has it that, as a coach load of Pompey fans from Leigh Park were making their way out of Liverpool, a young scally stepped up and threw a brick smashing one of the coach windows. The Loonies charged off the coach and grabbed the Scouser and dragged him onto the coach. They released their hostage, on the A27, five miles from Portsmouth.

The night at Liverpool is one of many that have entered Pompey folklore; other games that bring back great memories are away at Northampton on May 3rd 1980. Pompey needed a win and hope other results went for them elsewhere in order to gain promotion from Division 4. Pompey won 2-0 with goals from Steve Davey and Ian Purdie. Pompey fans had filled the ground and flooded onto the pitch at the end as news came in that their two-year stay in the basement Division was over. On the way home, thousands of Pompey fans took over Trafalgar Square as the celebrations continued.

The closest we came to a final was in the FA Cup in 1992. In the quarter final, we were at home to Nottingham Forest which finished with a 1-0 win. To be honest, Pompey had scored with a well-worked free kick in the opening minutes. Stuart Pearce had kicked the young Darren Anderton up in the air. It was one of those fouls an experienced pro does early on to let the young buck know that he is there. Today though, it would be Forest's undoing. The free kick came over and Alan McLaughlin got underneath it and the ball nestled into the back of the net. We spent the next 87 minutes on a gallant rearguard action as Forest poured everything forward. The reward was a semi-final tie against Liverpool at Highbury. That Sunday we were brilliant. Whether the Liverpool fans would care to admit it or not, other than a nervous opening twenty minutes, the blues played the reds off the park. Darren Anderton, known as Shaggy to the fans due to his uncanny resemblance to Scooby Doo's sidekick, was tremendous, sending us Pompey fans into dreamland when, during extra time, he was sent free. He ran through the Liverpool defence as if it wasn't there and slotted the ball past an on-rushing keeper. The remaining minutes ticked away, every second seemingly lasting an hour. We were within touching distance of Wembley and their first FA Cup final appearance since 1939 when Andy Awford brought down Steve Nichol. The resulting free kick came off the post and Ronnie Whelan was the first to react, poking in the equaliser in the last minute of extra time. The replay at Villa Park never reached the heights of the first match. Although Pompey battled hard, they couldn't break down the Liverpool defence but then Liverpool couldn't score either. The game finished 0-0 and, for the first time ever, an FA Cup semi-final would be settled on penalties. We knew that this was the end of the line; in fact, it was clear that this wasn't going to be our night when, during extra time, Alan McLaughlin rose above everyone else only to send his header crashing against the cross bar from only two yards out. Pompey lost the penalty shoot out 3-1 with a couple of their penalties more resembling back passes. We sung ourselves hoarse in both games, really getting behind the team but to no avail. One song during the replay riled the holier than thou Scouser supporters. After the first game, it transpired that their manager, Graeme Souness, needed heart surgery. Packed on the Holte End terrace, we started singing, 'Attack, attack, a Souness heart attack'. Liverpool beat Sunderland in the final in what was a terrible game.

Another match that is talked about is a First Division game away to Crewe during the 1997/98 season. Pompey were bottom of the league, eight points adrift and rapidly running out of games. We were 3-1 down and, as you looked across the pitch, it was obvious that some if not all the players had given up the ghost. In the stand, however we had other ideas. The chant was started off by just a handful but soon spread amongst the 1,500 Blues fans at Gresty Road. For the last half hour of the game, we were on our feet chanting. Alan Ball's blue and white army, over and over, without so much as a pause for breath. The following Tuesday, we played at home to Stockport County. That evening, the whole ground was on its feet for ninety minutes. Again non stop Alan Ball's blue and white army. The message to the players was clear; we are all in this together, you do your bit on the pitch and we'll do ours off it. Every game was the same. As word got out, the crowds got bigger and, as the crowds got bigger, the decibel levels grew. After getting narrowly beaten by promotion chasing Ipswich, their manager, when asked if he was planning to make any new signings, simply said that he would like to sign the Pompey fans due to all the noise they make. The season culminated in a last day-trip to Bradford. Somehow we had managed to get ourselves to a position where a victory would see us safe, a great feat considering the position we were in. The blues won 3-1 although, to be fair, Bradford were already on their holidays. Pompey were safe, meanwhile Manchester City were relegated at Stoke. At the end of the year, the BBC Southern region held its annual sports awards as well as the usual top sportsman and top team award. Pompey fans were given a special award for the way they got behind the team. Five years later to the day, we would again face a trip to Valley Parade on the final day of the season but how things would be different.

After the club went into receivership, American based Serbian Milan Mandaric who had made his fortune in the computer world stepped in and saved the club from going out of business altogether. Although we were now financially secure, we faired little better on the pitch. Last day victories for safety became the norm. As well as the Bradford match, we managed to beat Barnsley in the final fixture of the 1999/00 season. Under Mandaric, managers came and went. Tony Pullis lasted only months replaced by Steve Claridge as caretaker boss. Steve played just over 100 games for the club and is one of the few remaining characters left in football but unfortunately the results we were getting and the football we were starting to play left Mandaric with little choice to replace him with Graham Rix who managed to steer us away from relegation with the win against Barnsley. Rix was the next casualty the next season. He was replaced this time by the club's director of football, Harry Redknapp early in 2002. Former boss, Jim Smith, was instated as his assistant and, during the summer, 'Arry 'n' Jim set about building a side that would blend together and become arguably the best Pompey team for a couple of generations. Something old, Paul Merson in the twilight of his career, was signed on a free transfer from Aston Villa. Something new, left back Matthew Taylor, already a sensation in the lower leagues with Luton Town; Redknapp left Luton manager Joe Kinnear seething when he signed Taylor for a paltry £750,000. Something borrowed, Vincent Pericard the 19-year-old French striker on loan from Italian giants Juventus, all together in Pompey blue. Once the season was underway, we set off like a train hitting the top of Division One in August and unbelievably staying there until May. Could this be our year? Surely something will go wrong. After all, we're Pompey; something always goes wrong. As if to prove that point, we were home to Sheffield Wednesday who were cast adrift at the bottom of the table with little or no hope of surviving relegation. The script was written; three points would see us promoted to the Premiership; only the script was off. Wednesday stunned Fratton Park with a 2-1 win. The champagne would have to be kept on ice for a little longer. Pompey always have to do things the hard way, don't they? The following Tuesday, they had another bite of the cherry. This time against Burnley. For 73 minutes, it looked like we would go home frustrated yet again but then Svetoslav Todorov scored the goal that put Pompey in the Premier.

At the final whistle, there were wild celebrations as fans flooded onto the pitch. We were up and the party could start. Only twelve days later, we found ourselves in position to clinch the title. Earlier in the day, our only challengers, Leicester, had slipped up by drawing. Now victory would see us crowned champions. In anticipation of these events, the football league had bought the trophy to Fratton so the team could be awarded it straight after the match. For once, everything went to plan although, to their credit, Rotherham didn't lay down and die. It was a bit tense but Pompey held out for a 3-2 win. After the season ended, there was a civic reception with a open top bus tour ending on Southsea common. It poured with rain for most of the day but it didn't stop somewhere in the region of 60,000 turning out. I saw many old faces there that day. Many of them were regulars on away days back in the 1980's but, over the years, had dropped away from the 6.57 Crew scene, either giving up football altogether or on the whole preferring to attend with their own children who they had brought along on this day. All of them said that they just had to be there to see it. I reminisced with one or two of them, remembering going to places like Scarborough on a Tuesday night. All of those nightmare trips were worth it for a day like this and, despite the pouring rain, nothing would dampen our spirits as it was for days like this that we are football fans for.

When I see Pompey fans getting behind the team, I tend to think about some of the fans of other sides. We played Fulham at Fratton Park. The Londoners had won the First Division championship a few days before and, although they filled the Milton End with around 3,000 fans, you wouldn't have known that they were there. If that had been the other way around, I know Pompey would have filled Craven Cottage and it would have been party time for all. This is what happened when we travelled to Bradford. We had already won the First Division title but still everyone travelled to Yorkshire. Bradford saw their biggest gate of the season, a little under 20,000,. most of them making the long journey from the South coast even though the game was basically meaningless. I suppose you have to wonder how many of the Fulham fans that day at Fratton became lifelong long fans of the Cottagers (surely the most dubious nick name in football) the moment that Mr. Al Fayed arrived with his millions. Exactly how many of them were around when Fulham needed them most when they were in Division Four and broke? Most likely many have now moved onto to become life long fans of neighbours Chelsea now that they have a rich benefactor.

Harry Redknapp was a popular manager but there was constant snipeing going on in the media between him and Milan Mandaric; nobody really knows what went on between them but, when Redknapp resigned at the end of November 2004, most were disappointed. Given the job that he had done, we were tenth in the Premiership and things were looking up. At that point, a lot saw Mandaric as the bad guy forcing Redknapp out. Yet two weeks later, hero went to zero when Harry did the unthinkable. From the moment it was announced that he would be joining Southampton, everything that he achieved at Fratton Park went out of the window, overnight he became a Scummer and a Judas. Meanwhile, Velimir Zajec was appointed as temporary manager. It was the appointment of Zajec as director of football that had started the rumblings in the first place. Alain Perrin was put in full-time charge of the team and probably couldn't have gotten off to a better start. Seventeen days into his new job, Harry Redknapp brought his new side to Fratton Park. In just twenty six minutes, they had been destroyed. Lua Lua was in inspired form, scoring twice as we smashed them 4-1. To the taunts ringing in their ears, the Harry Redknapp and the Southampton team slunk away to stare relegation in the eye. Mainly due to our early season form, Pompey were safe by the time we went to West Brom on the final day but there was to be a final twist in the tale. If West Brom won, Southampton were down and as the Baggies scored twice, Pompey fans celebrated as much as the home supporters. Once more, we are the top dogs on the south coast.

Perrin's good run didn't continue. He seemed to lose the dressing room with his strict disciplinary code and results suffered. We once again found ourselves in relegation trouble, only this time, there looked little chance of us getting out of it. Perrin went the way of so many managers before him - out of door marked exit. The question now was who would take his place. Many names were tossed into the ring but rumours began to circulate that a shock move could be on the cards and Redknapp could be on his way back. Just a year after his walkout, we were all stunned when Harry Redknapp was reinstated as Pompey manager. Most of us, me included, would have welcomed the Luftwaffe back to the City of Portsmouth before Harry Redknapp but here he was. The appointment caused huge divisions between the Pompey supporters despite Redknapp's claims that Fratton Park was his spiritual home and that he wished that he had never left. Few were in the mood to forgive and forget but football is a results business and, with some astute January signings, he did put some fight back into the team. Unbelievably, we stayed up again but some will still never forgive him and I know some who refuse to go, all the time Redknapp is in charge.

CONCLUSION

I hope that you have found some of what I have had to say of some interest. I have no doubts that some of you reading this have thrown the book across the room, shouting that what I have written is a load of old bollocks. Football and the violence that sometimes surrounds it really is in the eye of the beholder. Neither is what I have put together here by any means meant as a definitive book on the 6.57 Crew. There are those that have many stories to tell of the years that they have followed Pompey. The same can be said of fans of just about any club in the country. I also know that, at some games, when whatever team you happen to support has been given the run around, you convince yourself and your mates by the time that the second or third pint has been sunk that you didn't do all that bad after all and, by the time the next game comes along, the previous weeks hiding has somehow turned into a real result even if it is only a moral one. How many times have you told yourself or had someone say to you 'If we had had our full firm out today....' Or 'I'll tell you what, they were lucky all those Old Bill turned up because, once we got them around the corner, we would have done 'em'. It is, of course, complete rubbish. Like I have said, everyone has at sometime or other been on the wrong end of a complete drubbing, some though don't like to see it that way.

A group of us were having a post match pint and the subject of football hooliganism was brought up. One of the guys asked the question 'What's the best firm you've come across over the years?' This is one of those questions like 'Who is pound for pound the best ever boxer?' As you can imagine, there were various thoughts and suggestions as to who was the best firm or worst depending on your point of view although the unanimous decision was it would have to be Millwall with Birmingham second. The third place was left undecided as just about everyone had their own thoughts and reasons why. For the record, my own thoughts on this subject are Millwall and Birmingham and then followed in no particular order by Cardiff, Chelsea, West Ham, Bristol City & Middlesbrough. This is not in anyway meant to be a conclusive list and, just as in the FA Cup, there is a little minnow capable of toppling one of the big boys on their day. Over the years, there are many firms that can be considered as among the best but I suppose we all have our own views depending on our own experiences against a particular mob. For instance, Tottenham's Yid Army are one of the most respected firms in the country who have been about for years doing it up and down England as well as abroad. We have clashed with them on a couple of occasions with differing results. They gave us a bit of a ragging at their place and have always had our respect. Leicester City on the other hand are another firm that some would say are good but, at Pompey, while we would give them credit for always making the effort, they never really gave us too many problems that we couldn't handle. Again it's how we all see things differently.

I also have no doubts that there are some who will be outraged by the contents of this book and will question whether books like this should be published. In the 1980's, the Portsmouth 6.57 Crew were in their prime but those days are now long gone. Back then, hundreds of lads following various clubs would travel across the country with the intention of doing battle with one another. This is by and large now only part of football's dark history. Football hooliganism is still in existence but those involved now aren't in the same league as those that waged war when the phenomena was at its height. It is nowhere near as bad as it once was but, any given Saturday during the football season, there are outbreaks of football related violence around the country. If you don't believe me, log onto the National Criminal Intelligence Service web site. There you will see a rundown of all the football violence related incidents that were reported to them during the past couple of seasons. Nowadays however, there is no place for football hooliganism. Back in the 1970's and 80's, football almost deserved what it got. In the same way that, if you provoke a dog enough, it will eventually bite so football and the authorities were bitten. Football fans were looked upon by many clubs as no more than a nuisance. Cramped terraces, very few amenities, at many places including Fratton Park not even a roof on the toilets, football needed to come of age and start to realise that even though those that came through the turnstiles loved their clubs, they still wanted to be treated decently and respectfully.

I was at Selhurst Park, watching Pompey play Crystal Palace. It was a particularly dull game and I had got bored with talking to the Palace lad on the terrace below the seats that we were in. This particular dreamer was telling us of all the teams that had been battered by Palace that season and, if we wanted it, where to go after the game. I have been to Palace countless times (it easily reaches into double figures) and can never recall seeing anything that resembles a firm, let alone it going off there. I went up a few rows of seats and asked an old guy with a radio what the score of the Liverpool v Nottingham Forest FA Cup semi-final was. 'It hasn't kicked off yet' came his reply; he continued, 'There's been some crowd trouble and there's loads of people on the pitch, there must be some hurt 'cause there's an ambulance on the pitch now'. I left the guy to his radio and returned to my mates; Paul was still winding up the Palace fan who was by now getting himself right at it, 'Yeah we ran Millwall right back to the station' I heard him say. I then told the lads the news that the old guy with the radio had told me. We thought no more about it and, after the match, went for our usual jaunt around the West End, ending up as always at the Queen Ann in Vauxhall before making our way to Waterloo and home. At Waterloo, we got the Sunday papers and couldn't believe what we saw. The full horror of the Hillsborough disaster unfolded. We sat stunned by what we were reading; we were in full agreement that this disaster, unlike the fire at Bradford, was bound to happen somewhere. There can't have been a football fan around that didn't see the terrible scenes at Hillsborough that day and think there but for the grace of God go I.

For me, it brought back memories of when Pompey played Tottenham in the league cup. We had drawn at White Hart Lane and the replay a week or so later for some reason wasn't an all ticket affair. The evening of the match saw a large crowd gather at Fratton. Outside the ground, at the Milton End/North Stand corner, became a bottleneck as thousands of fans tried to get into the ground. I was being pushed and pulled in every direction when a mate of mine had an idea. We pushed our way back out of the crowd and away from Fratton Park; we then walked down Rodney Road where the away coaches used to be parked to an alleyway that, at the time, led back to the ground at the Fratton End. The turnstile operators were twiddling their thumbs, chatting, it was that quiet. We told them what was happening at the other end of the ground. They couldn't believe it. That was how good communications were at Fratton Park then. I don't know how there wasn't a fatality that night or even how there weren't many serious injuries. I had been in crushes at football before but nothing like that. It was for a few moments very scary.

There were and still are many excuses for what happened at Hillsborough but, for me, it showed that football needed to get its act sorted. For years, the clubs Football league and Football Association had made money from the fans without putting anything back. Added to this of course was the practise of 'double clicking' where two of you would push in together for the price of one or you'd slip the turnstile operator a couple of quid and get in together. How many times have you ever been squeezed into a football ground only for the 'official' crowd to be announced as relatively low? There was a time I'm sure where a lot clubs skimmed thousands off the crowd in order to keep the cash. Football needed to be brought kicking and screaming into the Twentieth Century despite nearly being in the 21st. For years and years, football grounds had been left to rot without a penny spent to upgrade them. Hillsborough brought an end to this disgrace; it is a crying shame that it took the lives of 95 football fans for it to happen.

Many football grounds are now great. Fratton Park is one of those that is still lacking behind however. The club can't be blamed for this; they have tried just about everything they can to relocate only for their efforts, up to now, being thwarted. For this reason, Pompey have been loathe to spend too much on Fratton Park other than to keep it safe and who can really blame them. After promotion to the Premiership was achieved, the club squeezed in as many extra seats as was safely possible in order to maximise the capacity and earning ability of the ground, bringing the capacity up to little over 20,000, far too small for any club in the top league given the wage demands of top players. A few years ago, the old Fratton End had been rebuilt and this is where an awful lot of noise is generated on a match day but, other than that, the old place is pretty much the same as it was when my Dad first took me apart from there are now seats bolted onto the old terrace areas. I was pleased however when I read in a guide to football grounds that the author considered a game at Fratton Park as 'a proper day out at football'. I am pleased that the atmosphere at Fratton Park is intimidating for opposing teams to play in front of, rival players certainly know that they are away from home at our place so much so that Sky television pick out Pompey games to show live, knowing the atmosphere will come across great to the viewers. At the same time, I'm also pleased that, on the whole, opposing fans can visit Portsmouth in relative safety. Recently, figures were released that showed Pompey fans to be the worst in the Premiership. The survey was misleading as the numbers of arrests and the banning orders put in place on the whole resulted in one incident after the Southampton match. Sure, if a mob wanted to try and kick off, they would be able to find willing participants. In that sense, Portsmouth is no different from the majority of football grounds but those who just wish to come and have a good day out, can do so without fear. The age of the 6.57 Crew is now over and that's not a bad thing. The game of football is a very different sport to what it was when we first came about after all. Sure, there are those few fans who are still living in the dark ages of football, still living for the thrill of kicking off with the opposing firm. While they are living in a gone-by era, the police and courts aren't. Unlike when it should have been, now millions of pounds and resources are thrown at football. Police have powers now that, when they could have done with them, could have only dreamt about. Hand held video cameras, state of the art computer imagery, the lot. Also the courts are handing out punishments which, on the face of it, hardly fit the crime. When you look at how a football fan is dealt with compared with some crimes, it can be a bit harsh. However, the fans know this and, if they still carry on, then they can only blame themselves. Custodial sentences are now the norm whereas they used to be the exception, banning orders are thrown about for even the smallest of misdemeanours so much so that even though it has been a hard fought battle, taking some forty years, the tide has now turned in favour of the police. They bask in the glow of victory as does football itself.

In Portsmouth, football hooliganism has been on the decline since the mid 1990's mainly because it is no longer 'fashionable' and most just can't be bothered. Lads that were more than happy to get stuck in a few years back now attend with their families; they have steady jobs and the responsibilities that go with that. If you like, we have all grown up and can see no sense in serving 5 years in prison for having a punch up at football. Most of the original 6.57 Crew are from the same generation and, like Tony Adams and the rest of the famous Arsenal back line, grown old together. A few of the old lads are now successful business men, some of them are now very wealthy with very comfortable lifestyles that they would be very stupid to jeopardise by all that running up and down the street on a Saturday afternoon. Myself, I am no longer interested either and haven't been for some time. I'm self-employed and in business with my wife Linda and we are doing well for ourselves. On a

Saturday, I love going to watch Pompey although I don't travel away as much as I once did and my life no longer revolves around Saturdays. I still keep in touch with the old lads and see a lot of them on match days, after all we have all known each other for twenty odd years. The problem is down at Fratton Park, the police don't seem to realise that, for us, the war is over. They stand outside the pubs that we have used for years, filming.

I phoned a radio talk-in show about this very subject a little while ago. I can't remember the self-opinionated hosts name but what he was saying was (a) laughable and (b) showed he had no idea about the subject he was talking about. Basically, he was saying that football had rid itself of hooliganism because they had deliberately put the admission prices up in order to price the 'yobs' out of the market. I can only gather that this guy was thirty years out of date and still in a time when the skinhead in his Doctor Martins ruled the terraces. I tried to argue with the guy that, if your average football hooligan doesn't bat an eyelid when handing over £250 for a Stone Island jumper, does he really think that he cares that he has to pay between £20-£50 to watch his side play? The presenter refused to believe me when I pointed out that the image of the bovver boy died out along with the Bay City Rollers and that the football hooligan of today is as likely to work in a bank as he is to work on a building site. Neither would he except that even those who are regarded as 'football hooligans' are passionate and knowledgeable about their football and their club. There are many reasons that football hooliganism has died out. Since we have been in the Premiership, we have played Leeds, Chelsea, Spurs, Manchester United, Birmingham and others which all passed without any incident. In the past, games against these sides have led to very serious disorder but it is clear that trouble in the Premiership will not be tolerated under any circumstances! The Premiership is a brand that sells across the world and nothing will be allowed to tarnish the image. It's not a bad thing and I for one wouldn't have it any other way but it is clear that more money is thrown at policing football in the top division than elsewhere. Admission prices are what they are because clubs have to meet the wage demands of the top players. More and more clubs are targeting the corporate end of the market getting a business to buy a block of ten seats at a grand a time so that the Chief Executive can bring along some clients for hospitality. Before the game of course, he would of wined and dined these clients in the club restaurant, spending a fortune there as well. Don't get me wrong. I am all for football clubs getting this type of commercial business but as long as the 'man in the street' isn't priced out of it. I know plenty of guys who used to stand on the terraces of Fratton Park with their Fathers in exactly the way that I did who would love to take their sons and daughters to watch their beloved Pompey but they just can't afford it. Unfortunately, there are is a whole generation of youngsters that are growing up where the only football they see is on television but I suppose that is progress.

With Pompey now in the Premiership, the football on show is a joy to watch. Fans across the country are at a loss as to why Pompey fans make so much noise throughout the game. Maybe they have become too used to the sterile atmospheres that are usually the norm in England's top division. Whereas places such as Newcastle, Liverpool and Manchester United used to have wall-to-wall noise, now the fans sit and politely applaud at the appropriate moment. When we recently played at St. James' Park, in an attempt to create an atmosphere, each of the Geordies was given a black and white scarf. I thought that they were supposed to be this massive club with the best supporters in the land, don't make me laugh! Fratton Park for all its faults and to be fair there are many has an old-fashioned bear pit atmosphere. Fans and players alike know that they are away when they play at our place. With Pompey though, it is not necessarily the football that they are making all that noise for; more the fact, it's a celebration. The past few seasons have been great which was why the Pompey fans were applauding Thierry Henry and chanting his name at the end of an FA Cup game against Arsenal. Pompey fans are football fans and that day we were torn apart by some of the best football and best teams ever seen at Fratton Park and, when you've become used to being stuffed by Crewe Alexandra and being a lower league also ran, year after year, you begin to realise life ain't so bad.

Football hooligan books and videos are on the increase. Many of them attempt to reason why the hooliganism existed. While sociologists attempt to claim that it was all part of a working class backlash against the ruling classes and other such claptrap, they have basically missed the point. In my opinion, football hooliganism was the original extreme sport. The thrill of turning up on the other side of the country, mob handed and ready to go to war with like minded defenders, can only be experienced and not explained. In fact, all that riding BMX bikes down the side of a mountain is tame by comparison. Apparently, the idea of these so-called extreme sports is to push you to the limit and get the ultimate rush of adrenalin. However, if you really want to get the adrenalin pumping around your body and heart beating so fast you think its going to jump out of your chest, try walking down the Old Kent Road with only about a dozen or so mates when the natives are on the warpath - you'll certainly get a rush of something.

I know that there will be some who will argue that I am just trying to glorify football hooliganism by writing this book. I'm not. I'm purely trying to tell it like it really has happened. In years to come, Granddads across the city will sit impressionable youngsters on their knee and thrill them with stories of how, when they were younger, they used to follow this local football team, long before the European Super League was ever thought about. They will tell tales of how, back then, before dawn was breaking, hundreds of them would climb aboard what was known as a train; this army were bonded together behind a banner made of a Star and Crescent; they would drink together; they would laugh together and they would fight together. They would fight for their cause and their belief that was Portsmouth Football Club. They would engage in many battles; many they won, some they didn't but, regardless, they were a united band. Their name would be mentioned by their foes with revered respect. For they knew that, come Saturday, the legendary 6.57 Crew would come to town and, when they did, it would be ...

BUSINESS AS USUAL